Fodor's InFocus

CHARLESTON

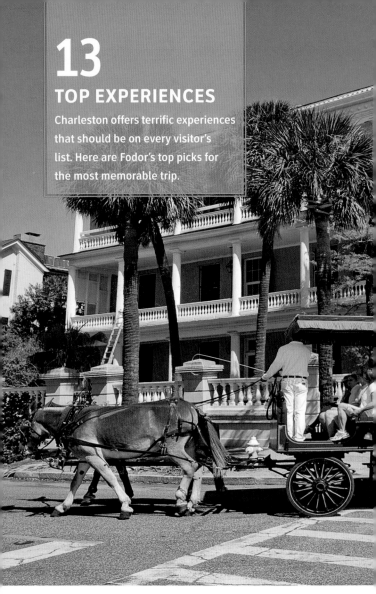

13
TOP EXPERIENCES
Charleston offers terrific experiences that should be on every visitor's list. Here are Fodor's top picks for the most memorable trip.

1 Carriage Ride
Get your bearings the fun way with a carriage ride through the historic district. You'll soak up history, lore, and architectural tidbits all while enjoying amazing views. *(Ch. 1)*

2 White Point Gardens and the Battery

The tip of Charleston's peninsula has been home to everything from strolling ladies in hoopskirts to booming Civil War cannons. Today the stunning view of the harbor remains, along with a regal oak allée. *(Ch. 2)*

3 Old Slave Mart Museum

Charleston was the main point of entry into America for enslaved people in the 18th and 19th centuries. Visit this museum (and one-time slave auction house) for a detailed telling of their journey. *(Ch. 2)*

4 Sullivan's Island

Drive 20 minutes north of town to this slow-paced island. Family friendly and mellow, the beaches are edged in dunes and maritime forests. *(Ch. 6)*

5 Sweetgrass Baskets

"Sewn" from sweet-smelling plants that line the Lowcountry's marshes, these baskets were first made to winnow rice. The designs can be traced to West African countries. *(Ch. 7)*

6 USS *Yorktown*

Charleston's naval history is long, and Patriot's Point on the Charleston Harbor offers three amazing (and retired) ships for tours: the aircraft carrier USS *Yorktown*, the destroyer USS *Laffey*, and the submarine USS *Clamagore*. *(Ch. 2)*

7 King Street

Shop for antiques, artisan candy, fashion, jewelry, and home goods at hip local boutiques and superior national chains on King Street. The two-mile mecca is Charleston's hottest shopping and dining area. *(Ch. 7)*

8 The Wreck of the Richard and Charlene

Named after an old shrimp boat, this seafood dive on Shem Creek is home to famed fried grits, red rice, okra, and fresh-off-the-docks crab, shrimp, and fish. *(Ch. 3)*

9 Drayton Hall

Head 40 minutes out of town to explore this rare, still-standing pre-Revolutionary plantation home on the banks of the Ashley River. *(Ch. 2)*

10 Fort Sumter National Monument

Take the boat tour to this fort in the harbor to see where the first shots of the Civil War were fired in 1861. You can also learn about the lives of the Federal and Confederate troops who occupied it. *(Ch. 2)*

11 Regional Cuisine

A national culinary destination, Charleston has talented chefs who offer innovative twists on traditional Lowcountry cuisine. Pull up a chair at Husk, where James Beard Award-winning Sean Brock wows diners. *(Ch. 3)*

12 Spoleto Festival USA

Visit in late May and early June for Spoleto Festival USA's flood of indoor and outdoor performances by international luminaries in opera, music, dance, and theater. *(Ch. 5)*

13 Nathaniel Russell House Museum

Go behind closed doors at this mansion-turned-museum to wander around grand parlors and drawing rooms, and learn about antebellum life in Charleston. *(Ch. 2)*

CONTENTS

About This Guide 10

**1 EXPERIENCE
CHARLESTON** 11
What's Where 12
Charleston Planner 14
When to Go 16
Perfect Days in Charleston. . . 17
If You Like 18
Kids and Families 22

**2 EXPLORING
CHARLESTON** 23
Exploring Charleston 25
Side Trips from Charleston. . . 48

**3 WHERE TO EAT IN
CHARLESTON** 57

**4 WHERE TO STAY IN
CHARLESTON** 87
Lodging Reviews 90

**5 NIGHTLIFE AND
PERFORMING ARTS** 105
Performing Arts 106
Nightlife 110

**6 SPORTS AND THE
OUTDOORS.** 117
Sports and Activities 119

7 SHOPPING 135
Shopping Districts. 137
Shopping Reviews 137

**8 HILTON HEAD AND THE
LOWCOUNTRY.** 151
Orientation and Planning . . .152
Hilton Head Island 158
Beaufort 191
Daufuskie Island 201

**TRAVEL SMART
CHARLESTON** 205
INDEX 215
ABOUT OUR WRITERS . . 226

MAPS

Downtown Charleston . . . 28–29
Greater Charleston 41
Where to Eat in
Downtown Charleston . . . 60–61
Where to Eat in
Greater Charleston 79
Where to Stay in
Downtown Charleston . . . 92–93
Where to Stay in
Greater Charleston 102
Hilton Head and the
Lowcountry 159
Hilton Head Island 161
Where to Eat on
Hilton Head Island 163
Where to Stay on
Hilton Head Island 170
Beaufort 193

segmentnavigation">**10 <**

ABOUT THIS GUIDE

Fodor's Ratings

Everything in this guide is worth doing—we don't cover what isn't—but exceptional sights, hotels, and restaurants are recognized with additional accolades. Fodor's Choice★ indicates our top recommendations. Care to nominate a new place? Visit Fodors.com/contact-us.

Trip Costs

We list prices wherever possible to help you budget well. Hotel and restaurant price categories from **$** to **$$$$** are noted alongside each recommendation. For hotels, we include the lowest cost of a standard double room in high season. For restaurants, we cite the average price of a main course at dinner or, if dinner isn't served, at lunch. For attractions, we always list adult admission fees; discounts are usually available for children, students, and senior citizens.

Hotels

Our local writers vet every hotel to recommend the best overnights in each price category, from budget to expensive. Unless otherwise specified, you can expect private bath, phone, and TV in your room. For expanded hotel reviews, facilities, and deals visit Fodors.com.

Restaurants

Unless we state otherwise, restaurants are open for lunch and dinner daily. We mention dress code only when there's a specific requirement and reservations only when they're essential or not accepted. To make restaurant reservations, visit Fodors.com.

Credit Cards

The hotels and restaurants in this guide typically accept credit cards. If not, we'll say so.

Top Picks
★ Fodor's Choice

Listings
⊠ Address
⊠ Branch address
🕮 Mailing address
☎ Telephone
🖷 Fax
⊕ Website
✉ E-mail

🎟 Admission fee
🕗 Open/closed times
Ⓜ Subway
⊹ Directions or Map coordinates

Hotels & Restaurants
🏨 Hotel
🛏 Number of rooms
🍴 Meal plans

✕ Restaurant
🍽 Reservations
🏛 Dress code
🗖 No credit cards
⑂ Price

Other
⇨ See also
☞ Take note
⛷ Golf facilities

1

EXPERIENCE CHARLESTON

WHAT'S WHERE

1 **North of Broad.** The main part of the Historic District, where you'll find the lion's share of the Historic District's homes, bed-and-breakfasts, and restaurants, is the most densely packed area of the city and will be of the greatest interest to tourists. King Street, Charleston's main shopping artery, is also here.

2 **South of Broad.** The southern part of the Historic District is heavily residential, but it has important sights and B&Bs, though fewer restaurants and shops than North of Broad. This is where you'll find the Battery.

3 **Mount Pleasant and Vicinity.** East of Charleston, on the other side of the Arthur Ravenel Jr. Bridge, which spans the Cooper River, is Mount Pleasant, an affluent suburb with some interesting sights (such as Boone Hall Plantation). There are several good hotels in Mount Pleasant itself.

4 **West of the Ashley River.** The area outside Charleston west of the Ashley River beckons to visitors with its three major historic plantations on Ashley River Road.

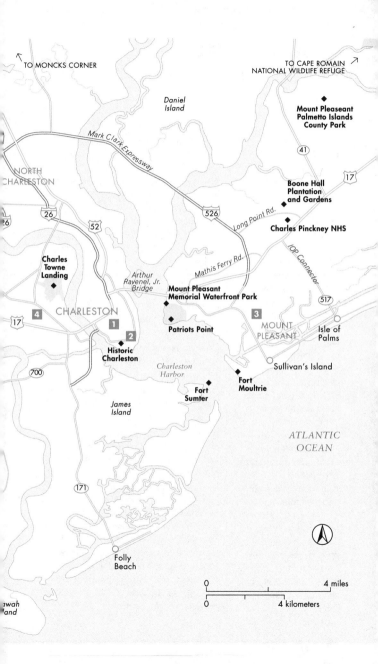

CHARLESTON PLANNER

Visitor Resources

The **Charleston Area Convention & Visitors Bureau** (*www.charlestoncvb.com*) is the best place to start piecing together your trip, whether in person or via their website. Other great resources include *Charleston City Paper* (*www.charlestoncitypaper.com*), a free weekly with events galore, and *Charleston* magazine (*www.charlestonmag.com*); check out both publications for their extensive online calendars. To find out more about Restaurant Week in this foodie city (January and September), look at the website for the **Charleston Restaurant Association** (*www.charlestonrestaurantassociation.com*). And to browse options for both home and garden tours, head to the websites of the **Preservation Society of Charleston** (*www.preservationsociety.org*) and **Historic Charleston Foundation** (*www.historiccharleston.org*).

Getting Here and Around

Fly to Charleston: Flying into the Charleston International Airport is a straightforward affair. American Eagle, United, Delta, US Airways, Southwest, and JetBlue all offer flights. (Another option is the inexpensive Spirit Airlines, which flies into Myrtle Beach International Airport, 90 miles north of Charleston.) Once you land, you'll have to take a taxi or shuttle into the city, about 15 minutes to downtown, unless you rent a car.

Hop a Train: Amtrak pulls into Charleston thanks to the Palmetto service, which spans New York City to Savannah, Georgia, with stops in Philadelphia, Washington, D.C., and other spots, including Charleston.

Drive In: Two main highways feed into Charleston—Highway 17 and Interstate 26. To gauge driving distance, the city is 265 miles from Atlanta, 173 miles from Charlotte, North Carolina, and 85 miles from Savannah, Georgia.

In the City: A car isn't a must in this walkable city, but for those who prefer not to hoof it, there are bikes, pedicabs, tour buses, taxis, water taxis, and trolleys, plus buses that go to the suburbs and beaches. Street parking is irksome, as meter readers are among the city's most efficient public servants. (But if you purchase a SmartCard from the Division of Motor Vehicles downtown, you can "deposit" meter money and credit it back to your card when you leave a metered spot.) Parking garages, both privately and publicly owned, charge approximately $1 an hour.

Planning Your Time

You can get acquainted with Charleston's Historic District at your leisure, especially if you can devote at least three days to the city, which will allow time to explore some of the plantations west of the Ashley River. With another day, you can explore Mount Pleasant, and if you have even more time, head out to the coastal islands.

Savings

You can bank on "high season" running year-round, with minor dips in the heat of late July through early September, and mid-January to Valentine's Day. But if you're motivated, there are deals to be found. Always look online to book hotel packages. Restaurant Week, where multicourse meals are offered at discounted prix fixe, hits twice, in January and September. Year-round, the city-run trolley service offers free hop-on, hop-off service along routes throughout downtown. If you must drive, know that metered parking is free from 6 pm to 9 am. And for those looking to hop on a carriage tour, be sure to raid your hotel's lobby rack cards for coupons offering a few dollars off. Freebie events include the City Farmers' Market, where food vendors, farmers, and artisans offer their wares; Piccolo Spoleto (late May to mid-June), where artists sell their work and musicians give gratis performances; *Charleston City Paper's* Movies in Marion Square in April; Artwalk in the French Quarter, where galleries offer late-night viewing, cocktail nibbles, and drinks every first Friday of the month; and Second Sundays on King, when King Street closes to traffic from Calhoun to Broad streets, and sales hit the sidewalks along with restaurants offering Sunday specials.

Reservations

High season is pretty much any season in Charleston, aside from maybe the hottest stretch of the year, from mid-July through early September. That means reservations are always a good idea at upscale restaurants and a must for downtown hotels. Although you can call around a few days ahead for most tables, top-tier eateries often require a week or more advanced booking for Friday or Saturday nights. Holidays (Thanksgiving, Christmas, New Year's Eve and Day, Valentine's Day, Mother's Day, or Easter brunch) demand reservations made a month or more prior. For those willing to fly by the seat of their schedules, deeply discounted same-day hotel reservations are available through the Lowcountry Reservation Service, operated at the Charleston Area Convention & Visitors Bureau, the Isle of Palms Visitor Center, and the North Charleston Visitors Center.

WHEN TO GO

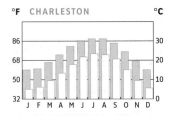

Spring and fall tend to be the most popular times to visit Charleston. The former sees courtyard gardens exploding in blooms and warm temperatures coaxing sundresses and seersucker suits out of local closets. The latter finds residents and tourists alike returning to the sidewalks to stroll, now that summer's most intense heat (and hair-curling humidity) is mellowing out. There are truly only two slightly slower times for tourism in Charleston (July to mid-September and January to mid-February), so those loath to brave crowds or vie for dinner reservations are best advised to visit during those months. Typically, airfare is pricey year-round, but discount airlines Southwest and JetBlue offer options that are easier on your bottom line. Book money-saving hotel packages online or make day-of reservations through Lowcountry Reservations Service at the Charleston Convention & Visitors Bureau.

Climate

Aside from the dog days of summer, where temperatures range from 80°F to 100°F and the humidity nears a stifling 100%, Charleston boasts mild temperatures and a semitropical climate. Expect afternoon rainstorms to blow in and out during summer months, but know that an umbrella is more than enough to keep you happily exploring outside. Come fall, pack light sweaters, and when winter rolls in from December to early February with low 50°F temps, pull on a coat if you're thin-blooded. Basically there are four seasons here, but summer and spring stretch out the longest.

Festivals and Events

The **Southeastern Wildlife Exhibition** in mid-February marks the first big annual event on Charleston's busy social calendar. Dog trials, birds-of-prey exhibits, and wildlife-art sales make it quite testosterone fueled, but it's fun for kids, too. Next up in March comes the **BB&T Charleston Wine + Food Festival** in Marion Square, where cook-offs, sampling, and special dinners reign. Spring home and garden tours hit in late March, and the catwalks are crawling with fashionistas for **Charleston Fashion Week**. The **Cooper River Bridge Run** welcomes some 44,000 runners and walkers for the 10K the last weekend in March, and some 30,000 attendees catch the tennis matches at the **Family Circle Cup** in early April. **Spoleto Festival USA** and **Piccolo Spoleto** both offer live performances and art exhibitions (combined, they total more than 700 options) from late May to mid-June. Charleston's African American and Caribbean heritage is celebrated with the **MOJA Arts Festival** in September and October, and fall home and garden tours rev up then as well.

PERFECT DAYS IN CHARLESTON

Here are a few ideas on how to spend a day in Charleston.

Tour Waterfront Park, South of Broad neighborhoods, the Battery, and City Market. To soak up Charleston best, you've either got to walk it, pedal it (via bike or pedicab), or cover it by carriage. The common thread: you've got to move slowly to see the intricate details in the gardens and architecture and to discover the sweet alleys. Start at Waterfront Park, and read the history markers there. Wander down to the Battery along East Bay and sit in White Point Gardens. Head up King or Church to gawk at the amazing antebellum residences, and then head over to the old City Market to shop for everything from sweets to sweetgrass baskets. Lunch at Husk is a good bet.

Shop King Street. King Street is Charleston's version of the Miracle Mile. On King Street, this amounts to beautifully renovated storefronts that look much like they have for the past few hundred years. Start at Broad and King streets and work your way north for the most comprehensive experience. Try breakfast at Bull Street Gourmet & Market, and then wander from Broad to Market streets, checking out antiques shops and fancy clothing boutiques. Continue shopping in central King, where you'll find chic chains as well as locally born shops like Hampden Clothing. Get lunch at 39 Rue de Jean while heading into the Upper King Area. North of Calhoun, things get funkier. Here's where you'll find Blue Bicycle. Dinner at the MacIntosh makes a lovely end.

Explore the Plantations. Charleston started as a port city in the late 1600s and later dominated in the rice, indigo, and even cotton trade until the Civil War. Many of the large plantations still exist outside the city. Whether you opt to visit Boone Hall Plantation in Mount Pleasant or one or two of three other such properties along Ashley River Road in West Ashley, you will get a better understanding of what built Charleston and helped the colonies break away from England so long ago.

Play at the Beach. Hit the shore at Folly Beach south of town if you like waves that you can surf, a rogue approach to living, a hopping village bar scene, and natural parks to wander. Head east from downtown to Sullivan's Island for kiteboarding and family-friendly beaches. And volleyball aficionados aim for Isle of Palms, where the sporting life and beach bars rule the surfside.

IF YOU LIKE

Exploring Living History

Time-travel to the 18th century with Charleston's wealth of markets, historic homes, and churches, and explore the agrarian side to the city via its outlying former plantations. Taken together, the sum tells the story of wars, wealth, collapse, and rebirth.

Aiken-Rhett House. This downtown estate includes slave quarters, a stable, and a remarkable (and threadbare) mansion.

Boone Hall Plantation and Gardens. This still-working plantation is the oldest of its kind in the Charleston area.

City Market. See where locals shopped for produce, seafood, and meat from the late 1700s to the early 1900s. Shop the souvenir stalls that now thrive there.

Drayton Hall. One of the few remaining plantation homes in the Lowcountry, Drayton Hall was completed in 1742 and lived in by descendants of original family until the 1970s.

Magnolia Plantation and Gardens. The gardens and trolley tour of rice paddies, slave quarters, and the swamp is the main draw at this popular destination.

Middleton Place. After viewing the house (once torched during the Civil War, its "gentlemen's wing" has been restored to its former glory), be sure to visit the estate's rolling green spaces, lively stable yard, and delightful Butterfly Lakes.

Nathaniel Russell House Museum. Built in 1808, this remains one of the nation's finest surviving examples of Adam-style architecture.

Old Slave Mart Museum. Explore the city's part of the slave trade, which was responsible for Charleston's grandeur and the eventual death of the Confederacy.

St. Philip's Church. The namesake of famous Church Street, this graceful late-Georgian structure dates from 1838.

Playing Outside

Water plays a major part in the recreation possibilities here, with the Atlantic Ocean and the Ashley and Cooper rivers, as well as myriad tidal creeks and estuaries. You can fish, especially in the Gulf Stream, go on dolphin-watching trips, and kayak. Back on land, tennis and golf are the top tickets.

Beaches. Head here for family-friendly beaches of Sullivan's Island and a view of Charleston from across the harbor.

Bike. Rent a bike from various outfitters downtown and beyond, and explore Charleston on two wheels.

Consider biking the **Cooper River Bridge**, or taking your bike to the trails at **James Island County Park** or **Palmetto Island County Park**, **Charlestowne Landing**, or **Magnolia Plantation and Gardens**. Those looking to log miles loop **Hampton Park** with its new mile-long bike and pedestrian lane.

Golf. Golfers rave about the links both on **Kiawah Island** (the 2012 PGA Championship was played on the Ocean Course there) and at **Wild Dunes** on Isle of Palms.

Run. Although all of downtown makes a great track, the **Cooper River Bridge** and Hampton Park's mile-long asphalt parcourse, half-mile garden circle, and mile-long bike-pedestrian lane are where the locals go.

Tennis. Wild Dunes Resort on Isle of Palms reigns for the best tennis camps in the area, and the **Family Circle Cup** takes place each spring on Daniel Island.

Learning Gullah and African American History

"Gullah" is the name given to the descendants of slaves in the Lowcountry. The term can refer to the people themselves, to their language, or to their culture, now regarded as one of the most distinctive regional cultures of African American history.

Avery Research for African American History and Culture. Part museum and part archive, this center began as a school in 1865, which trained freed slaves and people of color to be teachers. Today, see artifacts and documentation of the slave era here.

Boone Hall Plantation and Gardens. Take a self-guided tour through the *Black History in America* exhibition on view in eight original brick slave cabins, or attend a performance at the estate's outdoor Gullah Theater.

Gullah Tours. These tours cover Charleston, Beaufort, and Hilton Head, and give you a glimpse into the authentic history of the Gullah.

Middleton Place. Eliza's House, built in the 1870s for the freed slaves who stayed on at this plantation, has a fascinating *Beyond the Fields* exhibition that reveals how reliant this estate was on its former slaves.

MOJA Arts Festival. During the last week of September and first week of October, African heritage and Caribbean influences on African American culture are celebrated.

Mount Pleasant Memorial Waterfront Park. You can chat with Gullah locals selling their traditional baskets in the Sweetgrass Cultural Arts Pavilion at this beautiful park.

Shopping

Charleston has evolved into a shopper's haven. Most of the action happens on King Street, and Upper King has added the Design District, with a new wave of antiques, furniture, and home-fashion stores. Add to this more than two dozen art galleries, predominantly in the French Quarter, and there's plenty to browse and buy.

Ben Silver. A Charleston institution, this provider of preppie blazers and polo shirts keeps locals looking snappy.

Blue Bicycle Books. The only bookstore downtown sells used, rare, and new books with local ties.

City Market. Sweetgrass baskets, candies, T-shirts, bags, spices, and much, much more are for sale from the vendors here.

Copper Penny. Designers like Diane von Furstenberg, Trina Turk, and Millie are well represented on these racks.

Croghan's Jewel Box. This family-owned gem has sold wedding silver, engagement rings, anniversary presents, and jewelry galore to Charlestonians for more than 100 years.

George C. Birlant & Co. Silver, silver, and more silver abounds here.

Hamden Clothing. Find out why New York fashion editors consider this hipster paradise a must-see when they are anywhere in the South.

Heirloom Book Co. A foodie town deserves this bookstore specializing in vintage cookbooks.

King Street. This is the Rodeo Drive of Charleston, with all of the latest fashions in locally owned boutiques and well-known chains.

Getting Away from It All

Charleston itself is a little step off the beaten path, but for those looking to isolate and unwind further, there are options.

Inn at Middleton Place. A super-mod-style hotel in the woodlands adjacent to Middleton Place, this inn affords private access to the plantation grounds.

The Sanctuary at Kiawah Island. Luxury knows no bounds at this hotel with its acclaimed restaurant, spa, and nearby golf courses.

Wentworth Mansion. When celebrities want to stay downtown but out of the limelight, they head to this 1886 mansion with its spa, restaurant, and quiet neighborhood a few blocks from King Street.

Eating Out

You can't toss a plate for hitting a James Beard Award nominee or winner in Charleston these days. Take advantage of this and try some of these spots for fresh cuisine from Lowcountry farms and artisan purveyors.

Basil. Don't fret over the line at this popular Asian eatery in the heart of downtown. It's always worth the wait.

Charleston Grille. Chef Michelle Weaver runs one of the city's most popular eateries, known through the region for its groundbreaking New South cuisine.

Chez Nous. Head to the outdoor patio at this hard-to-find local eatery, the perfect place for dinner or brunch.

Cupcake. If you're in the mood for sweets, this darling little shop features more than 50 kinds of cupcakes. Peanut butter banana fluff, anyone?

Cypress Lowcountry Grille. Can't decide on a wine? You'll have trouble deciding at this popular eatery, which has a "wine wall" packed with 4,500 bottles.

FIG. Mike Lata's impeccable Lowcountry-accented dishes are born of perfectly sourced, perfectly prepared, and perfectly honest ingredients.

Husk and **McCrady's.** Chef Sean Brock brought the Southern locavore movement into the mainstream with the former and treats you to top-end white-linen dining with the latter.

Macaroon Boutique. Sweet treats that make for great gifts (or simple snacks) are the order of the day here.

Market Street Sweets. Hit this confectionary to sample cinnamon-and-sugar crusted pecans or benne wafers—a Charleston original.

Martha Lou's Kitchen. This palace of soul food is one of the best places to go for traditional fare.

Peninsula Grill. Break out the fancy clothes for supreme service and gourmet decadence at the Charleston institution. Don't leave without trying the coconut cake.

The Tattooed Moose. Homey eats like house-smoked barbecue brisket, chicken salad, jumbo chicken wings, and fried turkey breast are on offer at this unpretentious place.

Ted's Butcherblock. One-stop shopping for gourmet picnic provisions, Ted's is also a great place to hit for wine tastings.

Trattoria Lucca. Italian food never tasted so fine as it does at Chef Ken Vedrinski's friendly neighborhood kitchen.

KIDS AND FAMILIES

What kid wouldn't delight in a town that looks like a fairy tale, and has cobblestone streets and secret alleyways, horses pulling carriages, real-life pirate stories, and candy shops with free samples handed out daily? Charleston is made for kids, and exploring it is a great (and painless) way to get them to learn history, so bring on the family time.

Activities

As for entertainment, **carriage tours** (and the stables at Pinckney and Anson streets) captivate, as do rides on the **water taxis** and **pedicabs**. Rainy days are best passed in the **Children's Museum of the Lowcountry** (the interactive gravity and water exhibits and model shrimp boat are favorites), the **South Carolina Aquarium,** or at **Patriots Point** with its decommissioned destroyer, submarine, and aircraft carrier. Sunny days call for a visit to the blacksmith's shop and stableyard at **Middleton Place,** the petting zoo at **Magnolia Plantation and Gardens,** or a **Riverdogs** baseball game at the Joe downtown. If you're looking to cool off, any of the beaches are a good bet, or even the fountains at **Waterfront Park**. For shopping, try **Market Street Sweets** for goodies and **City Market** for souvenirs.

Dining

Kids are welcome everywhere in town—but they are expected to mind their manners. If your child needs a little schooling in that department, feel free to enroll them in etiquette camp or send them to a children's tea party for that purpose via the **Charleston School of Protocol and Etiquette** (*www.charlestonschoolofprotocol.com*). Manners aside, kids of all ages are especially welcome at **Taco Boy** and **Hominy Grill** (especially for weekend brunch).

Resorts

Kiawah Island Golf Resort and **Wild Dunes Resort** on Isle of Palms offer the most activities for kids. From tennis and golf lessons to swimming and crabbing and more, there are scores of ways to keep the junior set entertained. In town, **Embassy Suites** on Marion Square enchants with its castlelike appearance and sits in a primo location for all the events held on the square, from the Saturday Farmers' Market (with its jump castle and pony rides) to the Southeastern Wildlife Exposition (with its dog trials) to Piccolo Spoleto (with its children's arts activities).

EXPLORING
CHARLESTON

By Anna
Evans

WANDERING THROUGH THE CITY'S FAMOUS HISTORIC DISTRICT, YOU WOULD SWEAR IT IS A MOVIE SET. Dozens of church steeples punctuate the low skyline, and horse-drawn carriages pass centuries-old mansions and town houses, their stately salons offering a crystal-laden and parquet-floored version of Southern comfort. Outside, magnolia-filled gardens overflow with carefully tended heirloom plants. At first glance, the city may resemble a 19th-century etching come to life—but look closer and you'll see that block after block of old structures have been restored. Happily, after three centuries of wars, epidemics, fires, and hurricanes, Charleston has prevailed and is now one of the South's best-preserved cities.

Although it's home to Fort Sumter, where the bloodiest war in the nation's history began, Charleston is also famed for its elegant houses. These handsome mansions are show-cases for the "Charleston style," a distinctive look that is reminiscent of the West Indies, and for good reason. Before coming to the Carolinas in the late 17th century, many early British colonists first settled on Barbados and other Caribbean islands. In that warm and humid climate they built homes with high ceilings and rooms opening onto broad "piazzas" (porches) at each level to catch sea breezes. As a result, to quote the words of the Duc de La Rochefoucauld, who visited in 1796, "One does not boast in Charleston of having the most beautiful house, but the coolest."

Preserved through the hard times that followed the Civil War and an array of natural disasters, many of Charleston's earliest public and private buildings still stand. Thanks to a rigorous preservation movement and strict architectural guidelines, the city's new structures blend in with the old. In many cases, recycling is the name of the game—antique handmade bricks literally lay the foundation for new homes. But although locals do dwell—on certain literal levels—in the past, the city is very much a town of today.

Take, for instance, the internationally heralded Spoleto Festival USA. For 17 days every spring, arts patrons from around the world come to enjoy international concerts, dance performances, operas, and plays at various venues citywide. Day in and day out, diners can feast at upscale restaurants, shoppers can look for museum-quality paintings and antiques, and lovers of the outdoors can explore

Charleston's outlying beaches, parks, and waterways. But as cosmopolitan as the city has become, it's still the South, and just beyond the city limits are farm stands cooking up boiled peanuts, the state's official snack.

EXPLORING CHARLESTON

Everyone starts a tour of Charleston in downtown's famous Historic District. Roughly bounded by Lockwood Boulevard on the Ashley River to the west, Calhoun Street to the north, East Bay Street on the Cooper River to the east, and the Battery to the south, this fairly compact area of 800 acres contains nearly 2,000 historic homes and buildings. The peninsula is divided up into several neighborhoods, starting from the south and moving north, including the Battery, South of Broad, Lower King Street, and Upper King Street ending near the "Crosstown," where U.S. 17 connects downtown to Mount Pleasant and West Ashley.

You'll see no skyscrapers in the downtown area, because building heights are strictly regulated to maintain the city's historic setting. In the 1970s, most department stores decamped for suburban malls, turning King Street buildings into rows of (architecturally significant) empty shells. Soon, preservation-conscious groups began to save these beauties, and by the mid-1980s the shopping district was revived with the addition of the Omni Hotel (now Belmond Charleston Place). Big-name retailers quickly saw the opportunity in this attractive city and settled in as well. Lower King thrives and Upper King is booming, with many new businesses—hip bars and restaurants in particular—targeting the city's young, socially active population. Look up at the old-timey tile work at the entrances; inevitably it will have the names of the original businesses.

Beyond downtown, the Ashley River hugs the west side of the peninsula; the region on the far shore is called West Ashley. The Cooper River runs along the east side of the peninsula, with Mount Pleasant on the opposite side and Charleston Harbor in between. Lastly, there are outlying sea islands: James Island with its Folly Beach, John's Island, Wadmalaw Island, Kiawah Island, Seabrook Island, Isle of Palms, and Sullivan's Island. Each has its own appealing attractions, though John's and Wadmalaw have farms instead of beaches. Everything that entails crossing the bridges is best explored by car or bus.

NORTH OF BROAD

During the early 1800s, large tracts of land were available North of Broad—as it was outside the bounds of the original walled city—making it ideal for suburban plantations. A century later the peninsula had been built out, and today the resulting area is a vibrant mix of residential neighborhoods and commercial clusters, with verdant parks scattered throughout. The district comprises three primary neighborhoods: Upper King, the Market area, and the College of Charleston. Though there are a number of majestic homes and pre-Revolutionary buildings in this area (including the Powder Magazine, the oldest public building in the state), the main draw is the rich variety of stores, museums, restaurants, and historic churches.

As you explore, note that the farther north you travel (up King Street in particular), the newer and more commercial development becomes. Although pretty much anywhere on the peninsula is considered prime real estate these days, the farther south you go, the more expensive the homes become. In times past, Broad Street was considered the cutoff point for a coveted address. Those living in the area Slightly North of Broad were referred to as SNOBs, and, conversely, their wealthier neighbors South of Broad were nicknamed SOBs.

TOP ATTRACTIONS

FAMILY **Charleston Museum.** Although housed in a modern-day brick complex, this institution was founded in 1773 and is the country's oldest museum. To the delight of fans of *Antiques Roadshow,* the collection is especially strong in South Carolina decorative arts, from silver to snuffboxes. There's also a large gallery devoted to natural history (don't miss the giant polar bear). Children love the permanent Civil War exhibition and the interactive "Kidstory" area, where they can try on reproduction clothing in a miniature historic house. The Historic Textiles Gallery features rotating displays that showcase everything from uniforms and flags to couture gowns to antique quilts and needlework. Combination tickets that include the Joseph Manigault House and the Heyward-Washington House are a bargain at $22. ⊠ *360 Meeting St., Upper King* ☎ *843/722–2996* ⊕ *www.charlestonmuseum.org* ⊠ *$10, $22 ticket includes Joseph Manigault House and Heyward-Washington House* ⊙ *Mon.–Sat. 9–5, Sun. 1–5.*

Charleston Visitor Center. A 20-minute film called *Forever Charleston* makes a fine introduction to the city. ■TIP➔ **The first 30 minutes are free at the center's parking lot, making it a real bargain.** ⊠ *375 Meeting St., Upper King* ☎ *800/774–0006* ⊕ *www.charlestoncvb.com* ⚏ *Free* ☉ *Daily 8:30–5.*

FAMILY **Children's Museum of the Lowcountry.** Hands-on interactive environments at this top-notch museum will keep kids—from babies on up to age 10—occupied for hours. They can climb aboard a Lowcountry pirate ship, drive an antique fire truck, race golf balls down a roller coaster, and create masterpieces in the art center. ⊠ *25 Ann St., Upper King* ☎ *843/853–8962* ⊕ *www.explorecml.org* ⚏ *$10* ☉ *Tues.– Sat. 9–5, Sun. noon–5.*

Circular Congregational Church. The first church building erected on this site in the 1680s gave bustling Meeting Street its name. The present-day Romanesque structure, dating from 1890, is configured on a Greek-cross plan and has a breathtaking vaulted ceiling. While the church is not open to visitors except during Sunday morning service, you are welcome to explore the graveyard, which is the oldest in the city, with records dating back to 1696. ⊠ *150 Meeting St., Market area* ☎ *843/577–6400* ⊕ *www.circularchurch. org* ☉ *Graveyard open weekdays 8–6, Sun. 9–6.*

FAMILY **City Market.** Most of the buildings that make up this popular attraction were constructed between 1804 and the 1830s to serve as the city's meat, fish, and produce market. These days you'll find the open-air portion packed with stalls selling handmade jewelry, crafts, clothing, jams and jellies, and regional souvenirs. A major renovation transformed the market's indoor section, creating a beautiful backdrop for 20 stores and eateries. Local craftspeople are on hand weaving sweetgrass baskets—a skill passed down through generations from their African ancestors. From March through December, a night market on Friday and Saturday hosts local artists and food vendors. This shopping mecca's perimeters (North and South Market streets) are lined with restaurants and shops. ⊠ *N. and S. Market Sts. between Meeting and E. Bay Sts., Market area* ☎ *843/937–0920* ⊕ *www.thecharlestoncitymarket. com* ☉ *Jan. and Feb., daily 9–6; Mar.–Dec., Sun.–Thurs. 9–6, Fri. and Sat. 9–6 and 6:30–10:30.*

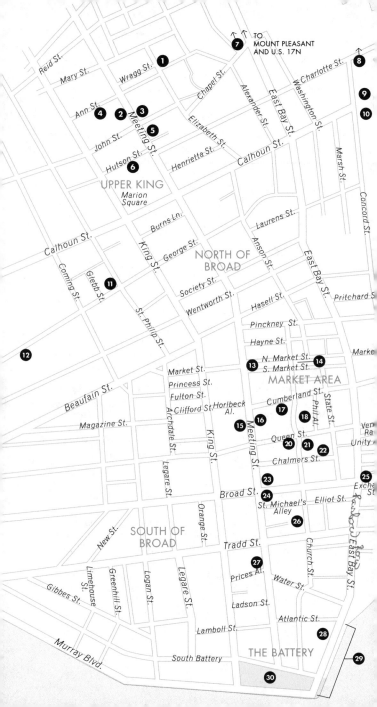

Charleston
Maritime Center

Downtown Charleston

31

Cooper River

Aiken-Rhett House, **1**	Gibbes Museum of Art, **15**
Avery Research Center for African American History and Culture, **12**	Heyward-Washington House, **26**
Battery, **29**	The *Hunley*, **8**
Charleston Museum, **3**	Joseph Manigault House, **5**
Charleston Visitor Center, **2**	Magnolia Cemetery, **7**
Children's Museum of the Lowcountry, **4**	Market Hall, **13**
Circular Congregational Church, **16**	Nathaniel Russell House, **27**
City Hall, **23**	Old Citadel, **6**
City Market, **14**	Old Exchange Building and Provost Dungeon, **25**
College of Charleston, **11**	Old Slave Mart Museum, **22**
Dock Street Theatre, **20**	Powder Magazine, **17**
Edmondston-Alston House, **28**	St. Michael's Church, **24**
Fort Sumter National Monument, **31**	St. Philip's Church, **18**
Fort Sumter Visitor Center, **10**	South Carolina Aquarium, **9**
French Protestant (Huguenot) Church, **21**	White Point Garden, **30**
	Waterfront Park, **19**

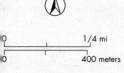

0   1/4 mi

0   400 meters

College of Charleston. With a majestic Greek revival portico, Randolph Hall—an 1828 building designed by Philadelphia architect William Strickland—presides over the college's central Cistern Yard. Draping oaks envelop the lush green quad, where graduation ceremonies and concerts, notably during the Spoleto Festival USA, take place. Scenes from films like *Cold Mountain* have been filmed on the historic campus of this liberal arts college, founded in 1770. ✉ *Cistern Yard, 66 George St., College of Charleston Campus* ☎ *843/805–5507* ⊕ *www.cofc.edu.*

Dock Street Theatre. Incorporating the remains of the Old Planter's Hotel (circa 1809), this theater is hung with green velvet curtains and has wonderful woodwork, giving it a New Orleans French Quarter feel. Charleston Stage Company performs full seasons of family-friendly fare, and the Spoleto Festival USA uses the stage for productions in May and June. ✉ *135 Church St., Market area* ☎ *843/720–3968* ⊕ *www.charlestonstage.com/dock-street-theatre.html.*

QUICK BITES. **Bakehouse Charleston.** Delicious seasonal desserts—heavenly sweet 'n' salty brownies, cheesecake bars, and whoopie pies—are baked at this popular spot. Soft as a pillow, the homemade marshmallows make great take-away treats. Looking for a heartier option? Have a breakfast sandwich or slice of quiche with a cup of locally roasted organic coffee. Craft beer is also available in this Wi-Fi hot spot, which has roomy booths and community tables as well as a few sidewalk seats. ✉ *160 East Bay St., Market area* ☎ *843/577–2180* ⊕ *www. bakehousecharleston.com.*

FAMILY Fodor's Choice ★ **Fort Sumter National Monument.** Set on a man-made island in Charleston's harbor, this is the hallowed spot where the Civil War began. On April 12, 1861, the first shot of the war was fired at the fort from Fort Johnson across the way. After a 34-hour battle, Union forces surrendered and Confederate troops occupied Fort Sumter, which became a symbol of Southern resistance. The Confederacy managed to hold it, despite almost continual bombardment from August 1863 to February of 1865. When it was finally evacuated, the fort was a heap of rubble. Today, the National Park Service oversees it, and rangers give interpretive talks.

To reach the fort, take a private boat or one of the ferries that depart from downtown's Fort Sumter Visitor Educa-

JOHN JAKES'S BEST BETS IN CHARLESTON

Renowned historical novelist John Jakes achieved the rare distinction of having 16 consecutive novels on the *New York Times* list of best sellers. Considered the contemporary master of the family saga, Jakes is best loved locally for his trilogy *North and South*, which was made into three miniseries for ABC in the 1980s and '90s. They focused on Charleston before and during the Civil War, with much of the filming done in the city. Less famous but equally entertaining and educational are his books and audiotapes, *Charleston* and *Savannah*, or a *Gift for Mr. Lincoln*. Jakes shared some suggestions for experiencing Charleston's historical sites with us:

"Fort Sumter. A boat ride to the famous Civil War fort is an attraction that shouldn't be missed by any visitor who appreciates history. Close your eyes just a bit and you can imagine Sumter's cannon blasting from the ramparts— maybe even spot a sleek, gray blockade-runner from Liverpool sneaking into the harbor at dusk.

Carriage Rides. We lived in the Lowcountry for years before I took one of the carriage rides that originate next to the outdoor market. I had a misguided scorn for such tours until I jumped impulsively into a vacant carriage one day. I found the young guide enormously informative, and learned a lot, even some years after writing the *North and South* trilogy. Caution: Carriage routes are determined by where they start from; try to avoid those that take you away from the real jewel featured in the others—the Historic District.

Boone Hall Plantation. This finely preserved property just a few miles north of the city stood in for Mont Royal, Patrick Swayze's home in the David L. Wolper miniseries *North and South*. The avenue of live oaks leading to the house is well worth the visit."
—John Jakes

tion Center and from Patriots Point in Mount Pleasant. There are six trips daily between mid-March and mid-August, fewer the rest of the year. ☎ 843/883–3123 ⊕ *www. nps.gov/fosu* ⌦ *Fort free; ferry $18* ☉ *Mid-Mar.–early Sept., daily 10–5:30; early Sept.–Nov. and early Mar., daily 10–4; Dec.–Feb. daily 11:30–4.*

Fort Sumter Visitor Education Center. Next to the South Carolina Aquarium, the visitor education center contains exhibits on the antebellum period and the causes of the Civil War.
This is a departure point for ferries headed to Fort Sumter.
✉ *340 Concord St., Upper King* ☎ *843/577–0242* ⊕ *www.
nps.gov/fosu* ⊠ *Free* ⊙ *Daily 8:30–5.*

HISTORY LESSON. **A ferry ride to Fort Sumter is a great way to sneak
in a history lesson for the kids. During the 30-minute ride, you
get a narrated journey that points out the historic sites and
explains how the Civil War began.**

French Protestant (Huguenot) Church. The circa-1845 Gothic-
style church is home to the nation's only practicing Huguenot congregation. English-language services are held Sunday
at 10:30, with a tour given to any visitors afterward at
11:15. ✉ *136 Church St., Market area* ☎ *843/722–4385*
⊕ *www.huguenot-church.org* ⊙ *Services Sun. 11:15; tours
mid-Mar.–mid-June and mid-Sept.–mid-Nov., Mon.–Thurs.
10–4, Fri. 10–1.*

★ Fodor'sChoice **Gibbes Museum of Art.** Housed in a beautiful
Beaux-Arts building, this museum boasts a collection of
10,000 works, principally American with a local connec-
tion. Different objects from the museum's permanent collection are on view in "The Charleston Story," offering a nice
overview of the region's history. ∎TIP→ **The museum will be
closed for major renovations until early 2016.** ✉ *135 Meeting
St., Market area* ☎ *843/722–2706* ⊕ *www.gibbesmuseum.
org* ⊠ *$9* ⊙ *Tues.–Sat. 10–5, Sun. 1–5.*

WHAT'S IN A NAME. **The Manigaults are descendants of the French
Huguenots who fled Europe because of persecution, and
are a golden example of the American dream fulfilled. They
became a wealthy rice-planting family and are still prominent
in Charleston; Manigaults own the daily newspaper, among
other businesses.**

★ Fodor'sChoice **Joseph Manigault House.** An extraordinary example of Federal architecture, this 1803 residence was designed
by Gabriel Manigault for his brother, Joseph. The National
Historic Landmark reflects the urban lifestyle of a well-
to-do rice-planting family and the African Americans they
enslaved. Engaging guided tours reveal a stunning spiral
staircase; rooms that have been preserved in period style;
and American, English, and French furniture from the

early 19th century. Outside, stroll through the artfully maintained period garden with a classical Gate Temple and interpretive signs that note where historical buildings once stood. ✉ *350 Meeting St., Upper King* ☎ *843/723–2926* ⊕ *www.charlestonmuseum.org/joseph-manigault-house* ✍ *$10* ⊙ *Mon.–Sat. 10–5, Sun. 1–5.*

Old Citadel. A fortresslike building on Marion Square became the first home of the Military College of South Carolina—now called the Citadel—in the 1840s. Today it houses a hotel, and you can stop into the lobby to see a case of interesting artifacts. The present-day Citadel is near Hampton Park on the Ashley River. ✉ *337 Meeting St., Upper King* ☎ *843/723–6900.*

FARMERS' MARKET. Set in Marion Square, at the intersection of King and Calhoun streets, the market runs from 8 am to 2 pm every Saturday from mid-April through mid-December. Here you can find organic produce, homemade jams, and handcrafted everything—from jewelry to decor and dog collars. Breakfast and lunch options are plentiful, too.

★ Fodor'sChoice **Old Slave Mart Museum.** This is thought to be the state's only existing building that was used for slave auctioning, a practice that ended here in 1863. It was once part of a complex called Ryan's Mart, which also contained a slave jail, kitchen, and morgue. It is now a museum that shares the history of Charleston's role in the slave trade, an unpleasant story but one that is vital to understand. Charleston was a commercial center for the South's plantation economy, and slaves were the primary source of labor both within the city and on the surrounding plantations. Galleries are outfitted with interactive exhibits, including push buttons that allow you to hear voices relating stories from the age of slavery. The museum sits on one of the few remaining cobblestone streets in town. ✉ *6 Chalmers St., Market area* ☎ *843/958–6467* ⊕ *www.charleston-sc.gov* ✍ *$7* ⊙ *Mon.–Sat. 9–5.*

★ Fodor'sChoice **St. Philip's Church.** Founded around 1680, St. Philip's didn't move to its current site until the 1720s, becoming one of the three churches that gave Church Street its name. The first building in this location (where George Washington worshipped in 1791) burned down in 1835 and was replaced with the Corinthian-style structure seen today. A shell that exploded in the churchyard while services were being held one Sunday during the Civil War didn't deter the minister from finishing his sermon (the congregation gathered elsewhere for the remainder of the war). Amble through the churchyards, where notable South Carolinians such as John C. Calhoun are buried. If you want to tour the church, call ahead, as open hours depend upon volunteer availability. ⊠ *142 Church St., Market area* ☎ *843/722–7734* ⊕ *www.stphilipschurchsc.org* ☉ *Churchyard weekdays 9–4.*

★ Fodor'sChoice **South Carolina Aquarium.** Get up close and per-
FAMILY sonal with more than 7,000 creatures at this waterfront attraction, where exhibits invite you to journey through distinctive habitats. Step into the Mountain Forest and find water splashing over a rocky gorge as river otters play. Enter the open-air Saltmarsh Aviary to feed stingrays and view herons, diamondback terrapins, and puffer fish. And gaze in awe at the two-story, 385,000-gallon Great Ocean Tank, home to sharks, jellyfish, and a loggerhead sea turtle. Kids love the Touch Tank and the 4-D Theater that shows films with special effects such as wind gusts and splashes of water. Tours of the Sea Turtle Hospital are well worth the extra $10. ⊠ *100 Aquarium Wharf, Upper King* ☎ *800/722–6455, 843/577–3474* ⊕ *www.scaquarium.org* ☞ *$24.95* ☉ *Mar.–Aug., daily 9–5; Sept.–Feb., daily 9–4.*

Waterfront Park. Enjoy the fishing pier's "front-porch" swings, stroll along the waterside path, or relax in the gardens overlooking Charleston Harbor. The expansive lawn is perfect for picnics and family play time. Two fountains can be found here: the oft-photographed Pineapple Fountain and the Vendue Fountain, which children love to run through on hot days. ⊠ *Vendue Range at Concord St., Market area* ☎ *843/724–7321* ☞ *Free* ☉ *Daily 6 am–midnight.*

ON THE CHEAP. **A $52.95 Charleston Heritage Passport, sold at the Charleston, North Charleston, and Mount Pleasant visitor centers, gets you into the Charleston Museum, the Gibbes Museum of Art, Drayton Hall, Middleton Place, and five historic houses for two consecutive days. Three- and seven-day passes are also available.**

WORTH NOTING

Aiken-Rhett House Museum. One of Charleston's most stately mansions, built in 1820 and virtually unaltered since 1858, has been preserved rather than restored, meaning visitors can see its original wallpaper, paint, and some furnishings. Two of the former owners, Governor Aiken and his wife, Harriet—lovers of all things foreign and beautiful—

bought many of the chandeliers, sculptures, and paintings in Europe. The carriage house remains out back, along with a building that contained the kitchen, laundry, and slave quarters, making this the most intact property to showcase urban life in antebellum Charleston. Take the audio tour, as it vividly describes both the ornate family rooms and the slave quarters, giving historical and family details throughout. ⊠ *48 Elizabeth St., Upper King* ☎ *843/723–1159* ⊕ *www.historiccharleston.org* ⊠ *$10; $16 with admission to Nathaniel Russell House Museum* ☉ *Mon.–Sat. 10–5, Sun. 2–5; last tour at 4:15.*

Avery Research Center for African American History and Culture. Part of the College of Charleston, this museum and archive was once a school for African Americans, training students for professional careers from approximately 1865 to 1954. The collections here focus on the civil rights movement, but also include slavery artifacts such as badges, manacles, and bills of sale, as well as other materials from throughout African American history. The free guided tours begin with a brief film. ⊠ *125 Bull St., College of Charleston Campus* ☎ *843/953–7609* ⊕ *avery.cofc.edu* ⊠ *Free* ☉ *Tours weekdays at 10:30, 11:30, 1:30, 2:30, and 3:30.*

The *Hunley*. In 1864, the Confederacy's *H. L. Hunley* sank the Union warship USS *Housatonic*, becoming the world's first successful submarine. Moments after the attack, it disappeared mysteriously into the depths of the sea. Lost for more than a century, it was found in 1995 off the coast of Sullivan's Island and raised in 2000. The *Hunley* is now being preserved and excavated in a 90,000-gallon tank, which you can see during an informative tour. A newly renovated exhibit area includes artifacts excavated from the sub and interactive displays. ⊠ *1250 Supply St., Old Charleston Naval Base, North Charleston* ☎ *843/743–4865, 877/448–6539 for tours* ⊕ *www.hunley.org* ⊠ *$12* ☉ *Sat. 10–5, Sun. noon–5.*

Market Hall. Built in 1841, this imposing landmark was modeled after the Temple of Wingless Victory in Athens. While City Market vendors occupy the ground floor, the second story contains the **Confederate Museum**, in which the United Daughters of the Confederacy mount displays of flags, uniforms, swords, and other Civil War memorabilia. Admission to the museum is $5. ⊠ *188 Meeting St., Market area* ☎ *843/723–1541* ⊕ *www.thecharlestoncitymarket.com* ⊠ *Free* ☉ *Tues.–Sat. 11–3:30.*

Powder Magazine. Completed in 1713, the oldest public building in South Carolina is one of few that remains from the time of the Lords Proprietors. The city's volatile—and precious—gunpowder was kept here during the Revolutionary War, and the building's thick walls were designed to contain an explosion if its stores were detonated. Today it's a small museum with a permanent exhibit focusing on colonial and revolutionary warfare. ⊠ *79 Cumberland St., Market area* ☎ *843/722–9350* ⊕ *www.powdermag.org* ☎ *$5* ☉ *Mon.–Sat. 10–4, Sun.1–4.*

BUILDING BOOM. Charleston grew apace with the plantation economy in the mid-1700s, thanks to the booming trade in South Carolina's rice, indigo, and cotton crops. Seeking a social and cultural lifestyle to match its financial success, the plantocracy entertained itself in style by using the talents of the local goldsmiths, silversmiths, gunsmiths, and cabinetmakers. More than 300 private residences were built between 1760 and 1770 alone, a surge reflective of Charleston's position as the wealthiest city in British North America at that time.

SOUTH OF BROAD

Locals jokingly claim that just off the Battery (at Battery Street and Murray Boulevard), the Ashley and Cooper rivers join to form the Atlantic Ocean. Such a lofty proclamation speaks volumes about the area's rakish flair. To observe their pride and joy, head to the point of the downtown peninsula. Here, handsome mansions and a large oak-shaded park greet incoming boats and charm passersby.

The heavily residential area south of Broad Street brims with beautiful private homes, many of which have plaques bearing brief descriptions of the property's history. Mind your manners, but feel free to peek through iron gates and fences at the verdant displays in elaborate gardens. Although an open gate once signified that guests were welcome to venture inside, that time has mostly passed—residents tell stories of how they came home to find tourists sitting in their front-porch rockers. But you never know when an invitation to have a look-see might come from a friendly owner-gardener. Several of the city's lavish house museums call this famously affluent neighborhood home.

TOP ATTRACTIONS

★ Fodor's Choice **Battery.** During the Civil War, the Confederate
FAMILY army mounted cannons in the Battery, at the southernmost
point of Charleston's peninsula, to fortify the city against
Union attack. Cannons and piles of cannonballs still line
the oak-shaded park known as White Point Garden—kids
can't resist climbing them. Where pirates once hung from
the gallows, strollers now take in the serene setting from
Charleston benches (small wood-slat benches with cast-iron
sides). Stroll the waterside promenades along East Battery
and Murray Boulevard and you can enjoy views of Charleston Harbor, the Ravenel Bridge, and Fort Sumter on one
side, with some of the city's most photographed mansions
on the other. You'll find locals dangling their fishing lines,
waiting for a catch. ⊠ *East Battery St., at Murray Blvd.,
South of Broad.*

OLD-FASHIONED WALK. In spring and summer, Charleston's gardens are in full glory. Then, in fall and winter, the homes are
dressed in their holiday finest. Twilight strolls are a Dickensian
experience, with houses lighted from within showing off one
cozy scene after another.

Heyward-Washington House. This Georgian-style double
house was the town home of Thomas Heyward, patriot
leader and signer of the Declaration of Independence. The
city rented the residence for George Washington's use during the President's weeklong stay in Charleston in 1791.
Inside, visitors find historic Charleston-made furniture,
notably the withdrawing room's Holmes Bookcase, considered to be one of the most exceptional examples of
American colonial furniture. Also significant is the 1740s
kitchen building, as it's the only one of its kind open to the
public in Charleston. Don't miss the formal gardens, which
contain plants commonly used in the area in the late 18th
century. ⊠ *87 Church St., South of Broad* ☎ *843/722–0354*
⊕ *www.charlestonmuseum.org/heyward-washington-house*
🖃 *$10* ☉ *Mon.–Sat. 10–5, Sun. 1–5.*

IF THE SHOE FITS. Wear good walking shoes, because the sidewalks,
brick streets, and even Battery Promenade are very uneven.
Take a bottle of water, or stop to sip from the fountains in White
Point Garden, as there are practically no shops south of Broad
Street—or public restrooms.

★ FodorsChoice **Nathaniel Russell House Museum.** One of the nation's finest examples of Federal-style architecture, the Nathaniel Russell House was built in 1808 and is restored to a 19th-century aesthetic. Its grand beauty is proof of the immense wealth Russell accumulated as one of the city's leading merchants. In addition to the famous "free-flying" staircase that spirals up three stories with no visible support, the ornate interior is distinguished by Charleston-made furniture as well as paintings and works on paper by well-known American and European artists, including Henry Benbridge, Samuel F. B. Morse, and George Romney. The extensive formal garden is worth a leisurely stroll. ⊠ *51 Meeting St., South of Broad* ☎ *843/724–8481* ⊕ *www. historiccharleston.org* ⌸ *$10; $16 with admission to Aiken-Rhett House Museum* ☉ *Mon.–Sat. 10–5, Sun. 2–5.*

St. Michael's Church. Topped by a 186-foot steeple, St. Michael's is the city's oldest surviving church. The first cornerstone was set in place in 1752 and, through the years, other elements were added: the steeple clock and bells (1764); the organ (1768); the font (1771); and the altar (1892). A claim to fame: George Washington worshiped in pew number 43 in 1791. Listen for the bell ringing band to ring changes before worship services. ⊠ *78 Meeting St., South of Broad* ☎ *843/723–0603* ⊕ *www.stmichaelschurch. net* ☉ *Weekdays 9–4:30, Sat. 9–noon.*

WORTH NOTING

City Hall. The intersection of Meeting and Broad streets is known as the Four Corners of Law, representing the laws of nation, state, city, and church. On the northeast corner is the Adam-style City Hall, built in 1801. Visitors enjoy viewing the historic portraits that hang in the second-floor council chamber (the second-oldest continuously used council chamber in the country), with highlights including John Trumbull's 1791 portrait of George Washington and Samuel F. B. Morse's likeness of James Monroe. ⊠ *80 Broad St., North of Broad* ☎ *843/577–6970* ⌸ *Free* ☉ *Weekdays 8:30–5.*

Edmondston-Alston House. In 1825, Charles Edmondston built this house in the Federal style on Charleston's High Battery. About 13 years later, second owner Charles Alston began transforming it into the Greek Revival structure seen today. Tours of the home—furnished with family antiques, portraits, silver, and fine china—are informative. ⊠ *21 E. Battery, South of Broad* ☎ *843/722–7171* ⊕ *www. edmondstonalston.com* ⌸ *$12; $49 ticket includes Middleton Place* ☉ *Tues.–Sat. 10–4:30, Sun. 1–4:30.*

PAT CONROY'S CHARLESTON

South Carolina's famed writer Pat Conroy describes Charleston in his 2009 novel, *South of Broad*: "I carry the delicate porcelain beauty of Charleston like the hinged-shell of some soft-tissued mollusk. . . . In its shadows you can find metal work as delicate as lace . . . it's not a high-kicking, glossy lipstick city."

"I know of no more magical place in America than Charleston's South of Broad," Conroy tells Fodor's. "I remember seeing this area near the Battery when I was a kid and I was stunned as to how beautiful it was. In meeting with my Doubleday publisher about writing this latest book, now entitled *South of Broad,* which is set there, she wanted to understand the big draw of this neighborhood. I said, 'It is the most beautiful area of this gorgeous city. It is what the Upper East Side is to Manhattan, what Pacific Heights is to San Francisco, or what Beverly Hills is to Los Angeles.' SOB is mysterious. It keeps drawing you back like a magnetic force. I am fortunate that my writer friend

Anne Rivers Siddons lets me stay in her carriage house there when I come to town. As a cadet at The Citadel, I would walk along the Battery and watch the ships come in and out of port. They looked so close you thought you could touch them."

Conroy talks of other Charleston favorites: "When my children come to town, I go to the aquarium with my grandchildren. It is small enough to take in. Aquariums always make me believe in God. Why? You see the incredible shapes of things and the myriad capacity for different forms of animals. And there is that wonderful outdoor area where you can look at the fish tanks and then look out to the river and see porpoises playing.

"Thanks to Mayor Riley [the city's mayor for more than 35 years], who has been like Pericles for Charleston, there are so many parks and open spaces. Waterfront Park is a great example.

"And one of the true joys of Charleston in these last decades is its restaurant renaissance."

Magnolia Cemetery. Ancient oak trees drip Spanish moss over funerary sculptures and magnificent mausoleums in this cemetery on the Cooper River. It opened in 1850, beautifully landscaped (thanks to the rural cemetery movement of the era) with paths, ponds, and lush lawns. The people of Charleston came not only to pay respects to the deceased, but also for picnicking and family outings. Similarly, visitors still find joy in the natural surroundings—and intrigue in the elaborate structures marking the graves of many prominent South Carolinians. All three crews of mariners who died aboard Civil War sub the *H.L. Hunley* are buried here, and more than 850 Confederate servicemen rest in the Soldiers' Ground. Walking maps are available in the front office. ⊠ *70 Cunnington Ave.* ☎ *843/722–8638* ⊕ *www. magnoliacemetery.net* ⊠ *Free* ⊙ *Daily 8–5.*

FAMILY **Old Exchange Building and Provost Dungeon.** Built as a customs house in 1771, this building once served as the commercial and social center of Charleston. It was the site of many historic events, including the state's ratification of the Constitution in 1788 and two grand celebrations hosted for George Washington (he remarked in his diary that 256 elegant ladies attended the ball). However, the place was also used by the British to house prisoners during the Revolutionary War, an ordeal detailed in one of the exhibits. Costumed interpreters bring history to life on guided tours, and kids are fascinated by the period mannequins on display in the dungeon. ⊠ *122 E. Bay St., South of Broad* ☎ *843/727–2165* ⊕ *www.oldexchange.org* ⊠ *$9* ⊙ *Daily 9–5.*

MOUNT PLEASANT AND VICINITY

East of Charleston, across the beautiful Arthur Ravenel Jr. Bridge, is the town of Mount Pleasant, named not for a mountain but for a plantation founded there in the early 18th century. In its Old Village neighborhood are antebellum homes and a sleepy, old-time town center with a drugstore where patrons still amble up to the soda fountain and lunch counter for egg-salad sandwiches and floats. Along Shem Creek, where the local fishing fleet brings in the daily catch, several seafood restaurants serve some of the area's freshest (and most deftly fried) seafood. Other attractions in the area include military and maritime museums, a plantation, and, farther north, the Cape Romain National Wildlife Refuge.

TOP ATTRACTIONS

★ Fodor'sChoice **Boone Hall Plantation and Gardens.** A drive through
FAMILY a ½-mile-long live-oak alley draped in Spanish moss introduces you to this still-functioning plantation, the oldest of its kind. Tours take you through the 1936 mansion, the butterfly pavilion, and the heirloom rose garden. Eight slave

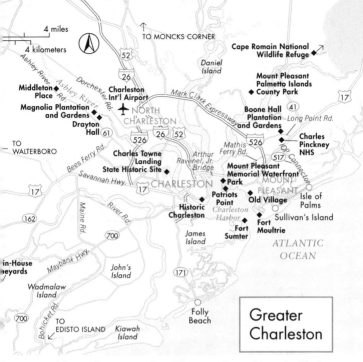

Greater Charleston

cabins on the property have been transformed into the Black History in America exhibit, displaying life-size figures, recorded narratives, audiovisual presentations, photos, and historical relics. Seasonal Gullah culture performances in the theater are perennial crowd favorites. Stroll along the winding river, or pluck in-season fruits (like strawberries, peaches, and pumpkins) from the fields. Across the highway is Boone Hall's Farm Market, with fresh local produce, a café, and a gift shop. *North and South, Queen,* and Nicholas Sparks's *The Notebook* were filmed here. ■TIP→ **Plan your visit to coincide with annual events like the Lowcountry Oyster Festival in January or the Scottish Games and Highland Gathering in September.** ⊠ *1235 Long Point Rd., off U.S. 17 N, Mount Pleasant, Charleston* ☎ *843/884–4371* ⊕ *www. boonehallplantation.com* ☝ *$20* ⊘ *Early May–Labor Day, Mon.–Sat. 8:30–6:30, Sun. noon–5; Labor Day–Dec., Mon.–Sat. 9–5, Sun. noon–5.*

FAMILY **Fort Moultrie.** A part of the Fort Sumter National Monument, this is the site where Colonel William Moultrie's South Carolinians repelled a British assault in one of the first patriot victories of the Revolutionary War. Completed in 1809, the fort is the third fortress on this site on Sullivan's

Island, 10 miles southeast of Charleston. Set across the street, the companion museum is an unsung hero. Although much is made of Fort Sumter, this smaller historical site is creatively designed, with figurines in various uniforms that make military history come alive. A 20-minute educational film that spans several major wars tells the colorful history of the fort. There's also an exhibit focusing on the slave trade and Sullivan's Island's role in it. ■TIP→ **Plan to spend the day bicycling through Sullivan's Island, where you'll find a cluster of century-old beach houses.** ⊠ *1214 Middle St., Sullivan's Island* ☎ *843/883–3123* ⊕ *www.nps.gov/fosu* ⊠ *$3* ☉ *Daily 9–5.*

★ **Fodor's**Choice **Mount Pleasant Memorial Waterfront Park.** Sprawl-

FAMILY ing beneath the Ravenel Bridge, this beautifully landscaped green space invites lounging on the grass with views of Charleston Harbor. You can also take a path up to the bridge for a stroll. Find helpful info in the visitor center, chat with Gullah locals selling traditional baskets in the Sweetgrass Cultural Arts Pavilion, and spend a quiet moment listening to the waterfall in the Mount Pleasant War Memorial. Kids love the playground modeled after the Ravenel Bridge, and parents appreciate that it's fenced, with benches galore. A 1,250-foot-long pier stretches into the water—grab a milk shake from the Snack Bar and Tackle Shop and a seat on one of the double-sided swings to watch folks fishing for their supper. ⊠ *71 Harry Hallman Blvd.* ☎ *843/884–8517* ⊕ *www.comeonovermp.com* ☉ *Daily 6 am–11 pm.*

FAMILY **Patriots Point Naval and Maritime Museum.** Climb aboard the USS *Yorktown* aircraft carrier—which houses the Congressional Medal of Honor Museum—as well as the submarine USS *Clamagore* and the destroyer USS *Laffey*. A life-size replica of a Vietnam support base camp showcases naval air and watercraft used in that military action. ⊠ *40 Patriots Point Rd., Mount Pleasant, Charleston* ☎ *843/884–2727* ⊕ *www.patriotspoint.org* ⊠ *$20* ☉ *Daily 9–6:30; last tickets sold at 5.*

BASKET MAKERS. **Drive along U.S. 17 North, through and beyond Mount Pleasant, to find the "basket makers" set up at roadside stands, weaving the traditional sweetgrass, pine-straw, and palmetto-leaf baskets for which the area is known. Be braced for high prices, although baskets typically cost less on this stretch** than in downtown Charleston. Each purchase supports the artisans, whose numbers are dwindling year by year.

WORTH NOTING

Cape Romain National Wildlife Refuge. Maritime forests, barrier islands, salt marshes, beaches, and coastal waterways make up this 66,287-acre refuge established in 1932 as a migratory bird haven. The **Sewee Visitor & Environmental Education Center** has information and exhibits on the property and its trails, as well as an outdoor enclosure housing four endangered red wolves. The refuge is aiding the recovery of the threatened loggerhead sea turtle, and a video details the work. ■TIP→ **From the mainland refuge, you can take a $40 ferry ride to Bulls Island.** ⊠ *Sewee Center, 5821 U.S. 17 N, Awendaw* ☎ *843/928–3368* ⊕ *www.fws.gov/caperomain* ☞ *Free* ☉ *Wed.–Sat. 9–5.*

Charles Pinckney National Historic Site. This site includes the last 28 acres of the plantation owned by Charles Pinckney, a drafter and signer of the U.S. Constitution. You can tour an 1820s coastal cottage, constructed after Pinckney's death, that features interpretive exhibits about the man, the Constitution, and slave life. A nature trail leads to the archaeological foundations of three slave houses. ⊠ *1254 Long Point Rd., off U.S. 17 N* ☎ *843/881–5516* ⊕ *www.nps.gov/chpi* ☞ *Free* ☉ *Daily 9–5.*

FAMILY **Mount Pleasant Palmetto Islands County Park.** With an observation tower, paved nature trails, and boardwalks extending over the marshes, this 943-acre park offers a day full of family fun. You can rent bicycles and pedal boats, set the kids loose in the playground, or pay an extra fee ($7.99) for entrance to the small Splash Island water park (open daily June through mid-August amd weekends in May and mid-August through Labor Day). ⊠ *444 Needlerush Pkwy.* ☎ *843/884–0832, 843/795–4386* ⊕ *www.charlestoncountyparks.com/picp* ☞ *$1* ☉ *Jan.–Apr. and Sept.–Dec., daily 8–sunset; May–Aug. daily 8–8.*

Old Village. The historic center of Mount Pleasant, this neighborhood is distinguished by white picket fences, storybook cottages, antebellum manses, tiny churches, and lavish waterfront homes. It's a lovely area for a stroll or bike ride, and Pitt Street offers a couple locally loved eateries and boutiques. Head south along Pitt Street to the Otis M. Pickett Bridge & Park, popular for picnicking, fishing, and sunset views. ⊠ *Pitt St. and Venning St.*

Cruising from Charleston

For almost 300 years Charleston, queen of port cities, has been primarily known for its commercial activity, but it recently became a port of embarkation for cruises. It started with two cruise lines and two ports of call. On today's port of call calendar you will see such names as Princess, Seabourne, Aida, and Carnival. Charleston's most frequent visitor is the *Carnival Fantasy,* going out year-round on five-, six-, and seven-day cruises.

City officials have gone to great lengths to accommodate the needs of cruise-line passengers, with plans in place for a grand new cruise terminal. Everyone should consider a pre- or post-cruise stay in Charleston, cited with several remarkable awards by cruisers, who have named the city one of the most romantic in the United States. Several hotels around the area offer free parking for the duration of their guests' cruise. For complete information on all ports of call, visit *www.scspa.com.*

WEST OF THE ASHLEY RIVER

Ashley River Road, Route 61, begins a few miles northwest of downtown Charleston, over the Ashley River Bridge. Sights are spread out along the way, and those who love history, old homes, and gardens may need several days to explore places like Drayton Hall, Middleton Place, and Magnolia Plantation and Gardens. Spring is a peak time for the flowers, although many of them are in bloom throughout the year.

TOP ATTRACTIONS

★ Fodor's Choice **Magnolia Plantation and Gardens.** Pick and choose
FAMILY from a variety of entertainments at Magnolia Plantation, established in the 1670s by Thomas Drayton after he moved from Barbados. The extensive garden—the oldest public one in the country—was begun in the late 17th century and has evolved into a Romantic-style green space overflowing with plants, including a vast array of azaleas and camellias, along with some themed areas (a biblical garden, for example). Take a train or boat to tour the grounds, or traverse more than 500 acres of trails by foot or bike (bring your own). The 60-acre Audubon Swamp Garden invites a good, long stroll on its network of boardwalks and bridges. Also here are a petting zoo, a nature center, and a reptile house. Five pre- and post-Emancipation cabins have been restored and serve as the

focal point of an interpreter-led tour called From Slavery to Freedom. And be sure to visit the 19th-century plantation house, which originally stood near Summerville. The home was taken apart, floated down the Ashley River, and reassembled here. ⊠ *3550 Ashley River Rd., West Ashley* ☎ *800/367–3517, 843/571–1266* ⊕ *www.magnoliaplantation.com* ⊠ *Grounds $15; house tour $8; tram $8; boat $8; From Slavery to Freedom exhibit $8* ⊗ *Apr.–Oct., daily 8–5:30; Nov.–Mar., daily 9–5.*

★ **Fodor's Choice Middleton Place.** This former plantation is home FAMILY to America's oldest landscaped gardens, begun in 1741 by Henry Middleton, second president of the First Continental Congress. From camellias to roses, blooms of all seasons form floral *allées* (alleys) along terraced lawns and around a pair of ornamental lakes that are shaped like butterfly wings. As for the house, a large part of the three-building residential complex was destroyed during the Civil War, but the "South flanker" that contained the gentlemen's guest quarters was restored. It now serves as a house museum, displaying impressive English silver, furniture, original paintings, and historic documents, including an early silk copy of the Declaration of Independence. In the stableyards, historic interpreters use authentic tools to demonstrate spinning, weaving, blacksmithing, and other skills from the plantation era. Heritage-breed farm animals, such as water buffalo and cashmere goats, are housed here, along with peacocks. If all this leaves you feeling peckish, head over to the cozy Middleton Place Restaurant for excellent Lowcountry specialties for lunch and dinner. Dinner guests can walk the gardens and stableyards from 5 until dusk. There is also a high-end (but not overpriced) museum gift shop that carries local arts and crafts, plus a Garden Market and Nursery with a lunch café. You can stay overnight at the contemporary Inn at Middleton Place, where floor-to-ceiling windows splendidly frame the Ashley River. Kayaking excursions depart from the inn, and the Middleton Equestrian Center offers trail rides. ⊠ *4300 Ashley River Rd., West Ashley* ☎ *800/782–3608, 843/556–6020* ⊕ *www.middletonplace.org* ⊠ *General admission $29, house tour $15, carriage tours $18; $49 combination ticket includes Edmonston-Alston House* ⊗ *Gardens daily 9–5; house museum Mon. noon–4:30, Tues.–Sun. 10– 4:30.*

WORTH NOTING

FAMILY **Charles Towne Landing State Historic Site.** There's plenty to see and do in this park marking the original 1670 settlement of Charles Towne, the first permanent European settlement in South Carolina. Begin with the visitor center's 12-room, interactive museum and exhibit hall that tells the history of Charles Towne. Kids will make a beeline for the Adventure, Charleston's only replica of the colonists' 17th-century tall ship. The park is threaded with paths through a wooded area that lead to the marshes, creek, and an Animal Forest where you can view a black bear, bobcat, bison, and more. All in all, there are 80 acres of gardens, including an elegant live oak alley. To best experience the site, take the $5 audio tour along the history trail. ✉ *1500 Old Towne Rd.* ☎ *843/852–4200* ⊕ *www.charlestownelanding.travel* 🎟 *$10* ⊗ *Daily 9–5.*

Drayton Hall. Considered the nation's finest example of Palladian-inspired architecture, Drayton Hall is the only plantation house on the Ashley River to have survived the Civil War intact. A National Trust Historic Site built between 1738 and 1742, it's an invaluable lesson in history as well as in architecture. The home has been left unfurnished to highlight the original plaster moldings, opulent hand-carved woodwork, and other ornamental details. Regular tours, with guides known for their in-depth knowledge, depart on the half hour and paint a vivid picture of the people who once inhabited this fabled house. Visitors can also see the African American cemetery and even take part in the 45-minute "Connections" program that uses maps and historic documents to trace the story of Africans from their journey to America, through slavery, and into the 20th century. ✉ *3380 Ashley River Rd., West Ashley* ☎ *843/769–2600* ⊕ *www.draytonhall.org* 🎟 *$20* ⊗ *Mon.–Sat. 9–3:30, Sun. 11–3:30.*

Irvin~House Vineyards. Located in idyllic countryside 40 minutes from downtown Charleston, Irvin~House boasts 11 acres of vineyards. Today it offers five varietals, all of which you can taste for $5 in the winery. Just across the patio is the owners' Firefly Distillery, which achieved notoriety for its sweet-tea vodka deftly seasoned with tea from a Low-country plantation. Sample this and their other vodkas for $6 in a barn that's also outfitted with everything country, from fried peanuts to preserves. ✉ *6775 Bears Bluff Rd., Wadmalaw Island* ☎ *843/559–6867* ⊕ *www.charlestonwine.com* 🎟 *Free* ⊗ *Tues.–Sat. 10–5.*

CLOSE UP

Charleston Preserved

When the Civil War ended in 1865, Charleston was left battered and bruised—both physically and economically. And because locals had little money for building new homes and businesses in the coming decades, they made do with those they had, effectively saving from destruction the grand structures seen today. As development in the city began to pick up in the early 1900s, many of these historic buildings could have been lost were it not for the spirit of community activism that sprang into being in the 1920s.

According to Jonathan Poston, author of *Buildings of Charleston,* the preservation movement took off when an Esso gas station was slated to take the place of the Joseph Manigault House. Irate citizens formed the Society for the Preservation of Old Dwellings (the first such group in the nation), whose efforts managed to save what is now a vastly popular house museum. By 1931, Charleston's City Council had created the Board of Architectural Review and placed a designated historic district under its protection as a means of controlling unrestrained development—two more national firsts. The Historic Charleston Foundation was established in 1947, and preservation is now second nature (by law).

As you explore, look for Charleston single houses: one room wide, they were built with the narrow end streetside with multistory Southern porches (called piazzas) to catch prevailing breezes. Wide-open windows allow the cool air that drifts across these shaded porches to enter the homes.

You'll see numerous architectural vestiges of the past on homes situated along Charleston's preserved streets. Many houses have plaques detailing their history; some exhibit Carolopolis Awards, which were received for responsible stewardship of historic architecture. Old fire insurance plaques are rarer; they denote the company that insured the home and that would extinguish the flames if a fire broke out. Notice the "earthquake bolts"—some in the shape of circles or stars and others capped with lion heads—that dot house facades along the Battery. These are attached to iron rods installed in the house to reinforce it after the great earthquake of 1886. Note also the iron spikes along the top of residential gates, doors, walls, and windows. Serving the same purpose as razor wire seen today atop prison fences, most of these *chevaux de frises* (French for "Frisian horses") were added to deter break-ins—or escapes—after a thwarted 1822 slave rebellion.

SIDE TRIPS FROM CHARLESTON

Gardens, parks, and the great outdoors are good reasons to travel a bit farther afield for day trips. As Charleston and the surrounding suburbs—particularly Mount Pleasant—keep on growing, it is good to know that Southern country towns still exist in the vicinity. Sit out on a screen porch after some good home cooking, paddle around a haunting cypress swamp, and take a hike through the towering pines of the Francis Marion National Forest. If the closest you have ever been to an abbey is watching *The Sound of Music,* you can visit Mepkin Abbey and see the simplicity of the religious life. Along the way, turn off the air-conditioning, breathe in the fresh air, and enjoy the natural beauty of these less-touristed parts of South Carolina.

MONCKS CORNER

30 miles northwest of Charleston on U.S. 52.

This town is a gateway to a number of attractions in Santee Cooper Country. Named for the two rivers that form a 171,000-acre basin, the area brims with outdoor pleasures centered on the basin and nearby Lakes Marion and Moultrie.

ESSENTIALS

Visitor Information **Santee Cooper Counties Promotion Commission and Visitors Center** ✉ *9302 Old Hwy. 6, Santee* P*803/854–2131* ⊕ *www.santeecoopercountry.org* ⊙ *Daily 8:30–4:30.*

EXPLORING

Cypress Gardens. Explore the inky swamp waters of this natural area in a flat-bottom boat, or walk along paths lined with moss-draped cypress trees, azaleas, camellias, daffodils, wisteria, and dogwoods. You can marvel at the clouds of butterflies in the butterfly house. The swamp garden was created from what was once the freshwater reserve of the vast Dean Hall rice plantation. The site is about 24 miles north of Charleston via U.S. 52, between Goose Creek and Moncks Corner. ✉ *3030 Cypress Gardens Rd.* ☎ *843/553–0515* ⊕ *www.cypressgardens.info* 🎫 *$10* ⊙ *Daily 9–5; last admission at 4.*

Francis Marion National Forest. Pack a picnic and your fishing poles, or hit the hiking, biking, horseback-riding, and motorbike trails in 260,000 acres of swamps, lakes, oaks, and pines. A canoe is a great way to see the natural landscape. ✉ *Francis Marion National Forest Ranger Station, 2967 Steed Creek Rd., Huger* ☎ *843/336–2200* ⊕ *www. fs.usda.gov/scnfs* ✆ *Free* ⊙ *Hrs vary by area.*

Mepkin Abbey. This active Trappist monastery overlooking the Cooper River is on the site of the former plantation home of Henry Laurens. It was later the home of noted publisher Henry Luce and his wife Clare Boothe Luce, who commissioned renowned landscape architect Loutrell Briggs to design a garden in 1937. That garden remains a stunning place for a serene walk or contemplative rest on a waterfront bench. You can take a guided tour of the church or even stay here for a spiritual retreat in the sleek, modern facility with individual rooms and private baths. Hearing the monks sing during their normal daily routine and attending the annual Piccolo Spoleto Festival concerts here are peaceful and spiritual experiences. The gift shop sells mushrooms and garden compost from the abbey's farm as well as candies, preserves, and creamed honey from other Trappist abbeys. ✉ *1098 Mepkin Abbey Rd., off Dr. Evans Rd.* ☎ *843/761–8509* ⊕ *www.mepkinabbey. org* ✆ *Free, tour brochure $5* ⊙ *Tues.–Sat. 9–4, Sun. 1–3. Tours Tues.–Sat. at 11:30 and 3 (no tours offered first Fri. of each month).*

FAMILY **Old Santee Canal Park.** Venture into the Charleston area's past at Old Santee Canal Park. Four miles of boardwalks and unpaved paths take you through Biggin Swamp and along the last portion of the country's first true canal. Prefer to explore by boat? Rent a canoe for $3 per half hour. An interpretive center details the history of the canal, which was used to transport goods from upstate South Carolina to the port of Charleston for the first half of the 19th century. The circa-1840 Stony Landing Plantation House is furnished with period reproductions, offering a glimpse into what a planter's secondary home might have been like in that era. Also on-site (and included in admission) is the Berkeley County Museum and Heritage Center, which tells the story of the county's cultural and natural history. ✉ *900 Stony Landing Rd., off Rembert C. Dennis Blvd.* ☎ *843/899–5200* ⊕ *www.oldsanteecanalpark. org* ✆ *$3* ⊙ *Daily 9–5; buildings close at 4:30.*

EDISTO ISLAND

44 miles southwest of Charleston via U.S. 17 and Rte. 174.

On rural Edisto (pronounced *ed*-is-toh) Island, find magnificent stands of age-old oaks festooned with Spanish-moss borders, quiet streams, and side roads; wild turkeys may still be spotted on open grasslands and amid palmetto palms. Twisting tidal creeks, populated with egrets and herons, wind around golden marsh grass. A big day on the island may include shelling and shark-tooth hunting.

The small "downtown" beachfront is a mix of public beach-access spots, restaurants, and old, shabby-chic beach homes that are a far cry from the palatial villas rented out on other area islands. The outlying Edisto Beach State Park is a pristine wilderness and camper's delight. There are a number of privately owned rental accommodations—condos, villas, and homes—and Wyndham Ocean Ridge Resort offers time-share units that can be rented when available. None are on the beach, however.

GETTING HERE AND AROUND

Edisto is connected to the mainland by a causeway. The only way here is by private car.

ESSENTIALS

Visitor Information Edisto Island Chamber of Commerce ✉ *430 Hwy. 174* ☎ *843/869–3867* ⊕ *www.edistochamber.com* ☉ *Weekdays 9–5.*

TOURS

Edisto Watersports & Tackle. Hop aboard one of Edisto Watersports & Tackle's two-hour sunset river cruises through the beautiful Ace Basin. With commentary on history and wildlife offered up along the way, the tour on a 24-foot Carolina Skiff costs $40. You can also charter a fishing boat, pick up an Otter Island shelling excursion, or opt for a kayak tour. ✉ *3731 Docksite Rd.* ☎ *843/869–0663* ⊕ *www.edistowatersports.net.*

The Pink Van Tour. An Edisto native leads tours full of history and facts entertainingly told. There are multiple stops of interest, from historic churches to a plantation, and the cost is $20 for 2½ hours. ✉ *Mains Market, 1084 Hwy. 174* ☎ *843/603–0967.*

EXPLORING

FAMILY **Edisto Beach.** Edisto's south side has 4 miles of public beach. At its western end, the beach faces St. Helena Sound and has smaller waves. There is beach access at each intersection along Palmetto Boulevard and free public parking along the road. The beach itself has narrowed because of erosion, so it's best to time your visit for low tide. These clean coastal waters teem with both fish and shellfish, and it's common to see people throwing cast nets for shrimp. It's a great beach for beachcombing. Alcohol is allowed as long as it is not in glass containers. There's little shade and no food stands, so be sure to pack snacks. **Amenities:** none. **Best for:** solitude; sunset; swimming. ⌂ *Palmetto Blvd., from Coral St. to Yacht Club Rd., Edisto Beach* ⊕ *www. townofedistobeach.com.*

★ **Fodor's**Choice **Edisto Beach State Park.** This 1,255-acre park
FAMILY includes a 1½-mile-long beachfront with some of the area's best shelling, marshland, and tidal rivers, and a lush maritime forest with a 7-mile trail running through it. The trail is hard-packed shell sand, suitable for bikes and wheelchairs. Overnight options include seven rustic, furnished cabins by the marsh. The park stays extremely busy, so you have to reserve these as far as 11 months in advance. The small ranger station has some fishing poles to lend and firewood for sale. Pets on leashes are allowed. The park's Environmental Learning Center is an entertaining way to explore the natural history of Edisto Island and the surrounding ACE Basin. ⌂ *8377 State Cabin Rd.* ☎ *843/869–2156* ⊕ *www.southcarolinaparks.com* ⌷ *$5* ⊙ *Daily 8–6.*

FAMILY **Edisto Island Serpentarium.** This top-notch operation features an indoor display of snakes from around the world, plus a meandering outdoor garden with habitats for snakes, turtles, and alligators. Educational programs and alligator feedings enrich the experience, and kids love the gift shop. Call ahead, as hours vary. ⌂ *1374 Hwy. 174* ☎ *843/869– 1171* ⊕ *www.edistoserpentarium.com* ⌷ *$13.95* ⊙ *Mon.– Sat. 10–6.*

Geechie Boy Market and Mill. Driving down Highway 174, look out for a giant red roadside chair. It welcomes folks to stop for a photo op and a trip inside a vintage-style grocery selling Geechie Boy's stone-ground cornmeal and grits (which you'll find served in many a fine Charleston restaurant). A 1945 grits separator presides over one side of the store; catch it in action during demos given on Saturday from 2 to 4. You can buy fresh produce from the family farm, tractor-churned ice cream, and cornmeal donuts. Crafts by area artists, cookbooks, and other gifts round out the offerings. ✉ *2995 Hwy. 174* ☎ *843/209–5220* ⊕ *www.geechieboymill.com* ⊘ *Mon.–Sat. 9–5.*

MYSTERY TREE. Truly unique, this tree across the highway (Route 174) from the entrance to Botany Bay Plantation is wildly decorated according to the season. A mystery person who prefers to be anonymous changes the tree's decorations during the night.

WHERE TO EAT

$$$ ✕ **Old Post Office Restaurant.** *Southern.* The old metal cages remain at this converted post office, but instead of mail you'll find Southern-inspired fare from Chef Cherry Smalls. Try the cherrywood-smoked Atlantic salmon with a sour cream and mustard-caper sauce for a taste of heaven. Local wild-caught shrimp are paired with grits for a classic Lowcountry dish. When there's a piano man in the upstairs bar, so much the better. $ *Average main: $24* ✉ *1442 Hwy. 174* ☎ *843/869–2339* ⊕ *www.theoldpostofficerestaurant.com* ⚇ *Reservations essential* ⊘ *Closed Sun. and Mon. No lunch. Closed in Jan.*

$ ✕ **Po' Pigs Bo-B-Q.** *Southern.* Step inside the Deep South at this restaurant—now in a spacious new location—for pork barbecue that's earned the attention of foodies from around the country. Sample the different sauces (sweet, mustard, tomato, or vinegar) and wash it all down with a tall glass of sweet tea. The buffet line is all about down-home sides like squash casserole, pork skins, lima beans and ham, creamed corn, and hushpuppies. The pulled turkey is a good option for those who prefer something more heart healthy. $ *Average main: $10* ✉ *487 Hwy. 174* ☎ *843/869–9003.*

$$$ ✕ **Pressley's at the Marina.** *Seafood.* To enjoy a meal with a view, head to this waterfront spot. The dinner menu (also available at lunch if you want more than tacos, sandwiches, or wraps) offers up fare from land and sea alike. Start off with hushpuppies served with sweet honey butter and a bowl of she-crab soup, then move on to the Edisto Creek shrimp basket or the fresh catch of the day. The deck opens for dinner, and there's live music on the weekends. Add a specialty cocktail to start and a slice of key lime pie to finish and you have vacation dining done right. $ *Average main: $20* ✉ *3702 Docksite Rd.* ☎ *843/869–9226* ⊕ *www.pressleysatthemarina.com* ⊘ *No lunch Mon. and Tues.*

WHERE TO STAY

$$ [H] **Prudential-Kapp/Lyons Realty.** *Rental.* Prudential's inventory of privately owned beach homes ranges from a two-bedroom apartment over a gallery to one-bedroom condos and six-bedroom manses smack on the beach. **Pros:** excellent staff is known for their efficiency, caring, and Southern hospitality; sparkling-clean, well-maintained properties; wide diversity of offerings. **Cons:** properties do not have resort amenities; if you are a group of singles looking to rent a hard-core party house, go elsewhere; units require that you empty your own trash and put away all dishes or be fined. [$] *Rooms from: $170* ✉ *440 Hwy. 174* ☎ *843/869–2516, 800/945–9667* 🌐 *www.kapplyons.com* 🛏 *160 units.*

$$$ [H] **Wyndham Ocean Ridge Resort.** *Resort.* If you're looking for high-end amenities in a get-away-from-it-all escape, you've found it here, at the only resort on the island. **Pros:** great choice for golfers; wonderful beach cabana; atmosphere is laid-back, unpretentious. **Cons:** no daily housekeeping services; hard to book at peak times; many units come with two to three flights of stairs. [$] *Rooms from: $219* ✉ *1 King Cotton Rd., Edisto Beach* ☎ *843/869–4516, 800/909–6155 for reservations* 🌐 *www.wyndhamoceanridge.com* 🛏 *250 units* 🍴 *No meals.*

SPORTS AND THE OUTDOORS

BIKING

Island Bikes & Outfitters. Since 1990, Island Bikes & Outfitters has been renting bikes to vacationers. Owners Sonya and Tony Spainhour will arm you with a map, orient you to the bike trails, and advise you on how to reach the section of the park that has a boardwalk network for bikers and hikers. Delivery is available. In addition, you can rent golf carts, kayaks, canoes, and paddleboards and buy bait. They sell beachwear, visors, boogie boards, beach chairs, and more. ✉ *140 Jungle Rd.* ☎ *843/869–4444* 🌐 *islandbikesandoutfitters.com* 🕓 *Mon.–Sat. 9–5, Sun. 9–noon.*

GOLF

The Plantation Course at Edisto. Sculpted from maritime forest by architect Tom Jackson in 1974, this course mirrors the physical beauty of the island's Lowcountry landscape. Although it's located within the island's only resort, Wyndham Ocean Ridge, it operates as a public course with memberships. The moderate rates are the same for all seasons, with special three-day cards and weekly unlimited-rounds specials. It offers pick-up service within the resort and from the nearby marina. ✉ *19 Fairway Dr.* ☎ *843/869–1111* ⊕ *www.theplantationcourseatedisto.com* ⛳ *$55–$65* ⛳ *18 holes, 6200 yards, par 70.*

WALTERBORO

44 miles west of Charleston via U.S. 17 and U.S. 64.

"Welcome Back to Let's Remember." This sleepy Southern town makes Charleston look like Manhattan. Its main drag, East Washington Street, still looks like it did in the 1950s. While continuing to embrace its endearing small-town ways, it is moving in a new, savvy direction. To wit, its marketing slogan is "Walterboro, the front porch of the Lowcountry," with a cherry-red rocking chair as its logo. Those rocking chairs can be found outside shops and restaurants, inviting passersby to sit awhile.

Walterboro has become a fun day trip for Charlestonians. The South Carolina Artisans Center has become a major draw, as have the moderately priced antiques and collectible stores. The annual events, which for decades included the Rice Festival on the last weekend in April and the Fall Plantation Tour in October, have been augmented by the Edisto Riverfest on the second weekend in June, the Walterboro Antiques, History & Arts Festival in mid-May, and the Downtown Walterboro Criterium International Bike Race in early May. A proliferation of inexpensive motels like Days Inn sprang up near the interstate, then limited-service chain hotels like Hampton Inn. Travelers wanting more local flavor opt for the homey bed-and-breakfasts in restored houses in the Historic District.

GETTING HERE AND AROUND
The downtown area is walkable and the town is great for bicycling, especially in the Walterboro Wildlife Sanctuary. There are no bike-rental shops, although some B&Bs do supply bikes.

ESSENTIALS
Walterboro-Colleton Chamber of Commerce ✉ *109C Benson St., Walterboro* ☎ *843/549–9595* ⊕ *www.walterboro.org* ⊙ *Weekdays 9–5.* **Walterboro Welcome Center** ✉ *1273 Sniders Hwy., Walterboro* ☎ *843/538–4353* ⊕ *www.walterborosc.org* ⊙ *Mon.–Sat. 9–5.*

2

EXPLORING

Colleton Museum & Farmers Market. This museum chronicles the history of a small Southern town, displaying everything from butter churns to the country's first anesthesia machine. Particularly charming is the small chapel complete with stained glass, pews, and century-old wedding gowns. There's a farmers' market outside on Tuesday and Saturday. ✉ *506 E. Washington St., Walterboro* ☎ *843/549–2303* 🌐 *www.colletoncounty.org* 🎟 *Free* 🕒 *Tues. noon–6, Wed.–Fri. 10–5, Sat. 10–2.*

Hiott's Pharmacy. Hiott's Pharmacy is one of those delightful throwbacks—a drug store with a soda fountain where the news of the day is discussed and young people share a Coca-Cola float. You can get a pimento cheese on white bread for $1.90. If you want a malted milk to go with it, that'll cost you $2.50. ✉ *373 E. Washington St., Walterboro* ☎ *843/549–7222* 🕒 *Weekdays 9–6, Sat. 9–1.*

Walterboro Wildlife Sanctuary. Boardwalks and hiking, biking, and canoe trails weave through this lovely 600-acre park. One of the paths traces the colonial-era Charleston-to-Savannah Stagecoach Road, where you can still see the cypress remnants of historic bridges. Serious hikers bring their gear and spend hours. It's a Southern swamp, so douse yourself with insect repellent and be on alert for reptiles. ✉ *399 Detreville St., Walterboro* ☎ *843/538–4353* 🌐 *www.walterborosc.org* 🎟 *Free* 🕒 *Daily dawn–dusk.*

South Carolina Artisans Center. This lovely center is a showcase for more than 250 South Carolina artists. Look for jewelry, sculptures, glass, woodwork, and more. The loomed shawls and silk scarves make great gifts, and the sweetgrass baskets are treasures. ✉ *318 Wichman St., Walterboro* ☎ *843/549–0011* 🌐 *www.scartisanscenter.com* 🎟 *Free* 🕒 *Mon–Sat. 9–5, Sun. 1–5.*

WHERE TO EAT AND STAY

$$$ ✕ **Carmine's Trattoria.** *Italian.* Although some locals call it the "fancy place," the only high-end furnishing is a baby grand, which is tickled by pianists on Friday and Saturday nights. Local clams come in a red tomato sauce, and the veal Marsala with fresh mushrooms is a tender treat. Lunch offerings include salads, panini, and pastas. [$] *Average main: $20* ✉ *242 E. Washington St., Walterboro* ☎ *843/782–3248* 🕒 *Closed Sun. No lunch Fri. and Sat.*

$ 🍴 **Main Street Grille.** *American.* Grab a window seat at this casual spot for a pleasant view of East Washington Street while you dig into shrimp and stone-ground grits, a Philly-style cheesesteak, or a juicy burger on a kaiser roll. Desserts like bourbon pecan pie are house made and served in generous portions. [$] *Average main: $12* ✉ *256 E. Washington St., Walterboro* ☎ *843/782–4774* 🕒 *Closed Sun. No lunch weekdays.*

$ 🏨 **The Hampton House Bed & Breakfast.** *B&B/Inn.* Built in 1912 by the patriarch of the prominent Fishburne family, this B&B has all of the accoutrements of a Lowcountry mansion, from its high ceilings to the charming literary nook, as well as modern-day luxuries like a crescent-shaped pool and a tennis court. **Pros:** caring and hospitable owners; small dogs allowed for extra fee; a must for doll lovers. **Cons:** not ideal for those seeking privacy; some areas could use a bit of freshening. [$] *Rooms from: $125* ✉ *500 Hampton St., Walterboro* ☎ *843/542–9498* 🌐 *www.hamptonhousebandb.com* 🛏 *3 rooms* 💳 *No credit cards* 🍽 *Breakfast.*

$ 🏨 **Nine O'Seven.** *B&B/Inn.* With hardwood floors, soaring ceilings, and an elongated front porch, this 1920s Walterboro cottage demonstrates excellent taste in its traditional decor. **Pros:** good value; exquisite interior decor; classy proprietress. **Cons:** no credit cards; relatively small house; long walk to downtown Washington Street. [$] *Rooms from: $75* ✉ *907 Hampton St., Walterboro* ☎ *843/542–2943* 🌐 *www.nineoseven.com* 🛏 *3 rooms, 1 suite* 💳 *No credit cards* 🍽 *Breakfast.*

SHOPPING

Bachelor Hill Antiques. David Evans displays an eclectic mix of fine furnishings, antiques, art, and '50s finds in inspiring roomlike tableaux. The fair prices mean items here move fast. In the back, a separate store called DIG (an acronym for "Design. Interiors. Gardens"), sells terrariums, garden statuary, wind chimes, and home accessories. ✉ *255 E. Washington St., Walterboro* ☎ *843/549–1300* 🌐 *www.bachelorhillantiques.com* 🕒 *Mon.–Sat. 9–6, Sun. 9–4.*

Choice Collectibles. On the site of the former Ritz Theater, Choice Collectibles is as retro as the sign for the theater's box office displayed over the cash register. You could get lost in time perusing the fascinating and inexpensive finds from decades past. ✉ *329 E. Washington St., Walterboro* ☎ *843/549–2617* 🕒 *Mon.–Sat. 9–5.*

WHERE TO EAT IN CHARLESTON

Updated
by Kinsey
Gidick

AS FAR AS FOOD IS CONCERNED, it's hard to beat Charleston. The city has been blessed with a bevy of Southern-inflected selections, from barbecue parlors to fish shacks to casual places serving Lowcountry fare like shrimp and grits. And if you'd like to sample something new, there are plenty of places serving updated versions of classic dishes. Before you leave, you'll definitely see why Charleston is considered one of the great food cities in the world.

And the city's status continues to rise, boosted by a group of James Beard Foundation repeat award winners. Robert Stehling of Hominy Grill, Mike Lata of FIG, and Sean Brock of Husk each earned the designation of Best Chef in the Southeast, in successive years. But the city boasts other prodigious talents, too: Jeremiah Bacon of the Macintosh, Craig Diehl of Cypress, Michelle Weaver of Charleston Grill, Ken Vedrinski of Trattoria Lucca, Frank Lee of Slightly North of Broad, Nico Romo of Fish, Josh Keeler of Two Boroughs Larder, and Jash Walker of Xiao Bao Biscuit. It's the establishment of the New South, circa now.

As for attire, Charleston invites a crisp yet casual atmosphere. Don't forget, Charleston was recognized as the Most Mannerly City in the union by Marjabelle Young Stewart. Which means that residents are slow to judge (or, at the least, that they're doing so very quietly). But on the whole, the city encourages comfort and unhurried, easy pacing. The result is an idyllic setting in which to enjoy oysters on the half shell and other homegrown delicacies from the land and sea that jointly grant the city its impressive culinary standing.

PRICES

Fine dining in Charleston can be expensive. One option to keep costs down might be to try several of the small plates that many establishments offer. To save money, drive over the bridges or go to the islands, including James and Johns islands.

WHAT IT COSTS				
	$	**$$**	**$$$**	**$$$$**
Restaurants	under $15	$15–$19	$20–$24	over $24

Restaurant prices are for a main course at dinner, not including taxes (7.5% on food, 8.5% tax on liquor).

NORTH OF BROAD

$$ 🍴 **39 Rue de Jean.** *French.* With a backdrop of classic French-bistro style—gleaming wood, cozy booths, and white-papered tables—Charleston's trendy set wines and dines until the wee hours here on such favorites as steamed mussels in a half dozen preparations. Order them with *pomme frites,* as the French do. Each night of the week there's a special, such as the popular bouillabaisse on Sunday. Rabbit with a whole-grain mustard sauce was so popular it jumped to the nightly menu, while the burgers have a well-established following. If you're seeking quiet, ask for a table in the dining room on the right. It's noisy—but so much fun—at the bar, especially since it has some of the city's best bartenders. [$] *Average main: $18* ✉ *39 John St., Upper King* ☎ *843/722–8881* 🌐 *www.39ruedejean.com* ✍ *Reservations essential.*

3

$$ 🍴 **Alluette's Cafe.** *Southern.* Alluette Jones has coined a new genre of cuisine—"holistic soul food"—which she prepares at her eponymous restaurant. It's simple, fresh, local, and organic, drawing from Geechee-Gullah origins, and has earned well-deserved praise. And guess what? You won't be able to find any pork products here. Her hearty soups (lima bean, for instance) contain nary a trace of the traditional Southern accoutrement: ham hock. Plus, Alluette cooks some of the city's best fried shrimp, which arrive butterflied and lightly battered after simmering in organic oil. It's a pleasant, newfound perspective on Southern food. [$] *Average main: $15* ✉ *80 Reid St.* ☎ *843/577–6926* 🌐 *www.alluettes.com.*

★ Fodor'sChoice 🍴 **Basil.** *Asian.* There's a reason that this corner

$$ restaurant in the heart of downtown has been lauded again and again for its Asian fare. Dinner hours generate extended wait times—no reservations allowed—as patrons angle for an outdoor or window table. From the exposed glassed-in kitchen emerge popular specialties such as *tom aban talay,* a hot-and-sour mixed seafood soup flavored with Kaffir lime leaves, lemongrass, and button mushrooms; red curry duck, a boneless half bird, deep-fried; and the tilapia served with shrimp and ginger sauce. And seriously, don't fret over the line. It's always worth the wait. But if you're farther afield, try hitting Basil's other location in Mount Pleasant. [$] *Average main: $16* ✉ *460 King St., Upper King* ☎ *843/724–3490* 🌐 *www.eatatbasil.com.*

$$$$ 🍴 **Blossom.** *Southern.* Exposed rafters, wood-paneled walls, and unadorned tables make this place casual and yet upscale. The terrace has a view of St. Philip's majestic spire, and the dining room and bar are heavily populated

Where to Eat in Downtown Charleston

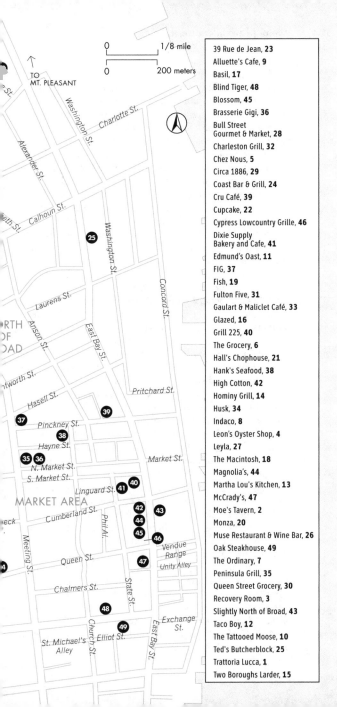

TO MT. PLEASANT

0   1/8 mile

0   200 meters

Charlotte St.

Washington St.

Charlotte St.

St.

Alexander St.

Calhoun St.

eth St.

Washington St.

Laurens St.

Concord St.

RTH
OF
DAD

Anson St.

East Bay St.

ntworth St.

Hasell St.

Pritchard St.

Pinckney St.

Hayne St.

N. Market St.

S. Market St.

Linguard St.

MARKET AREA

Cumberland St.

eck

Phil Al.

Meeting St.

Queen St.

Chalmers St.

State St.

Church St.

St. Michael's
Alley

Elliot St.

East Bay St.

Exchange St.

Vendue Range

Unity Alley

39 Rue de Jean, **23**
Alluette's Cafe, **9**
Basil, **17**
Blind Tiger, **48**
Blossom, **45**
Brasserie Gigi, **36**
Bull Street
Gourmet & Market, **28**
Charleston Grill, **32**
Chez Nous, **5**
Circa 1886, **29**
Coast Bar & Grill, **24**
Cru Café, **39**
Cupcake, **22**
Cypress Lowcountry Grille, **46**
Dixie Supply
Bakery and Cafe, **41**
Edmund's Oast, **11**
FIG, **37**
Fish, **19**
Fulton Five, **31**
Gaulart & Maliclet Café, **33**
Glazed, **16**
Grill 225, **40**
The Grocery, **6**
Hall's Chophouse, **21**
Hank's Seafood, **38**
High Cotton, **42**
Hominy Grill, **14**
Husk, **34**
Indaco, **8**
Leon's Oyster Shop, **4**
Leyla, **27**
The Macintosh, **18**
Magnolia's, **44**
Martha Lou's Kitchen, **13**
McCrady's, **47**
Moe's Tavern, **2**
Monza, **20**
Muse Restaurant & Wine Bar, **26**
Oak Steakhouse, **49**
The Ordinary, **7**
Peninsula Grill, **35**
Queen Street Grocery, **30**
Recovery Room, **3**
Slightly North of Broad, **43**
Taco Boy, **12**
The Tattooed Moose, **10**
Ted's Butcherblock, **25**
Trattoria Lucca, **1**
Two Boroughs Larder, **15**

with young professionals. The exhibition kitchen adds to the high-energy atmosphere. Lowcountry seafood is a specialty, including potato-crusted yellowfin tuna and pan-roasted mahimahi. The bar menu is available as late as 1 am on Friday and Saturday nights. $ *Average main: $25* ✉ *171 E. Bay St., Market area* ☎ *843/722–9200* 🌐 *www.magnolias-blossom-cypress.com.*

$$ 🍴 **Brasserie Gigi.** *French.* In the Market area, this French restaurant offers a respite from the tourist buzz. Chef Frank McMahon, who spent years honing his craft at Le Bernardin, opened Brasserie Gigi and named it after his wife. The expansive bar, tile floors, and wooden tables call to mind the casual eateries of Paris. The fried oyster salad with caramelized red onions, the steamed mussels accompanied by crispy fries, and the shrimp with linguine in a white wine sauce are standouts on the approachable menu. $ *Average main: $18* ✉ *102 N. Market St., Market area* ☎ *843/722–6393* 🌐 *brasseriegigi.com* ✍ *Reservations essential.*

$ 🍴 **Bull Street Gourmet & Market.** *American.* Don't let the name steer you wrong—this gourmet market on King Street remains a distinguished purveyor of sandwiches, meats, cheeses, and wines. Dean & Deluca is the favored comparison, and the exposed ceiling and ceramic tiles set the decor. Though the restaurant offers seared scallops and other delicious dishes for dinner, its lunchtime lineup of sandwiches served on local Normandy Farm breads earn top billing. Recommendations include the chicken salad, smoked salmon BLT, and smoked duck club. $ *Average main: $11* ✉ *120 King St., Lower King* ☎ *843/722–6464* 🌐 *www.bullstreetgourmetandmarket.com.*

★ $$$$ Fodor'sChoice 🍴 **Charleston Grill.** *Southern.* Quite simply, this restaurant provides what many regard as the city's highest gastronomic experience. Chef Michelle Weaver creates the groundbreaking New South cuisine, while sommelier Rick Rubel stocks 1,300 wines in his cellar, with many served by the glass. The dining room is a soothing backdrop, highlighted by pale wood floors, flowing drapes, and elegant Queen Anne chairs. A jazz ensemble adds a hip, yet unobtrusive, element. The menu continues to be divided into four quadrants: Simple, Lush (foie gras and other delicacies), Cosmopolitan, and Southern. A nightly tasting menu offers a way to sample it all. $ *Average main: $30* ✉ *Charleston Place Hotel, 224 King St., Market area* ☎ *843/577–4522* 🌐 *www.charlestongrill.com* ✍ *Reservations essential* 🕒 *No lunch.*

CLOSE UP

Best Bets for Charleston Dining

With hundreds of restaurants to choose from, how will you decide where to eat? Fodor's writers and editors have selected their favorite restaurants by price, cuisine, and experience in the Best Bets lists *below*. The Fodor's Choice properties represent the "best of the best" in every price category. You can also search by neighborhood for excellent eats—just peruse our reviews on the following pages.

Fodor's Choice: Charleston Grill, Chez Nous, Cupcake, Cypress Lowcountry Grille, FIG, Fish, The Grocery, Husk, Indaco, The Macintosh, Martha Lou's Kitchen, McCrady's, Moe's Tavern, Peninsula Grill, Perfectly Frank's, Recovery Room, Sesame Burgers & Beer, The Tattooed Moose, Tomato Shed Cafe, Trattoria Lucca, Tristan, Two Boroughs Larder, Xiao Bao Biscuit

Best American: The Grocery, Heart Woodfire Kitchen, Jack's Cosmic Dogs, Moe's Tavern, Ted's Butcherblock, Two Boroughs Larder

Best Asian: Xiao Bao Biscuit

Best Brunch: The Glass Onion, High Cotton, Hominy Grill

Best Budget Eats: Alluette's Cafe, Glazed, The Glass Onion, Hominy Grill, Jack's Cosmic Dogs, Martha Lou's Kitchen, Perfectly Frank's, The Tattooed Moose

Best Business Dining: Slightly North of Broad

Best French: 39 Rue de Jean, Chez Nous, Gaulart & Maliclet Café

Best Italian: Trattoria Lucca

Best Lunch: The Glass Onion, Poe's Tavern, Tomato Shed Cafe

Best Southern: FIG, Hominy Grill, Husk, McCrady's, Red Drum, Tristan

Child-Friendly: Cupcake, Jack's Cosmic Dogs, Perfectly Frank's, The Wreck of the Richard & Charlene

Great View: Bowen's Island, Fleet Landing, The Wreck of the Richard & Charlene

Hotel Dining: Charleston Grill

Hot Spots: Basil, Hall's Chophouse, The Macintosh, Taco Boy,

Late-Night Dining: Recovery Room, Voodoo Tiki Bar & Lounge

Most Romantic: Cypress Lowcountry Grille, Fulton Five

Outdoor Seating: Poe's Tavern

$$$ ✕**Chez Nous.** *French.* The menu may be illegible, the space miniscule, and the tucked-away location like finding Waldo, but the food—ah yes, the food. Chef Jill Mathias writes down her menu daily, and her lovely calligraphy is often hard to read, but no matter, because the attentive staff is happy to explain all the offerings. Each night only two appetizers, two entrées (like snapper with a *vin jaune* sauce

or gnocchi with chanterelles), and two desserts are offered. Sharing all of them typically makes the most sense. Owners Fanny and Patrick Panella monitor the dining room, bringing more of the delicious French bread should you run low. The dining room might feel too snug, in which case you should head to the outdoor patio, perfect for dinner or brunch. [$] *Average main: $24* ✉ *6 Payne Ct., off Coming St., Upper King* ☎ *843/579–3060* 🌐 *cheznouschs.com* ✍ *Reservations essential* ⊗ *Closed Mon.*

$$$$ 🍴 **Circa 1886.** *Southern.* Near Wentworth Mansion, this former residential home is full of hand-carved marble fireplaces and stained-glass windows. The award-winning eatery sets a sophisticated tone with low lighting and yellow roses atop each table. Executive Chef Marc Collins emphasizes seasonal offerings, highlighted by the menu's heirloom tomato salad, a deconstructed BLT made with bacon gelée, romaine lettuce foam, and white-grain toast. Collins also shows off his Texan extraction, serving an antelope dish, the free-range game procured from the Broken Arrow Ranch in Texas hill country. The tender variation spiced with horseradish is a must-eat for the adventurous. For those looking for an intimate, romantic meal, the quiet comfort of Circa 1886 is hard to top. [$] *Average main: $28* ✉ *149 Wentworth St., Lower King* ☎ *843/853–7828* 🌐 *www.circa1886.com* ✍ *Reservations essential* ⊗ *Closed Sun. No lunch.*

$$$ 🍴 **Coast Bar & Grill.** *Seafood.* Off a little alley in a restored indigo warehouse, Coast Bar & Grill has a stripped-down look with exposed brick walls and wood columns. Fried fare and heavy sauces are staples, but lighter dishes like fish tacos and ceviche make it a standout. Highlights include braised grouper served with tasty herbs, shiitake mushrooms, and decadent bacon-and-cheese grits, as well as the lobster and crab gratin, which comes complete with Parmesan mashed potatoes. The place can be noisy, but it's always fun. (It transforms into a boisterous bar in the later hours.) You can watch the cooks in the heat of the open kitchen in the front room or go in the back dining room where it is cooler. There are usually half-price wine specials, and there's live music on Sunday evening. [$] *Average main: $20* ✉ *39D John St., Upper King* ☎ *843/722–8838* 🌐 *www.coastbarandgrill.com* ⊗ *No lunch.*

$$$ 🍴 **Cru Café.** *Southern.* The sunny wraparound porch in this 18th-century house lures people to this eatery, but it's the inventive menu that keeps them coming back. Fried chicken breasts are topped with poblano peppers and mozzarella, and duck confit is served with caramelized pecans and goat cheese, topped with fried shoestring onions, and dressed with port-wine vinaigrette. No wonder there are lines—especially at lunch —out the door. Chef John Zucker, who got his start at Spago in Beverly Hills, goes heavy on the starches, and his flavorful whipped potatoes are made with real cream. Meat dishes are laced with sauces featuring green peppercorns, port wine, pear sherry, chipotle peppers, and horseradish cream. The four-cheese mac is a big favorite. [$] *Average main: $24* ✉ *18 Pinckney St., Market area* ☎ *843/534–2434* 🌐 *www.crucafe.com* ✍ *Reservations essential* ⏲ *Closed Sun. and Mon.*

3

★ Fodor's Choice ✕ **Cupcake.** *Bakery.* Better than Baskin-Robbins, this cute shop features more than 50 flavors of cupcakes. A daily flavor chart reveals the collection of pocket-sized pleasures on offer. Favorites include carrot cake, lemon-blueberry, peanut butter banana fluff, praline, pumpkin, red velvet, strawberry cheesecake, and death by chocolate. If you're wandering around on King Street, look for the station wagon parked outside with a large pink cupcake on top. Cupcake also has a sister property in Mount Pleasant at 600 Long Point Road. [$] *Average main: $3* ✉ *433 King St., Upper King* ☎ *843/853–8181* 🌐 *www.freshcupcakes.com.*

$ FAMILY

★ Fodor's Choice ✕ **Cypress Lowcountry Grille.** *Eclectic.* In a renovated 1834 brick building with striking contemporary decor, this eatery has leather booths, a ceiling with light sculptures that change color, and a "wine wall" packed with 4,500 bottles. The cuisine is high-end Southern-American, with fresh local ingredients accented with exotic flavors, notably from the Pacific Rim. Executive Chef Craig Deihl has gained recognition in the culinary world for his simple yet elegant fare, especially for his charcuterie, which is worth ordering for the table to share. Try fabulous salads, like the hearts of palm and baby greens with local goat cheese topped with a walnut vinaigrette. The sorghum-glazed pork chop is exceptional, and if you arrive on a night when the signature chicken and waffles is on the menu, say yes. [$] *Average main: $35* ✉ *167 E. Bay St., Market area* ☎ *843/727–0111* 🌐 *www.magnolias-blossom-cypress.com* ✍ *Reservations essential* ⏲ *No lunch.*

$$$$

$ ✕ **Dixie Supply Bakery and Cafe.** *Southern.* It might be buttressed by a Lil' Cricket convenience store, but don't be fooled by the size of Dixie Supply Bakery and Cafe. It belongs to an old Charlestonian family (and by old, we mean they arrived here in 1698 or so) that seeks to honor its roots through food. It's here you'll find Lowcountry and Southern classics: shrimp and creamy stone-ground

LOWCOUNTRY CUISINE

Although you can find Lowcountry cuisine along most of coastal South Carolina all the way down to Savannah, its foundation feeds off the Holy City of Charleston, where, several centuries ago, European aristocrats would share kitchens with their African slaves. The result was a colonial European fusion with Caribbean and West African, otherwise known as Gullah, influences.

Hoppin' John. This rice-and-bean concoction is not only a favorite Lowcountry dish but a lucky one at that. Families throughout the Lowcountry prepare hoppin' John on New Year's Day for lunch or dinner in hopes that it will provide them with a year's worth of good luck. It's all in the classic Lowcountry ingredients: black-eyed peas symbolize pennies (a side of collard greens adds to the wealth in the new year). Rice, chopped onions, bacon (or ham), and peppers are added to the peas. Add garnishes like a spoonful of salsa or a dollop of sour cream for an interesting Southwest spin.

Perlau. South Carolina takes great pride in its perlau (aka perloo), more lovingly known at the dinner table as chicken bog. This rice-based dish is cooked with chunks of tender chicken and sausage slices, simmered in the chef's choice of classic Southern seasonings. For more than 30 years, in fact, the tiny town of Loris has been hosting its annual Loris Bog-Off Festival, where hundreds of chefs compete to be awarded with the best bowl of bog.

She-Crab Soup. Rich and creamy, with lumps of crabmeat and a splash of dry sherry, she-crab soup is to the Lowcountry as chowder is to New England. The "she" of this signature dish actually comes from the main ingredient, a female crab's orange crab roe. It is delicious as an appetizer, and quite filling as an entrée.

Shrimp and Grits. If you're not convinced that South Carolina is serious about grits, consider this: in 1976, it declared grits the official state food. To be truly decadent, you need to finish this starch off with heavy cream and a slab of butter. Each chef has his or her own guarded recipe, but traditionally, local wild shrimp is sautéed with onions, garlic, and fresh tomatoes. Today, foodies will delight in discovering the dish to be dressed up with everything from sausage, bacon, and Cajun seasoning to cheese, gravy, and tomato-based sauces.

grits, fried chicken, and a mighty fine tomato pie. Daily blue-plate specials abound, including fried green tomatoes, shrimp from nearby Wadmalaw Island, summer-squash-and-ricotta ravioli, and a steady assortment of locally plucked vegetables. If you only want a bite, the biscuits are worth grabbing to go. ⓢ *Average main: $7* ⊠ *62 State St., Market area* ☎ *843/722–5650* ⊕ *www.dixiecafecharleston. com* ⊘ *No dinner.*

★ Fodor'sChoice ✕ **FIG.** *Southern.* Spend an evening here for $$$$ fresh-off-the-farm ingredients cooked with unfussy, flavorful finesse. Executive chef Jason Stanhope has taken over in the kitchen, and the young maverick has only burnished the restaurant's stellar reputation. The menu changes frequently, but the family-style vegetables might be as simple as young beets in sherry vinegar served in a plain white bowl. The main dishes get more complex: there's the must-have chicken liver pâté, slow baked red porgy with Carolina Gold grits, and perfectly executed pan-roasted golden tilefish. Hit the lively bar scene for a nightcap. ⓢ *Average main: $30* ⊠ *232 Meeting St., Market area* ☎ *843/805–5900* ⊕ *www.eatatfig.com* ⊘ *No lunch.*

★ Fodor'sChoice ✕ **Fish.** *Eclectic.* Savvy foodies were the first to $$$ embrace Chef Nico Romo's inventive French-Asian cuisine, and the rest of the city. (No wonder Romo is the youngest person to earn the title of Master Chef of France.) Start with the dim sum appetizer; it's more beautiful than a flower arrangement. Or try the sweet-chili calamari that gives the menu a kick. The bouillabaisse with coconut-lemongrass broth and ginger croutons is one-of-a-kind. Although it's easy to overlook this cozy spot, it's well worth adding to your itinerary because the service is always friendly and the meals are imaginative. ⓢ *Average main: $22* ⊠ *440–442 King St., Upper King* ☎ *843/722–3474* ⊕ *www.fishrestaurantcharleston.com* ⌂ *Reservations essential* ⊘ *Closed Sun. No lunch Sat.*

$$$$ ✕ **Fulton Five.** *Italian.* Tucked away in the antiques district, this romantic restaurant is appropriately decorated with chartreuse walls studded with brass accents. In warm weather you can opt for a seat on the second-floor terrace. Wherever you sit, the northern Italian specialties are worth savoring. Mushroom risotto with sweet corn accompanies beef with porcini mushrooms. There's also pappardelle with rabbit, and spinach gnocchi with crabmeat and tarragon-laced butter. ⓢ *Average main: $34* ⊠ *5 Fulton St., Lower King* ☎ *843/853–5555* ⊕ *www.fultonfive.com* ⌂ *Reservations essential* ⊘ *Closed Sun. and late Aug.–early Sept. No lunch.*

$ 🍴 **Glazed.** *Bakery.* Three words: maple bacon doughnuts. If that's not enough to get you in the door, any number of other creative options—think raspberry Nutella or berries and mascarpone—should do the trick. Allison Smith and Mark Remi opened their sweetheart of a store because they suspected there was an untapped enthusiasm for artisanal doughnuts. The verdict? Unqualified success. There are 7 to 10 varieties daily, filled with homemade jam and other flavors. Just name your flavor. [$] *Average main: $3* ✉ *481 King St., Upper King* ☎ *843/577–5557* 🌐 *www.glazedgourmet.com.*

$$$$ 🍴 **Grill 225.** *Steakhouse.* This atmospheric establishment has been stockpiling accolades over the years, and it's never been better. The cuisine—combined with a staggering array of excellent wines and professional, caring service—make Grill 225 a popular special-occasion spot. Take the opportunity to dress up; the elegant wood floors, white linens, and red-velvet upholstery call for it. If you enjoy red meat, indulge in the wet-aged steaks; the fillet with foie gras bathed in a fig demi-glace is equally excellent. But don't miss sharing a side or two, such as the mashed sweet potatoes with Boursin cheese. Presentation is at its best with appetizers like the towering tuna tartare. Expect hefty portions, but save room for the pastry chef's shining creations, which include a contemporized version of baked Alaska with a nutty crust, flambéed table-side. [$] *Average main: $40* ✉ *Market Pavilion Hotel, 225 E. Bay St., Market area* ☎ *843/266–4222* 🌐 *www.marketpavilion.com.*

★ Fodor's Choice 🍴 **The Grocery.** *Modern American.* Executive
**$$$$** Chef and owner Kevin Johnson's restaurant sits in impressive quarters near the corner of Cannon and King streets. The high wainscoting and tall shelving filled with jams and jellies, pickled vegetables, and vintage kitchenware project an earthy, unassuming presence. Similarly, the menu suggests a humble, considerate approach, as the dishes represent local flavors: the wood-roasted carrots come with feta, raisins, and pistachio crumble, while the wood-roasted black bass is delivered with salsa verde. A cassoulet of decadent chorizo, pork belly, and duck confit easily feeds two. If you visit during the hot months, try the beets and berries with crème fraîche. It tastes like summer in a bowl. [$] *Average main: $25* ✉ *4 Cannon St., Market area* ☎ *843/302–8825* 🌐 *www.thegrocerycharleston.com* ⏲ *No lunch.*

★ Fodor's Choice 🍴 **Hall's Chophouse.** *Steakhouse.* In the old Art-
$$$$ ist and Craftsman Supply building on King Street, Hall's Chophouse displays a different brand of craftsmanship:

WORD OF MOUTH

"We will be in Savannah for 2 nights and Charleston for 4 nights. I am looking for a non-touristy restaurant in Charleston or surrounding area that serves good southern fried chicken and/or good barbeque." —shellyk

"On the West Ashley side of Charleston, the Glass Onion is known for its fried chicken. You need to make reservations at least 24 hours

ahead. And, the atmosphere is most definitely casual."
—kathleen

"Look at Seewee and Page's Okra Grill, both in Mount Pleasant." —suewoo

"If you want good (i.e. great) BBQ, then go to Wiley's Championship BBQ. It was the best BBQ I have ever tasted, bar none. "
—Orlando_Vic

3

28-day aged USDA steaks. The two-story restaurant quickly established itself as one of the top steak houses in town (Oak and Grill 225 being the others). Recommended are the 28-ounce Tomahawk rib eye, the New York strip, and the slow-roasted prime rib. The bustling bar is a good place to rub shoulders with a variety of locals. A heads-up: The service borders on excessive, or is it obsessive? The staff takes uncommon heed of its guests, though the lavishly prepared steaks offer the restaurant's greatest source of hospitality. $ *Average main: $55* ⊠ *434 King St., Upper King* ☎ *843/727–0090* ⊕ *www.hallschophouse.com* ⚲ *Reservations essential* ⊗ *No lunch.*

$$$$ ✕ **Hank's Seafood.** *Seafood.* With a community table flanked by paper-topped private tables, this lively spot harks back to an earlier time in Charleston's culinary history. The kitchen reinvents recipes from the famed Henry's, a longtime favorite that used to grace the Market. This upscale fish house serves such Southern adaptations as Lowcountry bouillabaisse and seafood platters that come with sweet-potato fries and coleslaw. The atmosphere retains an authentic vibe under longtime chef Frank McMahon, with waiters in long white aprons buzzing about. With a location just off the Old Market, the sister restaurant to the fancy-pants Peninsula Grill is a noteworthy landmark on the dining scene. $ *Average main: $28* ⊠ *10 Hayne St., at Church St., Market area* ☎ *843/723–3474* ⊕ *www. hanksseafoodrestaurant.com* ⊗ *No lunch.*

CLOSE UP

Fodor's Interview with Eric Doksa

Eric Doksa is the food critic for *Charleston City Paper*, a barbecue nut, and a self-proclaimed beer nerd. Here, he talks with Fodor's about some of his favorite places in the Holy City.

Q: She-crab soup is probably the most iconic Charleston dish. Where do you go for the best version?

A: When I think of she-crab soup, **The Wreck of the Richard & Charlene** (✉ *106 Haddrell St., Mount Pleasant* ☎ *843/884-0052*) immediately comes to mind. It's quintessentially Shem Creek, low key, but makes a great she-crab.

Q: Where do you go for the best shrimp and grits?

A: It's a tie for me. **Husk** (✉ *76 Queen St., Market area* ☎ *843/577-2500*) and **Hominy Grill** (✉ *207 Rutledge Ave.* ☎ *843/937-0930*).

Q: Are there any new places that you're excited about?

A: **Edmund's Oast** (✉ *1081 Morrison Dr., North Central* ☎ *843/727-1145*). It's such a great concept and it touches all the bases—beer, food, atmosphere.

Q: Do you have a favorite local's joint?

A: **Dave's Carryout** (✉ *42 Morris St., Upper King* ☎ *843/577-7943*). It's a hole-in-wall seafood spot.

$$$$ × **High Cotton.** *Southern.* This place remains unchanged by time: lazily spinning paddle fans, lush palm trees, and exposed brick walls. Chef Shawn helms the kitchen, serving up regional classics like Lowcountry boil and bacon-wrapped, stuffed rabbit loin. If you want a traditional dinner, there are thick cuts of steaks and chops with your choice of sauce and side dishes like fried brussels sprouts and creamy white corn grits. For dessert, the pecan pie baked with bourbon brown sugar caramel and the high-rising peanut butter pie are like rich Southern blessings. And don't miss brunch, which is one of the best in town. [$] *Average main: $30* ✉ *199 E. Bay St., Market area* ☎ *843/724-3815* 🌐 *www.mavericksouthernkitchens.com/highcotton* ✍ *Reservations essential* ⏲ *No lunch weekdays.*

$ × **Hominy Grill.** *Southern.* Thanks to a tasteful renovation, this Lowcountry landmark now can seat many more hungry patrons. The wooden barber poles from the last century still frame the door of this small, homespun café. Chalkboard specials are often the way to go here, whether you are visiting for breakfast, lunch, or dinner. Chef Robert Stehling is a Carolina boy who lived in New York; that dichotomy shows in his "uptown" comfort food. Enjoy the perfect soft-shell-crab sandwich with homemade fries, but leave room for the tangy buttermilk pie or the chocolate peanut butter pie. The bottom line: Whatever Stehling cooks tastes good. [$] *Average main: $14* ✉ *207 Rutledge Ave., Canonboro* ☎ *843/937–0930* 🌐 *www.hominygrill.com* ⏲ *No dinner Sun.*

★ Fodor's Choice ✕ **Husk.** *Southern.* With an abundance of acco-
$$$$ lades, Husk serves an ambitious menu steeped in the South—and the South alone. Seriously. Celebrated Chef Sean Brock forbids the inclusion of items from other regions or provinces, even olive oil. A large chalkboard lists the ever-changing artisanal dishes available, as the menu sometimes varies twice daily. Supper favorites include seafood such as snapper, catfish, and flounder, frequently paired with heirloom vegetables. Try the Southern fried chicken skins or skillet of smoky bacon corn bread, too—both are terrifically popular. The building itself, balcony intact, dates to the late 19th century, and the freestanding bar beside the restaurant is lined with 100-year-old exposed brick and several Kentucky bourbons and whiskeys. If you can't score a reservation, Husk Bar next door is arguably just as good for intimate drinks and a burger. [$] *Average main: $29* ✉ *76 Queen St., Market area* ☎ *843/577–2500* 🌐 *www.huskrestaurant.com.*

$$$ ✕ **Indaco.** *Italian.* For sophisticated Italian fare in a vibrant (and sometimes boisterous) setting, this hip spot on Upper King is the place. A modern aesthetic of exposed wood and an open kitchen may drive the design, but the food isn't putting on airs. Start with the burrata cheese served with crisp flatbread, then dive into one of the many unique salads—the spring vegetable salad, with a cornucopia of seasonal veggies, is recommended. Chef Michael Perez makes his own pastas, and they are strikingly original. Don't miss the black-pepper tagliatelle crowned with a soft-boiled egg yolk. [$] *Average main: $24* ✉ *526 King St., Upper King* ☎ *843/727–1228* 🌐 *www.indacocharleston.com* ✍ *Reservations essential* ⏲ *No lunch.*

$$ ✕ **Leon's Oyster Shop.** *Southern.* This might have been just another oyster spot, but Leon's is an entirely different affair: casual, quirky, and a tad Wes Andersony, what with the kitschy ambience and blues soundtrack. Though a tad twee, this combination works wonderfully, and the dishes speak for themselves. Fried chicken sammies come towering, dressed in fresh slaw and nestled on perfectly prepared rolls. The oysters are from near or far, depend-

ing on the season. Rather than a formal bar, guests have to stand, encouraging conversation. One glitch: Beer is served in water glasses but costs the same as a pint. That said, it's hard to complain. Don't forget to ask for a soft-serve ice cream before you go; you can grab it at the window outside the former auto repair shop. Ⓢ *Average main: $15* ✉ *698 King St., Upper King* ☎ *843/531–6500* ⊕ *www. leonsoystershop.com.*

★ **Fodor's**Choice ✕ **Leyla.** *Lebanese.* This Lebanese restaurant
$$$ brings the authentic flavors of the Middle East to Charleston. The fragrance of beef, lamb, and chicken shawarma wafts from the glass front doors. While the prices are a bit high, the generous portions more than make up for them, and the service is friendly and informative. Adventurous eaters can find beef tongue and frogs' legs on the huge menu. Go for the $17 lunch special, stay for the meghli rice flour pudding bedecked in cloves, coconut, and cinnamon. Ⓢ *Average main: $22* ✉ *298 King St., Market area* ☎ *843/501–7500* ⊕ *www.leyla-charleston.com.*

★ **Fodor's**Choice ✕ **The Macintosh.** *American.* Here's another
$$$$ name to tuck into your sweetgrass basket filled with great Charleston chefs: Jeremiah Bacon. And what a perfect name, right? Bacon shows off his fondness for the little-regarded deckle—a highly marbled, delicious piece of rib eye—plus local cobia, clams, and grouper, as well as bone marrow bread pudding. His latest concoction has tongues wagging (and drooling)—seafood charcuterie. The Macintosh, often ranked among the country's best new restaurants, offers comfy quarters and homespun victuals to a stylish crowd. Exceedingly popular, the Mac's taken its place among Charleston's best. Ⓢ *Average main: $25* ✉ *478 King St., Upper King* ☎ *843/788–4299* ⊕ *www. themacintoshcharleston.com* ⊘ *No lunch.*

$$$$ ✕ **Magnolias.** *Southern.* The theme here is evident in the vivid paintings of creamy white blossoms that adorn the walls. A visit from Oprah Winfrey revived the reputation of "Mags," a pioneer here of innovative Lowcountry cuisine. (Many locals, particularly the younger ones, prefer its more youthful siblings, Cypress and Blossom.) Executive chef Don Drake refreshes classic dishes like fried green tomatoes with white cheddar grits, caramelized onions, and country ham. Sunday brunch is a more affordable way to sample the fare; the free parking helps defray the cost. Ⓢ *Average main: $26* ✉ *185 E. Bay St., Market area* ☎ *843/577–7771* ⊕ *www.magnolias-blossom-cypress.com* ⌕ *Reservations essential* ⊘ *No lunch.*

CHITTERLINGS. Do not be afraid, be informed. Chitterlings, better known as chitlins (and sometimes chit'lins), can be sampled from several soul food establishments in Charleston, including Martha Lou Gadsden's eponymous restaurant. A quick primer: Chitterlings are made up of the small intestines of a pig, and usually served fried or steamed after being boiled for several hours. They're not for everyone, but try to withhold judgment before tasting (possibly with cider vinegar or hot sauce).

★ Fodor'sChoice × **Martha Lou's Kitchen.** *Southern.* As plenty of local and national publications have professed, Martha Lou's is an institution. Martha Lou Gadsden has made her pink cinder-block building into a palace of soul food. And although the building is quirky, with a huge mural of the owner visible from a mile down the road, the food quickly convinces skeptics what all the fuss is about. The chicken comes perfectly cooked to golden brown, and those fried pork chops aren't bad, either. The tireless octogenarian works all day, preparing collard greens, giblet rice, lima beans, and, yes, even chitterlings. Just a chat with Miss Martha Lou is enough to make the trip worthwhile. Ⓢ *Average main: $8* ⊠ *1068 Morrison Dr.* ☎ *843/577–9583* ▭ *No credit cards* ⊘ *Closed Sun.*

★ Fodor'sChoice × **McCrady's.** *American.* Originally constructed in 1788, McCrady's features heart pine flooring, two fireplaces, exposed brick walls, and a pair of handsome brick archways. Its impressive legacy is supported by cuisine ranking among Charleston's best. Bear witness to the short ribs served with sweet corn and green tomatoes, or the beef tartare featuring small disks of egg yolk, ramps, and frisée. Or enjoy fresh fish from local waters, such as grilled cobia or flounder crusted with green peppercorn. Meats include Berkshire pork so tender your fork leaves indentions, and aged duck roasted on the bone. A four-course menu featuring smaller dishes allows diners to taste several items. The unswerving McCrady's still delivers, thanks to talented chef Daniel Heinze and his crackerjack staff. Ⓢ *Average main: $30* ⊠ *2 Unity Alley, Market area* ☎ *843/577–0025* ⊕ *www.mccradysrestaurant.com* ⌕ *Reservations essential* ⊘ *No lunch.*

★ Fodor'sChoice × **Moe's Tavern.** *American.* First things first: No, it's not a burrito joint—far from it. Moe's Tavern is decidedly old school, earning a perennial place on the area's best-burger list. The big, half-pound, Angus beef chuck patties are cooked to order. And they're not even the best things on the menu. Give it up for Moe's BLT, containing a sizable disc of mozzarella cheese, fried tomato, and, of course, plenty of bacon. The downtown branch is at 5 Cumberland Street. Ⓢ *Average main: $8* ✉ *714 Rutledge Ave., Hampton Park* ☎ *843/722–3287* ⊕ *www.moestaverns.com.*

$ ✕**Monza.** *Pizza.* An homage to the Italian city of the same name, Monza provides genuine Neapolitan-style pizza and an introduction to one of the world's most historic motor-sport racing circuits: the Autodromo Nazionale Monza. The restaurant takes its cue after several Formula One greats, naming its pizzas for Emilio Materassi, Felice Nazzaro, Giuseppe Campari, Wolfgang Von Trips, Ronnie Peterson, and "El Maestro," Juan Manuel Fangio. Like the sport the restaurant celebrates, the service is lightning fast, the setting modern. The pizza—baked in a wood-fired oven, in traditional style—boasts a thin, crisp crust and toppings like house-made sausage, pepperoni, eggplant, roasted red peppers, and locally farmed eggs. For those needing a lighter lunch, the salads are equally delish. Ⓢ *Average main: $14* ✉ *451 King St., Upper King* ☎ *843/720–8787* ⊕ *www. monzapizza.com.*

$$$ ✕**Muse Restaurant & Wine Bar.** *Mediterranean.* Set in a pale yellow building on Society Street, Muse lays bare Mediterranean stylings in sophisticated, relaxed quarters. The bar functions as a drawing room, permitting easy introductions and closer inspection of the restaurant's impressive, 100-plus-bottle wine list. Nature provides ideal lighting, as sunlight spills into the dining rooms during evenings in spring and summer. The restaurant serves standout plates, such as tuna carpaccio, sweetbreads, swordfish, and its signature dish: a delicious, scarcely fried sea bass, served with head and tail intact, over saffron rice and roasted-pepper puree. Ⓢ *Average main: $24* ✉ *82 Society St., Lower King* ☎ *843/577–1102* ⊕ *www.charlestonmuse.com* ⌖ *Reservations essential* ◌ *No lunch.*

$$$$ ✕**Oak Steakhouse.** *Steakhouse.* In a 19th-century bank building, this dining room juxtaposes antique crystal chandeliers with contemporary art. Reserve a table on the third floor for the full effect and the best vistas. It's pricey, but the filet mignon with foie-gras-and-black-truffle butter is excellent, and the side dishes, like creamed spinach, are perfectly executed. Favorite appetizers include beef carpaccio and Gorgonzola fondue. The service is professional and cordial under the leadership of Executive Chef Jeremiah Bacon. Ⓢ *Average main: $40* ✉ *17 Broad St., Market area* ☎ *843/722–4220* ⊕ *www.oaksteakhouserestaurant.com* ◌ *No lunch.*

$$$$ 🍴 **The Ordinary.** *American.* Award-winning Chef Mike Lata delivers every possible type of underwater delight, from Capers Inlet clams to jumbo blue crab Louie. The two-story dining room of this former bank building fills up fast, but you can always belly up to the stunning bar while you wait and enjoy a variety of clever cocktails like the Ting Collins (Old Tom gin, Cocchi Americano Rosa, Stiegl Radler, and lemon), or the Echo, Echo (Beefeater gin, Chartreuse, and grapefruit). Perhaps the best seat is at the oyster bar, where the freshest of bivalves await. And if you're looking for optimum indulgence, ask for the seafood tower. The triple decker will set you back $125, but spilling over with fruits de mer, it is worth every penny. [$] *Average main: $28* ✉ *544 King St., Market area* ☎ *843/414–7060* 🌐 *www.eattheordinary.com* ✍ *Reservations essential* 🕒 *Closed Mon. No lunch.*

★ Fodor's Choice 🍴 **Peninsula Grill.** *Southern.* Chef Graham Dailey incorporates Lowcountry produce and seafood into traditional Peninsula dishes, at once eyeing the past and the future. The dining room looks the part: the walls are covered in olive-green velvet and dotted with 18th-century-style portraits, and the ceiling supports wrought-iron chandeliers. These fixtures serve as an excellent backdrop for "sinfully grilled" Angus steaks, as well as jumbo sea scallops and Berkshire pork chops. Finish with the homemade sorbet, or try the signature three-way chocolate dessert that comes with a shot of ice-cold milk. The servers, who work in tandem, are pros; the personable sommelier makes wine selections that truly complement your meal, anything from bubbly to clarets and dessert wines. The atmosphere is animated and convivial, and the famous coconut cake still graces the menu. [$] *Average main: $35* ✉ *Planters Inn, 112 N. Market St., Market area* ☎ *843/723–0700* 🌐 *www.peninsulagrill.com* ✍ *Reservations essential* 🕒 *No lunch.*

$$$$

$ 🍴 **Queen Street Grocery.** *American.* For crepes and cold-pressed coffee, most folks turn to a venerable Charleston institution: Queen Street Grocery. Built in 1922, the corner building has served many purposes throughout the years: butcher shop, candy shop, and late-night convenience store. The restaurant's owners call to mind the place's roots as a neighborhood grocery store by sourcing much of the produce and other goods from local growers. Don't pass up the sweet and savory crepes, named for the islands surrounding Charleston. The place still operates as a charming bodega, perfect for picking up a bottle of wine on the way to a picnic in White Point Gardens. [$] *Average main: $9* ✉ *133 Queen St., Market area* ☎ *843/723–4121* 🌐 *www.queenstreetgrocerycafe.com.*

★ $ Fodor's Choice ✕ **Recovery Room.** *American.* The graffiti-splashed walls and tongue-in-cheek name make the Recovery Room a favorite for hipsters. In addition to cans of Pabst Blue Ribbon, this watering hole under the U.S. Highway 17 bridge serves up brunch, lunch, a late-night menu, and even amateur pole dancing on Monday night. Go for the tater tachos (tater tots covered in shredded cheeses, jalapeños, tomatoes, and onions) or the wings available in a dozen different sauces. The windows may be few and the view muted, but look at it this way: at least nobody will see you scarf down an order of "chicken biscuits"—fried chicken tenders sopping with honey or gravy over a homemade biscuit. [$] *Average main: $6* ✉ *685 King St., Upper King* ☎ *843/722–4220* 🌐 *www.recoveryroomtavern.com.*

$$$$ ✕ **Slightly North of Broad.** *Southern.* This former warehouse with atmospheric brick-and-stucco walls has a chef's table that looks directly into the open kitchen. It's a great place to perch if you can "take the heat," as Chef Frank Lee, who wears a baseball cap instead of a toque, is one of the city's culinary characters. He is known for his talent in prepping game, and his venison is exceptional. Many of the specialties are served as small plates, which makes them perfect for sharing. The braised lamb shank with a ragout of white beans, arugula, and a red demi-glace is divine. Lunch can be as inexpensive as $9.95 for something as memorable as mussels with spinach, grape tomatoes, and smoked bacon. [$] *Average main: $28* ✉ *192 E. Bay St., Market area* ☎ *843/723–3424* 🌐 *www.mavericksouthernkitchens.com/snob* ⏲ *No lunch weekends.*

$ ✕ **Taco Boy.** *Mexican.* Accommodating locals and out-of-towners alike, Taco Boy delivers tasty Mexican-American treats to a bustling patio crowd. The ambience is half the allure of this eclectic outpost featuring rehabbed or reclaimed materials—right down to the bar counter, carved from a fallen North Carolina walnut tree, and the funky Mexican folk art adorning every inch of wall space. It's a forward-thinking and fun joint, perfect for downing margaritas and *micheladas* (beer with lime juice, tomato juice, and chilies) or sharing a sampler trio of house-made guacamole and two types of salsa. For beach-bound travelers, Folly Beach—south of downtown Charleston—boasts the original restaurant on Center Street. [$] *Average main: $8* ✉ *217 Huger St., North of Broad* ☎ *843/789–3333* 🌐 *www.tacoboy.net.*

★ Fodor'sChoice ✕ **The Tattooed Moose.** *American.* If it looks like a cross between a veterans' hall and a dive bar, that's because the Tattooed Moose is going for a decidedly unpretentious vibe. With 90-plus beers on the menu, and a large moose head behind the counter, the place cuts a distinctive figure. The bar's famous duck club is a menu showstopper. Priced at twice as much as the other sandwiches, it relies on duck confit, apple-smoked bacon, garlic aioli, and ripened tomatoes bounded by sweet Hawaiian bread. Homey eats like house-smoked barbecue brisket, chicken salad, jumbo chicken wings, and fried turkey breast round out the offerings. And if you're looking for a swinging late-night scene off the main King Street drag, the Moose has a rotating lineup of live music. [$] *Average main: $10* ✉ *1137 Morrison Dr., Market area* ☎ *843/277–2990* 🌐 *www.tattooedmoose.com.*

$$

$ ✕ **Ted's Butcherblock.** *American.* Land at Ted's on a lucky evening and you'll likely be conferred a memorable greeting: the scent of smoked meat drifting from a grill perched near the entrance. Happy day, indeed. Ted's operates as a one-stop butcher shop, supplying beef, game, seafood, and homemade sausages to complement its selection of artisanal cheeses, wine, and other specialty foods. The shop also maintains a first-rate deli counter, drawing praise from *Bon Appetit* and other publications. Among the favored offerings: the house-roasted Wagyu beef panini and the ever-changing bacon-of-the-month BLT. [$] *Average main: $8* ✉ *334 E. Bay St., Market area* ☎ *843/577–0094* 🌐 *www.tedsbutcherblock.com.*

MUSTARD SAUCE. **So, you've sampled rich, tomato-based sauces in Kansas City or Memphis, spiked your barbecue with vinegar-flavored concoctions in eastern North Carolina, and maybe even tried the white, mayonnaise-based sauce of Alabama. Now, about that mustard sauce. . . . It can be traced to the state's German forebears, and is often called Orangeburg mustard in deference to the city of the same name, situated about 80 miles north of Charleston. Colored golden, the sauce is made up of mustard (naturally), brown sugar, and molasses and is certainly worth pouring over pulled pork or smoked chicken.**

★ Fodor'sChoice ✕ **Trattoria Lucca.** *Italian.* Chef Ken Vedrinski may have opened his incredible Italian seafood spot Coda del Pesce on Isle of Palms last year, but locals still rave about his first wonder, Trattoria Lucca. Come in for the warm

$$$$

cauliflower *sformatino* (with farm-fresh eggs, pancetta, and parmigiano cheese), stay for the pasta dishes made with locally milled organic semolina. On Sunday evening, family-style suppers with communal seating are a treat. New additions to the dining room have made it more quiet and intimate. $ *Average main: $26* ✉ *41 Bogard St., North of Broad* ☎ *843/973–3323* 🌐 *www.luccacharleston.com* ✍ *Reservations essential* ⏲ *No lunch.*

★ $$$ Fodor's Choice 🍴 **Two Boroughs Larder.** *American.* Husband and wife Josh and Heather Keeler ventured down from Philadelphia to open up their restaurant and market in the Cannonborough-Elliotborough neighborhoods. The menu changes daily, featuring an eclectic but irrepressible mix. You can opt for a breakfast sandwich any time of the day, only with *pepperonata* and egg, Neueske's bacon, or pork scrapple—a traditional heap of pork mush from Pennsylvania Dutch and Amish descent. But the restaurant supplies other pleasing mains, too, like grouper *brodetto*, oven-roasted trout, and veal sweetbreads, along with such plentiful sides as marrow-roasted cauliflower, braised heirloom beans, and buffalo pig tails. $ *Average main: $20* ✉ *186 Coming St., Cannonborough* ☎ *843/637–3722* 🌐 *www.twoboroughslarder.com.*

SOUTH OF BROAD

$ 🍴 **Blind Tiger.** *American.* One of Charleston's oldest speakeasies, the Blind Tiger can go toe-to-toe with any newcomer. Name the beer, name the backdrop, and the Tiger can deliver in spades, starting with two indoor bars and a historic, handsome outdoor patio. The kitchen also turns out solid bar food—the bacon-and-blue burger and the fried pickles make this a regular lunch spot for Broad Street attorneys. $ *Average main: $10* ✉ *36–38 Broad St., South of Broad* ☎ *843/577–0088* 🌐 *www.blindtigercharleston.com.*

$$ 🍴 **Gaulart and Maliclet Café.** *French.* This local favorite, also known as Fast and French, has celebrated 30—that's right, 30—years in business. And it's all thanks to the consistent food and the esprit de corps of the staff that keeps regulars coming back. Sharing family-style tables for breakfast, lunch, or dinner leads to camaraderie. Thursday brings a crowd for fondue. The cheese version can be disappointing, but the seafood, which you cook in broth yourself, is better. Opt to get your cheese fix with the wonderful Bucheron cheese salad. Nightly specials, such as bouillabaisse, are reasonably priced and come with a petite glass of wine. The subtly sweet chocolate-mousse cake is the best way to end

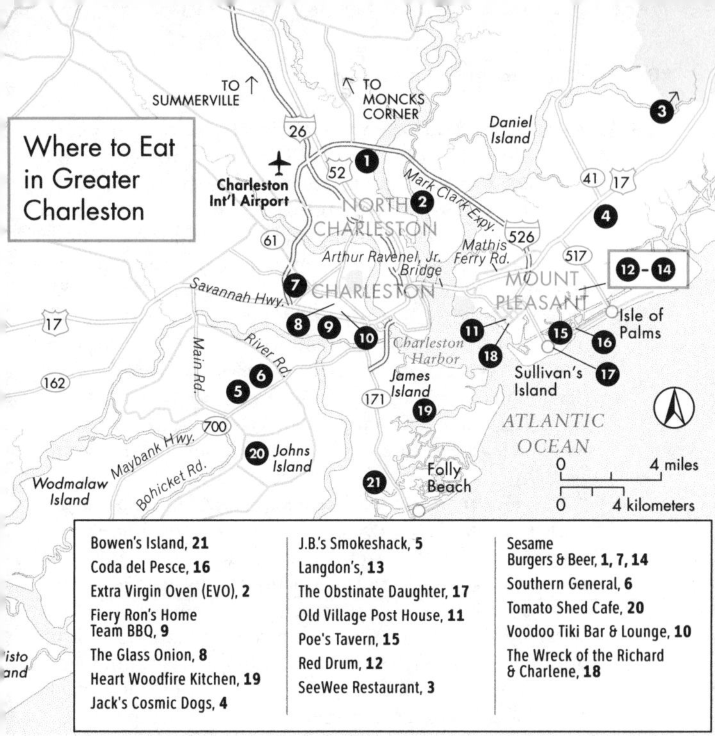
Where to Eat in Greater Charleston
TO SUMMERVILLE
TO MONCKS CORNER
Daniel Island
Charleston Int'l Airport
NORTH CHARLESTON
Mark Clark Expy.
Mathis Ferry Rd.
Arthur Ravenel, Jr. Bridge
CHARLESTON
MOUNT PLEASANT
Savannah Hwy.
Isle of Palms
River Rd.
Main Rd.
Charleston Harbor
James Island
Sullivan's Island
ATLANTIC OCEAN
Maybank Hwy.
Bohicket Rd.
Johns Island
Wodmalaw Island
Folly Beach
0 4 miles
0 4 kilometers
Bowen's Island, 21
Coda del Pesce, 16
Extra Virgin Oven (EVO), 2
Fiery Ron's Home Team BBQ, 9
The Glass Onion, 8
Heart Woodfire Kitchen, 19
Jack's Cosmic Dogs, 4
J.B.'s Smokeshack, 5
Langdon's, 13
The Obstinate Daughter, 17
Old Village Post House, 11
Poe's Tavern, 15
Red Drum, 12
SeeWee Restaurant, 3
Sesame Burgers & Beer, 1, 7, 14
Southern General, 6
Tomato Shed Cafe, 20
Voodoo Tiki Bar & Lounge, 10
The Wreck of the Richard & Charlene, 18

your meal. $ *Average main: $15* ✉ *98 Broad St., South of Broad* ☎ *843/577–9797* 🌐 *www.fastandfrenchcharleston.com* ⏲ *Closed Sun. No dinner Mon.*

MOUNT PLEASANT AND VICINITY

Although most of the region's best-know eateries are within the city limits, you won't have trouble finding a great meal when you're traveling to the more far-flung destinations. Mount Pleasant, in particular, is a foodie favorite.

$$$$ ✕**Langdon's.** *Modern Hawaiian.* Langdon's only drawback is that it's in a nondescript strip mall across the Cooper River Bridge. Otherwise, the restaurant and wine bar belonging to Mount Pleasant native son Patrick Owens triumphs, earning a teetering pile of awards. Owens merges local cuisine with Pan-Asian flavors, exacting a rich menu composed of Hawaiian tuna, local shrimp and grouper, and black-skillet beef tenderloin, along with sides like succotash, smoked-tomato-and-Brie grits, and leek-and-corn risotto. $ *Average main: $30* ✉ *778 S. Shelmore Blvd., Mount Pleasant* ☎ *843/388–9200* 🌐 *www.langdonsrestaurant.com.*

$$$$ 🍴 **Old Village Post House.** *Southern.* If you've been on the road too long, this circa 1888 inn will provide warmth and sustenance. Many residents of this tree-lined village consider this their neighborhood tavern. The second, smaller dining room is cozy, and the outdoor space under the market umbrellas is open and airy. Expect contemporary takes on Southern favorites like lump crab cakes, shrimp and grits, and especially the fresh vegetables, like a butter beans mélange. From the open kitchen, the chefs can perfectly sauté the catch of the day. Here, pork tenderloin may have a ginger-peachy glaze. In season, plump soft-shell crabs are deftly fried. Frank Sinatra serenades as you cleanse your palate with a tart key lime pie with a crunchy crust and passion-fruit coulis. [$] *Average main: $26* ✉ *101 Pitt St., Mount Pleasant* ☎ *843/388–8935* 🌐 *www.mavericksouthernkitchens.com* 🕒 *No lunch Mon.–Sat.*

$$$$ 🍴 **Red Drum.** *Southwestern.* Locals and visitors alike tend to overlook this Mount Pleasant staple in favor of the more stylish picks downtown. That's their loss. Chef Ben Berryhill leans on his Texas roots to formulate a South-by-Southwest approach, cooking venison sausage, double-cut pork chops, and rib-eye steaks on a wood-burning grill he calls "The Beast." Also sample savory beef empanadas or large "fork and knife" tacos from the bar, and head out to the outdoor patio for a beer or beverage. The nightlife here is lively. [$] *Average main: $25* ✉ *803 Coleman Blvd., Mount Pleasant* ☎ *843/849–0313* 🕒 *No lunch.*

$$ 🍴 **SeeWee Restaurant.** *Southern.* This former general store is about 20 minutes from downtown, but it's worth the trip for the Southern-style flashback. You pull open the screen door and find shelves that are still lined with canned goods with a scattering of tables. Outdoors on the screened porch is more seating and a spot where bands perform (really good blues, bluegrass, and so on) on warm Saturday nights. The veteran waitresses will call you "hon" and recommend their favorites, a lot of which are Southern-fried: pickles, green tomatoes, chicken, oysters, and fresh local shrimp. The blackboard lists more contemporary, less caloric dishes. For breakfast or lunch, opt for the lovely traditional shrimp and grits. [$] *Average main: $18* ✉ *4808 Hwy. 17 N, Awendaw* ☎ *843/928–3609* 🕒 *No dinner Sun.*

★ $$$ Fodor's Choice 🍴 **The Wreck of the Richard & Charlene.** *Seafood.* At first glance, the odd name appears to refer to this waterfront restaurant's exterior, topped off with a shabby screened-in porch. In actuality, the *Richard and Charlene* was a trawler that slammed into the building during a hurricane in 1989. But looks aren't the thing here—it's all about the food. Located in the old village of Mount Pleasant, the kitchen serves up Southern tradition on a plate: boiled peanuts, fried shrimp, and stone-crab claws. The best option is the most expensive: the mixed seafood platter with fried flounder, shrimp, oysters, and scallops. Get here early, as the place closes by 8:30 Tuesday through Thursday, and at 9:15 on Friday and Saturday night. $ *Average main: $22* ⊠ *106 Haddrell St., Mount Pleasant* ☎ *843/884–0052* ⊕ *www.wreckrc.com* ⚓ *Reservations not accepted* ▭ *No credit cards* ⊗ *No lunch. Closed Sun. and Mon.*

GREATER CHARLESTON

$$ ✕**Bowen's Island.** *Seafood.* This seafood shack has survived hurricanes, fires, and the onslaught of trendy restaurants hitting downtown. Littered with oyster shells and graffiti, the funky spot serves dinner in an enclosed dock house, on a covered deck, and inside the main building. The menu is the constant: big ol' shrimp, fried or boiled; shrimp and grits; hush puppies; and the biggie—all the steamed oysters you can eat for about $20. At this "fish camp," you might be entertained by musician Smokin' Weiner or Juke Joint Johnny. This local landmark sits on an island just before Folly Beach, about 15 minutes from downtown. When you see the sign, head down the dirt road until you see water. $ *Average main: $16* ⊠ *1871 Bowen's Island Rd., James Island* ☎ *843/270–7050* ⊕ *www.bowensislandrestaurant.com* ▭ *No credit cards* ⊗ *No lunch. No dinner Sun. and Mon.*

$$$$ ✕**Coda del Pesce.** *Italian.* On Isle of Palms, Ken Vedrinski's homage to the sea is not to be missed. Sure, it's a hike from downtown, but it's worth it because the chef's take on seafood is—dare we say it—seaworthy. The crudo (raw fish) with tangerines, wine vinegar, and pickled garlic makes an excellent starter before you dive into blue crab with parsley, lemons, and bread crumbs or clams with preserved tomatoes and spicy peppers. (Local waterman Clammer Dave provides the main ingredient.) If the chef is around, he'll be more than happy to make wine recommendations and provide some entertaining conversation. A bonus: This tiny restaurant has one of the rare ocean views from its second-story patio. $ *Average main: $28* ⊠ *1130 Ocean Blvd., Isle of Palms* ☎ *843/242–8570* ⊕ *www.codadelpesce. com* ⊗ *No lunch.*

$$$$ 🍴 **Edmund's Oast.** *Southern.* A short drive from King Street, this place is worth the trek if you're a brew aficionado. With 40 beers on tap, owners Rich Carly and Scott Shor (also owners of the Charleston Beer Exchange) weren't kidding when they said they were opening a brew pub. But it's not just what's in the pint glasses that has locals raving. Chef Andy Henderson (whose culinary career includes San Francisco's Local Mission Eatery) has proved himself in the kitchen, dishing up heritage chicken and Carolina Gold rice porridge, roasted grouper with cowpea and fennel salad, and braised lamb meatballs. The atmosphere is chic yet comfortable with large booths, canvased chairs, and a huge bar, and an outdoor patio invites you to sip in the sunshine. [$] *Average main: $25* ✉ *1081 Morrison Dr., North Central* ☎ *843/727–1145* 🌐 *edmundsoast.com* ⏲ *No lunch.*

$ 🍴 **Extra Virgin Oven.** *Pizza.* The Park Circle neighborhood of North Charleston is home to one of the area's top pizzerias, which doles out Neapolitan-style pies with super-thin and crunchy crusts. The Food Network chose EVO's pistachio pesto pie—containing goat, mozzarella, and Parmesan cheese on a pesto base whipped up with olive oil, salt, and pistachios—as the state's best slice. As for the locals, they tend to go for the pork trifecta pizza, a meat-tastic dish made with house-made sweet sausages, pepperoni, and smoked bacon. EVO also relies on local and regional purveyors for produce like grape and heirloom tomatoes and lettuce. There's a bonus: you're guaranteed a nice variety of craft brews like Holy City's Chucktown Follicle Brown and Westbrook's White Thai witbier. [$] *Average main: $14* ✉ *1075 E. Montague Ave., North Charleston* ☎ *843/225–1796* 🌐 *www.evopizza.com* ⏲ *Closed Mon. No lunch Sat.*

$ 🍴 **Fiery Ron's Home Team BBQ.** *Southern.* This bar and restaurant has swiftly earned the endorsement of even the old-school barbecue set (the restaurant's newfangled pork tacos notwithstanding). And Home Team has done so with time-honored adherence to the oft-preferred technique of low-and-slow grilling, producing St. Louis–style ribs, and traditional smoked pork and chicken. Dress up your meal with three tableside sauces, including vinegar flavored, tomato tinged, and a mustard-based concoction, befitting South Carolina's German heritage. Side offerings are a good measuring stick for any barbecue joint, and Home Team delivers with mashed potatoes, collard greens, red rice, baked beans, poppy-seed slaw, and potato salad. There's a second location on Sullivan's Island. [$] *Average main: $8* ✉ *1205 Ashley River Rd., West Ashley* ☎ *843/225–7427* 🌐 *www.hometeambbq.com.*

$ ✕ **The Glass Onion.** *Southern.* Established by a trio of Louisiana ex-pats, the Glass Onion fashions a taut bond between Charleston and New Orleans, dishing up *beaucoup* Southern eats. Take a peek at the menu: deviled eggs, meat loaf, fried catfish po'boys, and overstuffed pimiento-cheese sandwiches, along with sweets like bread pudding with whiskey sauce. Yep, it's decidedly Southern, and decidedly dreamy. The Saturday brunch is a must, with fluffy buttermilk biscuits and gravy, and savory pork tamales, but get there early, as they often sell out. The meals are set on sheets of brown paper that drape the restaurant's wooden tabletops, another clever touch. [$] *Average main: $12* ✉ *1219 Savannah Hwy., Johns Island* ☎ *843/225–1717* 🌐 *www.ilovetheglassonion.com.*

3

$$ ✕ **Heart Woodfire Kitchen.** *American.* On James Island, Heart Woodfire Kitchen turns out perfect skewered meats, roasted vegetables, and flatbreads aboard its open-flame rotisserie and wood-fired oven. Housed inside a former burrito joint in the suburbs, the restaurant's best feature is its outdoor patio. The pricing—cocktails included—checks in at a reduced rate compared with the rest of downtown, allowing a stylish but affordable night out. The heavenly cheeseburger, on a bun baked on the premises, remains one of the best around. The sides are tasty and seasonal, including kale, grits, apple-celery root, and creamed mustard greens. [$] *Average main: $15* ✉ *1622 Highland Ave., James Island* ☎ *843/718–1539* 🌐 *www.heartkitchenji.com.*

$ ✕ **Jack's Cosmic Dogs.** *American.* Searching for a good hot
FAMILY dog? The Galactic, Krypto, Orbit City, and Neutron varieties at Jack's Cosmic are otherworldly excellent, with blue-cheese slaw, spicy mustard, sauerkraut, zippy onion relish, and Jack's own sweet-potato mustard, all swaddled in Pepperidge Farms split-top buns. Akin to a diner, Jack's serves milk shakes and sundaes, real custard soft-serve ice cream, draft root beer, and hand-cut fries. Kids love it here. It's the perfect intersection of the '50s—the 1950s and 2050s. [$] *Average main: $5* ✉ *2805 N. Hwy 17, Mount Pleasant* ☎ *843/225–1817* 🌐 *www.jackscosmicdogs.com.*

$ ✕ **JB's Smokeshack.** *Southern.* If you're hankering for a country barbecue joint, JB's will do ya. When you spot the sign of the pig (along with other rudimentary signs stuck in the ground), you'll know you've arrived. At this funky find, you'll find everything from beat-up pickup trucks to shiny BMWs in the parking lot. Most patrons choose the reasonably priced buffet, which consists of barbecue pork, apple-wood-smoked chicken, a selection of Southern veggies—usually including okra gumbo, butter beans, and coleslaw—and desserts like banana pudding. Barbecue connoisseurs know that JB's takes the big prizes at the competitions and that the ribs and the Angus beef brisket are top-shelf. To further flavor the smoky meats, sauces are served on the side. Arrive early, because dinner is over by 8:30. [$] *Average main: $9* ✉ *3406 Maybank Hwy., Johns Island* ☎ *843/577–0426* 🌐 *www.jbssmokeshack.com* ⏲ *Closed Sun.–Tues.*

$$ 🍴 **The Obstinate Daughter.** *Italian.* Known for his fine Italian cuisine at Wild Olive on John's Island, Chef Jaques Larson has moved to the Obstinate Daughter on Sullivan's Island, where he's once again been a wild success. In the charming blue-and-white space—nautically styled, of course—the music is vintage R&B and the vibe is relaxed. Larson's Mepkin Abbey mushrooms is the best of the starters. From there you can play it safe with the excellent gnocchi or fat strands of spicy bucatini pasta. Or dive into some grilled octopus with white beans, collard flower kimchi, and charred green onion, or scallops and squid fra diavolo. [$] *Average main: $17* ✉ *2063 Middle St., Sullivan's Island* ☎ *843/416–5020* 🌐 *theobstinatedaughter.com* ✍ *Reservations essential.*

$ 🍴 **Poe's Tavern.** *American.* Sullivan's Island has played host to history, accommodating an important battle of the American Revolution and, in the late 1820s, a certain author named Edgar Allan Poe. The writer enlisted in the army and wound up at Fort Moultrie, at the western end of the island. His stint inspired "The Gold Bug," a short story about a magical beetle, and then much later, Poe's Tavern. The bar and restaurant is beloved among visitors and locals for its fish tacos and gourmet burgers, all named after Poe stories. To wit: The Tell-Tale Heart, containing fried eggs, apple-wood bacon, and cheddar cheese; the Amontillado, with guacamole, jalapeño jack cheese, pico de gallo, and chipotle sour cream; and naturally, the Gold Bug Plus, done up in a variety of cheeses. Come early to enjoy the clever treats, as Poe's has a line year-round. [$] *Average main: $8* ✉ *2210 Middle St., Sullivan's Island* ☎ *843/883–0083* 🌐 *www.poestavern.com.*

★ $ Fodor's Choice 🍴 **Sesame Burgers & Beer.** *American.* This burger-and-beer joint makes just about everything on the premises—from its house-ground burgers right down to the mustard, ketchup, and mayonnaise. Among the don't-miss burgers are the South Carolina, topped with homemade pimiento cheese; the Southwestern, with guacamole and chipotle sour cream; or the Park Circle, with cheddar cheese, coleslaw, barbecue sauce, and tomatoes. Also garnering special mention: Blue's corn on the cob, which is charred on the grill, then slathered in chipotle butter and Cotija cheese. Sesame's devotion to beer is strong, too, with selections running at least 30-deep. Two other locations can be found in North Charleston at 4726 Spruill Avenue and in Mount Pleasant at 675-E Johnny Dodds Boulevard. [$] *Average main: $10* ✉ *2070 Sam Rittenberg Blvd.* ☎ *843/766–7770* 🌐 *www.sesameburgersandbeer.com.*

$ ✕ **Southern General.** *Southern.* This no-frills strip mall spot puts the word "sandwich" to shame. The Southern General's 16 options include meaty masterpieces like the Super Butt, house-braised pork with smoked sweet onions and potato cream cheese, as along with healthier options like the Southern Shrimp Salad flavored with cucumber, dill, and tomato. They all come with what are arguably the best pickles in town and a choice of homemade fries or chips. The beer list is hearty as well. If you're en route to Kiawah Island and get stuck in traffic, the Southern General makes an excellent stop. [$] *Average main: $9* ✉ *3157 Maybank Hwy., Upper King* ☎ *843/640–3778* 🌐 *www.thesoutherngeneral.com.*

★ $ Fodor's Choice ✕ **Tomato Shed Cafe.** *Southern.* Open only for lunch on weekdays, the Tomato Shed Cafe presents a banquet of locally raised delicacies. Owners and farmers Pete and Babs Ambrose maintain a 135-acre farm on Wadmalaw Island, sourcing grounds for the restaurant. The menu emphasizes seasonal choices, allowing for fresh butter beans, cabbage, collards, cucumber salad, and rutabaga casserole. These veggies sit well with the Tomato Shed's other offerings, such as peel-and-eat shrimp from local waters, crab cakes, and roast pork. Be sure to grab a bag of boiled peanuts on your way out. [$] *Average main: $10* ✉ *842 Main Rd., Johns Island* ☎ *843/599–9999* 🌐 *www.stonofarmmarket.com* ⊗ *Closed Sun.*

★ $ Fodor's Choice ✕ **Voodoo Tiki Bar & Lounge.** *Eclectic.* Who would you rather share a Mai Tai with—Bruce Lee, Elvis, or Wile E. Coyote? At Voodoo, no choice is needed. All three are set in velvet portraits and framed in the dining room, directly opposite the portholes and gold curtains. The decor helps doll up this fantastical (albeit a bit fraying) tiki hut and lounge, situated in Charleston's Avondale neighborhood, west of the Ashley River. Of course, the pu pu platter—lobster corndogs, teriyaki Spam kabobs, and cheeseburger spring rolls—adds a bit of Polynesian flair. Try an order of tacos: flavors range from bacon cheeseburger to BBQ duck, and they're half-price on Sunday. $ *Average main: $8* ✉ *15 Magnolia Rd., West Ashley* ☎ *843/769–0228* 🌐 *www.voodootikibar.com* 🕓 *No lunch.*

4

WHERE TO STAY
IN CHARLESTON

By Stratton
Lawrence

CHARLESTON HAS A WELL-EARNED REPUTATION, BOTH NATIONALLY AND INTERNATIONALLY, not only as one of the most historic and beautiful cities in the country, but also as one that offers superior accommodations. It is a city known for its lovingly restored mansions that have been converted into atmospheric bed-and-breakfasts, as well as deluxe inns, all found in the residential blocks of the Historic District. World-class hotels share space in the heart of downtown with boutique hotels that provide an intimate, one-of-a-kind experience. Most are within walking distance of the shops, restaurants, and museums spread throughout the nearly 800-acre district.

Chain hotels pepper the busy, car-trafficked areas like Meeting Street. In addition, there are chain properties in the nearby areas of West Ashley, Mount Pleasant, and North Charleston, where you'll find plenty of Holiday Inns, Hampton Inns, Marriott Courtyards, and La Quinta Inns. Mount Pleasant is considered the most upscale suburb; North Charleston is the least, but if you need to be close to the airport, are participating in events at the Coliseum complex, or aim to shop the outlet malls there, it is a practical, less expensive alternative.

Overall, a visit to Charleston is a lifetime memory, and to know it is to love it. The city's scorecard for repeat visitors is phenomenal. Charleston is a port of embarkation for cruise ships, and most cruisers wisely plan on a pre- or postcruise stay. The premier wedding and honeymoon destination also draws many couples back for their anniversaries.

BED-AND-BREAKFAST AGENCIES

Historic Charleston Bed & Breakfast. Rent a carriage house behind a private home in downtown's Historic District through this reservation service. Handsomely furnished, these properties can be less expensive than many hotel rooms. Each one has a private entrance and is required to offer free parking. ☎ 843/722–6606, 800/743–3583 ⊕ *www.historiccharlestonbedandbreakfast.com.*

VACATION HOME RENTALS

Dunes Properties. For a wide selection of house and condo rentals on Folly Beach and Isle of Palms (including Wild Dunes Resort), call the Isle of Palms branch of locally owned Dunes Properties. ✉ *1400 Palm Blvd., Isle of Palms* ☎ *843/886–5600* ⊕ *www.dunesproperties.com.*

Wyndham Vacation Rentals. For condo and house rentals on Kiawah Island, Seabrook Island, and Isle of Palms (including Wild Dunes Resort), contact Wyndham Vacation Rentals. ✉ *554 Freshfields La., Johns Island* ☎ *800/247–5050* ⊕ *www.wyndhamvacationrentals.com.*

PRICES

Charleston's downtown lodgings have three seasons: high season (March to May and September to November), mid-season (June to August), and low season (late November to February). Prices drop significantly during the short low season, except during holidays and special events like the Southeastern Wildlife Exposition each February. High season is summer at the island resorts; rates drop for weekly stays and during the off-season. Although prices have gone up at the B&Bs, don't forget that a full breakfast for two is generally included, as well as an evening wine reception, which can take the place of happy hour and save on your bar bill. You should factor in, however, the cost of downtown parking; if a hotel offers free parking, that is a huge plus. In the areas "over the bridges," parking is generally free. Depending on when you arrive—such as a Saturday night, staying Sunday—you can try to find on-street metered parking, as there is no charge after 6 pm and all day Sunday.

■TIP➔ **If you're on a budget, consider lodgings outside the city limits, which tend to be less expensive.** Also remember that longer stays sometimes translate into a better per-night price.

WHAT IT COSTS				
	$	$$	$$$	$$$$
Hotels	under $150	$150–$200	$201–$250	over $250

Prices are for two people in a standard double room in high season, excluding tax.

LODGING REVIEWS

Listed alphabetically within neighborhoods. The following reviews have been condensed for this book. Please go to Fodors.com for full reviews of each property.

DOWNTOWN CHARLESTON

NORTH OF BROAD

★ FodorsChoice **1837 Bed & Breakfast.** *B&B/Inn.* A hospitable staff helps give you a sense of what it would be like to live in one of Charleston's grand old homes. **Pros:** a very good concierge will help you plan your days; reasonable rates; free parking. **Cons:** limited on-site parking. *[$] Rooms from: $129 ✉ 126 Wentworth St., Market area ☎ 843/723–7166, 877/723–1837 🌐 www.1837bb.com 🛏 8 rooms, 1 suite 🍴 Breakfast.*

$

$$ **Andrew Pinckney Inn.** *B&B/Inn.* Nestled in the heart of Charleston, this West Indies–inspired inn offers a range of accommodations, from charming rooms perfect for couples to two-level suites big enough for the whole family. **Pros:** the town houses are ideal for longer stays; afternoon gourmet tea and coffee service with fresh-baked cookies; iPod docks in every room. **Cons:** elevator access for standard rooms only; bustling neighborhood and nearby horse stables can be noisy. *[$] Rooms from: $199 ✉ 40 Pinckney St., Market area ☎ 843/937–8800, 800/505–8983 🌐 www.andrewpinckneyinn.com 🛏 33 rooms, 3 town houses, 5 suites 🍴 Breakfast.*

★ FodorsChoice **Ansonborough Inn.** *B&B/Inn.* At this boutique hotel you can relax in your comfortable suite or indulge in evening wine and cheese on the rooftop terrace while enjoying views of the city and Cooper River. **Pros:** lots of period details; 24-hour upscale supermarket across the street; easy walking distance to the Market. **Cons:** not that close to King Street shops; some rooms open to a central atrium directly over the lobby. *[$] Rooms from: $169 ✉ 21 Hasell St., Market area ☎ 843/723–1655, 800/723–1655 🌐 www.ansonboroughinn.com 🛏 45 suites 🍴 Breakfast.*

$$

★ FodorsChoice **Belmond Charleston Place.** *Hotel.* Even casual passersby enjoy gazing up at the immense handblown Murano glass chandelier in the hotel's open lobby, clicking across the Italian marble floors, and browsing the gallery of upscale shops that completes the ground-floor offerings of this hotel. **Pros:** full of antiques from Sotheby's; on the best shopping street in the Historic District; pet-friendly. **Cons:** rooms aren't as big as one might expect for the

$$$$

CLOSE UP

Best Bets for Charleston Lodging

We've compiled our picks for every price range, from the best budget beds to the most sophisticated lodgings. The very best have a Fodor's Choice symbol.

Fodor's Choice: 1837 Bed & Breakfast, Ansonborough Inn, Charleston Place, Kiawah Island Golf Resort, Market Pavilion Hotel, Mills House, Planters Inn, Restoration on King, Two Meeting Street Inn, The Vendue, Wentworth Mansion, Wild Dunes Resort, Zero George

Best B&Bs: The Governor's House Inn, John Rutledge House Inn, Two Meeting Street Inn

Best Beaches: Kiawah Island Golf Resort, Seabrook Island, Wild Dunes Resort

Best Beds: John Rutledge House Inn, Restoration on King, Wentworth Mansion

Best Budget Stay: Aloft Charleston Airport & Convention Center, Old Village Post House

Best for Kids: DoubleTree by Hilton Hotel & Suites Charleston–Historic District, Wild Dunes Resort, Charleston Harbor Resort & Marina

Best for Romance: John Rutledge House Inn, Wentworth Mansion

Best Grand Dame Hotels: Francis Marion Hotel, Wentworth Mansion

Best Gym: Charleston Place, Kiawah Island Golf Resort

Best Hotel Bars: Ansonborough Inn, Charleston Place, Market Pavilion Hotel, The Vendue

Best Interior Design: Restoration on King, The Sanctuary at Kiawah Island (at Kiawah Island Golf Resort)

Best-Kept Secret: 1837 Bed & Breakfast, Restoration on King, William Aiken House Cottage and Lowndes Grove

Best Location: Charleston Place, Francis Marion Hotel

Best Pools: Charleston Place, Hilton Garden Inn Charleston Waterfront, Market Pavilion Hotel

Best Service: Charleston Place, Market Pavilion Hotel, Planters Inn

Best Views: HarbourView Inn, Two Meeting Street Inn, Wentworth Mansion

Business Travel: Charleston Marriott, Charleston Place, HarbourView Inn

Great Concierge: Courtyard by Marriott Charleston Historic District, Francis Marion Hotel, Mills House

Hipster Hotels: Aloft Charleston Airport & Convention Center, Restoration on King, Zero George

Pet-Friendly: Charleston Place, Indigo Inn, Inn at Middleton Place

Remarkable Architecture: Wentworth Mansion, William Aiken House Cottage and Lowndes Grove

4

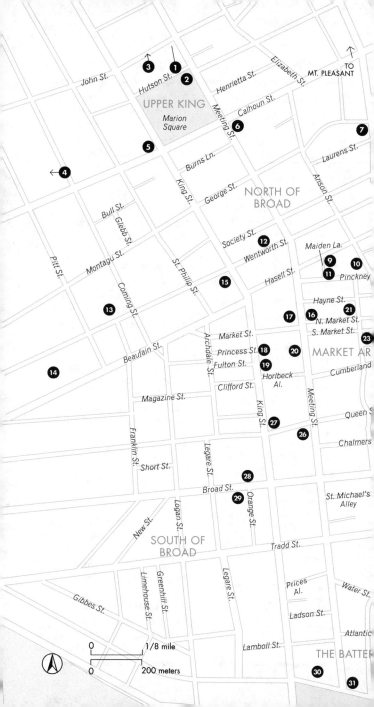

Where to Stay in Downtown Charleston

Concord St.

Pritchard St.

Market St.

22

25
Vendue
24 Range
Unity Alley

Exchange
St.

St.

East Bay St.

Cooper River

1837 Bed & Breakfast, **13**

1843 Battery
Carriage House Inn, **30**

Andrew Pinckney Inn, **10**

Ansonborough Inn, **8**

Belmond
Charleston Place, **17**

Courtyard by Marriott
Charleston Historic District, **6**

DoubleTree by Hilton Hotel &
Suites—Charleston Historic
District, **21**

The Elliott House Inn, **27**

Embassy Suites Historic
Charleston, **2**

Francis Marion Hotel, **5**

French Quarter Inn, **23**

Fulton Lane Inn, **18**

The Governor's House Inn, **29**

Hampton Inn–Historic
District, **1**

HarbourView Inn, **25**

Indigo Inn, **11**

Jasmine House Inn, **9**

John Rutledge House Inn, **28**

Kings Courtyard Inn, **19**

Lowndes Grove, **4**

Market Pavilion Hotel, **22**

Meeting Street Inn, **20**

Mills House, **26**

Planters Inn, **16**

Renaissance Charleston
Historic District Hotel, **12**

Restoration on King, **15**

Two Meeting Street Inn, **31**

The Vendue, **24**

Wentworth Mansion, **14**

William Aiken
House, **3**

Zero George, **7**

price; hosts lots of conference groups in shoulder seasons; built in 1986, it lacks the charm of more historic properties. ⓢ *Rooms from: $279 ⊠ 205 Meeting St., Market area* ☎ *843/722–4900, 888/635–2350* ⊕ *www.belmond.com/charleston-place* ⚡ *435 rooms, 48 suites* ⓞ *No meals.*

$$ ▦ **Courtyard by Marriott Charleston Historic District.** *Hotel.* Step off the historic streets of Charleston into the high-tech lobby of this hotel—looks for a tucked-away media center with a big-screen TV, a boarding-pass printing station, and a sleek bistro that offers coffee, cocktails, and breakfast and dinner fare. **Pros:** concierge Kevin McQuade gets rave reviews for his excellent recommendations; families will be right at home in the suites with comfortable seating and kitchenettes. **Cons:** many views are obstructed by other buildings; breakfast not included; at the corner of a very busy intersection. ⓢ *Rooms from: $159 ⊠ 125 Calhoun St., Upper King* ☎ *843/805–7900* ⊕ *www.marriott.com/hotels/travel/chshd-courtyard-charleston-historic-district* ⚡ *168 rooms, 8 suites* ⓞ *No meals.*

$$$ ▦ **DoubleTree by Hilton Hotel & Suites Charleston–Historic District.**
FAMILY *Hotel.* With a beautifully restored entrance portico from 1874, this former bank building offers spacious suites with nice touches like antique reproductions and canopy beds. **Pros:** an easy walk to King Street shopping and a charming stroll to the South of Broad residential area; family-friendly vibe. **Cons:** no free breakfast, although there is an on-site café; lacks the historic atmosphere of an independent inn. ⓢ *Rooms from: $209 ⊠ 181 Church St., Market area* ☎ *843/577–2644* ⊕ *www.doubletree.com* ⚡ *47 rooms, 165 suites* ⓞ *No meals.*

$$$$ ▦ **The Elliott House Inn.** *B&B/Inn.* Listen to the chimes of nearby churches as you sip wine in the greenery-laden courtyard of this inn, then retreat to a cozy room with period furnishings and four-poster beds, or bubble away some social time in the whirlpool tub that can (and often does) hold a dozen people. **Pros:** the helpful staff is generous with recommendations and advice; free bikes and Wi-Fi access; nightly wine-and-cheese reception. **Cons:** street-view rooms can be noisy; no roll-away beds for the kids; complimentary breakfast offerings are limited. ⓢ *Rooms from: $269 ⊠ 78 Queen St., Market area* ☎ *843/518–6500* ⊕ *www.elliotthouseinn.com* ⚡ *25 rooms* ⓞ *Breakfast.*

$$ ▦ **Embassy Suites Historic Charleston.** *Hotel.* A courtyard where cadets once marched is now a soaring atrium—complete with a glass ceiling, frilly palm trees, and a babbling fountain—in this 1822 building that once served as the Old

PROPERTY TYPES IN CHARLESTON

Charleston's lodgings run the gamut from intimate inns to sophisticated hotels to beach-front resorts where you can pretend you're miles away from civilization.

B&Bs: Bed-and-breakfasts conjure up the image of a mom 'n' pop operation with Mother at the stove flipping pancakes. In Charleston, the concept has been taken to a higher level; although they may be owned by a couple, most B&Bs also employ a small staff. Most are within the Historic District and often were former grand residences, such as the Governor's House Inn or the John Rutledge House Inn.

Inns. In this town, a fine line divides true inns from B&Bs. They are usually larger than B&Bs and often have more professional staff, including a concierge (as at the Planters Inn). The breakfast and evening offerings are often a step above those of B&Bs, and they may even have a restaurant, as does the Wentworth Mansion.

Boutique Hotels: Though small by international hotel standards, Charleston's boutique hotels offer a pampering staff in a small setting. Those who stay here can experience the good life by day and at night slumber in a sumptuous bed dressed with Egyptian-cotton sheets and cashmere blankets. The Market Pavilion Hotel is perhaps the city's best-known boutique hotel, but a newer kid on the boutique hotel block, Restoration on King, is quickly gaining notoriety and a solid fan base as well.

Full-Service Hotels: In a city known for atmospheric B&Bs, there are visitors who prefer the amenities and privacy of a large, world-class property (Charleston Place) or a well-known American chain hotel (such as the Charleston Marriott). And in a city where the temperatures trend high during the summer months, it may be worth trading historic charm for a hotel pool and vigorous air-conditioning.

Island Resorts: The barrier islands surrounding the city of Charleston are the sites for three major, self-contained resorts: Kiawah Island Golf Resort, its neighbor Seabrook Island, and the Wild Dunes Resort on the Isle of Palms. All three have 18-hole golf courses, with Kiawah's being the most famous and most costly (the PGA Championship was played there in 2012), and each has excellent tennis facilities. Seabrook has no hotel accommodations (just villas and condos); Wild Dunes is the most family-friendly.

Citadel. **Pros:** near the Saturday farmers' market; close to Upper King's hip business and retail district; complimentary manager's reception nightly in the bar and lobby. **Cons:** the suites lack charm; some rooms have little or no natural light. [$] *Rooms from: $199* ✉ *337 Meeting St., Upper King* ☎ *843/723–6900, 800/362–2779* 🌐 *www.embassysuites.com* 🛏 *153 suites* 🍴 *Breakfast.*

$$ 🏨 **Francis Marion Hotel.** *Hotel.* Wrought-iron railings, crown moldings, and decorative plasterwork speak of the elegance of 1924, when the Francis Marion was the largest hotel in the Carolinas. **Pros:** in the midst of the peninsula's best shopping; on-site day spa; some of the best city views. **Cons:** rooms are small, as is closet space; on a busy intersection. [$] *Rooms from: $169* ✉ *387 King St., Upper King* ☎ *843/722–0600, 877/756–2121* 🌐 *www.francismarioncharleston.com* 🛏 *218 rooms, 17 suites* 🍴 *No meals.*

SOMETHING EXTRA. **Charleston isn't regularly voted among the most romantic cities in the country for nothing. When you book your room, ask about special packages. Extras that are often available include romantic carriage rides, dinners, interesting guided tours, and champagne or other goodies delivered to your room. This goes for most properties downtown.**

$$ 🏨 **French Quarter Inn.** *Hotel.* You'll appreciate the lavish seasonal breakfasts with freshly baked pastries (and mimosas and other beverages on weekends), the afternoon wine-and-cheese receptions, and evening cookies and milk at this friendly boutique hotel. **Pros:** a quiet haven in the heart of the Market area; champagne at check-in; free bike rentals. **Cons:** no pool or fitness area; neighborhood can be noisy and crowded; parking is pricey and valet only. [$] *Rooms from: $199* ✉ *10 Linguard St., Market area* ☎ *843/722–1900, 866/812–1900* 🌐 *www.fqicharleston.com* 🛏 *33 rooms, 17 suites* 🍴 *Breakfast.*

$$$ 🏨 **Fulton Lane Inn.** *B&B/Inn.* This inn is both lovely and quirky: its Victorian-dressed rooms (some with four-poster beds, handsome fireplaces, and jetted tubs) are laid out in a bit of a floor-creaking maze, but it adds to the inn's individuality. **Pros:** location is tops; charming choice of rooms; breakfast can be delivered to your room. **Cons:** what's character to one guest can be annoying to another; street noise does seep in. [$] *Rooms from: $219* ✉ *202 King St., Lower King Street* ☎ *843/720–2600* 🌐 *www.fultonlaneinn.com* 🛏 *45 rooms* 🍴 *Breakfast.*

$$ 🏨 **Hampton Inn Charleston–Historic District.** *Hotel.* Hardwood floors, a central fireplace, and leather furnishings in the lobby of what was once an 1800s warehouse help elevate this chain hotel a bit above the rest. **Pros:** hot breakfast; located near numerous restaurant and nightlife options. **Cons:** a long walk to the Market area; rooms are smallish; no views. [$] *Rooms from: $199* ✉ *345 Meeting St., Upper King* ☎ *843/723–4000, 800/426–7866* 🌐 *www.hamptoninn.com* 🛏 *170 rooms* 🍴 *Breakfast.*

$$$$ 🏨 **HarbourView Inn.** *Hotel.* This is the only hotel facing Charleston Harbor, and if you ask for a room with a view or even a private balcony, and you can gaze out onto the kid-friendly fountain at the center of Waterfront Park. **Pros:** Continental breakfast can be delivered to your room or the rooftop; location is tops; service is notable. **Cons:** rooms are off long, modern halls, giving the place more of a chain-hotel feel. [$] *Rooms from: $279* ✉ *2 Vendue Range, Market area* ☎ *843/853–8439* 🌐 *www.harbourviewcharleston.com* 🛏 *52 rooms* 🍴 *Breakfast.*

$$ 🏨 **Indigo Inn.** *B&B/Inn.* Repeat guests are the norm thanks to the convenient setting of the family-owned Indigo Inn, a former warehouse that's known for its particularly welcoming and helpful front-desk staff. **Pros:** excellent location; pets allowed in some rooms; quality bottles of wine can be purchased from the front desk. **Cons:** rooms are not large and some are dark; although renovations are ongoing, decor can be a little tired. [$] *Rooms from: $189* ✉ *1 Maiden La., Lower King* ☎ *843/577–5900* 🌐 *www.indigoinn.com* 🛏 *40 rooms* 🍴 *Breakfast.*

$$ 🏨 **Jasmine House Inn.** *B&B/Inn.* Walking down the quiet, tree-lined street and coming upon this glorious 1843 Greek-revival mansion—yellow with white columns—you simply want to make your way inside. **Pros:** complimentary beverages (hot and cold in the kitchen); evening wine-and-cheese spreads on the sideboard; several rooms have working fireplaces; a wide front porch features comfortable rocking chairs. **Cons:** children are not allowed. [$] *Rooms from: $199* ✉ *64 Hassell St., Market area* ☎ *843/577–5900* 🌐 *www.jasminehouseinn.com* 🛏 *8 rooms, 2 suites, 1 apartment* 🍴 *Breakfast.*

$$$ 🏨 **Kings Courtyard Inn.** *B&B/Inn.* The three delightful courtyards at this centrally located circa-1853 inn are great places to enjoy your continental breakfast, afternoon sherry, or evening wine and cheese in the open air. **Pros:** ideal location for walking to shops and restaurants; pets are allowed in four rooms; double-paned windows muffle street noise. **Cons:** walls are thin; guests from Fulton Lane Inn share in the evening receptions, creating a sometimes-bustling atmosphere. $ *Rooms from: $219* ✉ *198 King St., Lower King Street* ☎ *843/723-7000, 800/845–6119* 🌐 *www.kingscourtyardinn.com* 🛏 *37 rooms, 4 suites* 🍴 *Breakfast.*

★ Fodor'sChoice 🏨 **Market Pavilion Hotel.** *Hotel.* The hustle and
$$$$ bustle of one of the city's busiest corners vanishes as soon as the uniformed bellman opens the lobby door of the Market Pavilion Hotel to reveal wood-paneled walls, antique furnishings, and chandeliers hung from high ceilings; it resembles a European grand hotel from the 19th century, and you feel like you're visiting royalty. **Pros:** opulent furnishings; architecturally impressive, especially the tray ceilings; conveniently located for everything. **Cons:** the gym is small; some may find the interior over the top. $ *Rooms from: $279* ✉ *225 E. Bay St., Market area* ☎ *843/723–0500* 🌐 *www.marketpavilion.com* 🛏 *61 rooms, 9 suites* 🍴 *Breakfast.*

$$ 🏨 **Meeting Street Inn.** *B&B/Inn.* Guest rooms in this 1874 stucco house with porches on the second, third, and fourth floors overlook a lovely courtyard with fountains and a heated spa tub. **Pros:** some of the more expensive rooms have desks and other extras; bathrooms sport nice marble fixtures. **Cons:** decor could use some updating; some rooms overlook an adjacent parking lot; parking is pricey. $ *Rooms from: $159* ✉ *173 Meeting St., Market area* ☎ *843/723–1882, 800/842–8022* 🌐 *www.meetingstreetinn.com* 🛏 *56 rooms* 🍴 *Breakfast.*

★ Fodor'sChoice 🏨 **Mills House.** *Hotel.* A favorite local landmark
$$ that serves as a departure point for several historic tours, the Mills House is the modern iteration of the original 1853 hotel by the same name, where General Robert E. Lee once slept. **Pros:** convenient to Historic District; a popular Sunday brunch spot; a concierge desk so well regarded that locals call for neighborly assistance and advice. **Cons:** rooms are rather small, which is typical of hotels of this time period; it's on a busy street; parking is valet only and expensive. $ *Rooms from: $179* ✉ *115 Meeting St., Market area* ☎ *843/577–2400, 800/874–9600* 🌐 *www.millshouse.com* 🛏 *199 rooms, 16 suites* 🍴 *No meals.*

★ Fodor'sChoice 🏨 **Planters Inn.** *B&B/Inn.* Part of the Relais
$$$$ & Châteaux group, this boutique property with well-appointed and beautifully maintained rooms is a stately sanctuary amid the bustle of Charleston's Market. **Pros:** double-pane and interior shuttered windows render the

rooms soundproof; front-desk staff knows your name upon arrival; exceptional full breakfast (included only as part of a package). **Cons:** no pool; no fitness center; parking is pricey and by valet only. [$] *Rooms from: $399* ✉ *112 N. Market St., Market area* ☎ *843/722–2345, 800/845–7082* 🌐 *www.plantersinn.com* 🛏 *58 rooms, 6 suites* 🍴 *No meals.*

$$$$ 🏨 **Renaissance Charleston Historic District Hotel.** *Hotel.* If you want to park your car and explore the city by foot, this upscale property is the place for you. **Pros:** located in the King Street shopping district; lounge and restaurant completely renovated in 2013; friendly and helpful staff. **Cons:** rooms have a chain-hotel feel; charge for in-room Wi-Fi; small pool. [$] *Rooms from: $299* ✉ *68 Wentworth St., Ansonborough* ☎ *843/534–0300* 🌐 *www.renaissancecharlestonhotel.com* 🛏 *163 rooms, 3 suites* 🍴 *No meals.*

★ Fodor'sChoice 🏨 **Restoration on King.** *B&B/Inn.* Charleston
$$$$ architect Neil Stevenson designed this boutique hotel to be swank and suave to the hilt, even featuring a rooftop terrace with sleek sofas and prime views. **Pros:** complimentary passes to nearby workout facilities; room service comes via neighboring restaurants; free bike and beach chair rentals. **Cons:** no gym on the premises, but there are within easy walking distance; prices are steep. [$] *Rooms from: $299* ✉ *75 Wentworth St., Market area* ☎ *843/518–5100* 🌐 *www.restorationonking.com* 🛏 *16 suites* 🍴 *Breakfast.*

ZEN DOG. **If you have brought your dog along but don't want to leave him in your room all day, call Zen Dog, run by Pet Vet Animal Hospital in Mount Pleasant. Their cageless daycare includes a backyard for playtime.** ✉ ***307 Mill St., Mount Pleasant*** ☎ ***843/884–7387.***

★ Fodor'sChoice 🏨 **The Vendue.** *B&B/Inn.* A $4.8 million renova-
$$$$ tion transformed the Vendue into an art-filled space that feels as much like a contemporary art museum as it does a boutique hotel. **Pros:** free bike rentals; soundproofing masks street noise; great restaurant and coffee shop. **Cons:** no complimentary breakfast. [$] *Rooms from: $275* ✉ *19 Vendue Range, Market area* ☎ *843/577–7970, 800/845–7900* 🌐 *www.thevendue.com* 🛏 *86 rooms.*

★ Fodor'sChoice 🏨 **Wentworth Mansion.** *B&B/Inn.* The grandest
$$$$ inn in town features Second Empire antiques and reproductions, elaborate woodwork, and original stained-glass windows, as well as the sweeping views from the rooftop cupola. **Pros:** each room has a whirlpool tub and iPod docking station; three rooms are pet-friendly; free parking.

Cons: style can strike some people as forbidding; outside the tourist areas. $ *Rooms from: $420 ⊠ 149 Wentworth St., College of Charleston Campus ☎ 843/853–1886 ⊕ www. wentworthmansion.com ⌨ 21 rooms ⦿ Breakfast.*

$$ ▣ **William Aiken House.** *Rental.* One of the city's most picturesque, historic, and popular wedding sites has suites where you can spend the night in a National Historic Landmark. **Pros:** filled with museum-quality art; steeped in history; ideal for those who crave privacy. **Cons:** not for guests who want or need a lot of attention; suites don't have kitchens and are equipped with only a minirefrigerator and microwave. $ *Rooms from: $175 ⊠ 456 King St., Upper King ☎ 843/853–1810 ⊕ www.pphgcharleston.com ⌨ 7 suites ⦿ No meals.*

★ **Fodor'sChoice** ▣ **Zero George.** *Hotel.* Five restored 19th-century
$$$$ residences have been joined together to create this hideaway in the heart of Charleston's leafy Ansonborough neighborhood that's surrounded by well-heeled homes, and just a short walk from East Bay restaurants, City Market, and Liberty Square. **Pros:** comfortable style; convenient and quiet location; attentive service; local charm; free Wi-Fi and breakfast. **Cons:** it's a bit of a walk to the Market and to King Street. $ *Rooms from: $299 ⊠ 0 George St., Ansonborough ☎ 843/817–7900 ⊕ www.zerogeorge.com ⌨ 18 studios and suites ⦿ Breakfast.*

SOUTH OF BROAD

$$$ ▣ **1843 Battery Carriage House Inn.** *B&B/Inn.* Facing White Point Gardens, this 19th-century house has views of Fort Sumter and Charleston Harbor from the front steps. **Pros:** quiet and romantic location; high level of service; each room is individually decorated. **Cons:** most rooms are small and modest; children staying here must be at least 12 years old; no full breakfast (light continental instead). $ *Rooms from: $229 ⊠ 20 S. Battery, South of Broad ☎ 843/727–3100 ⊕ www.batterycarriagehouse.com ⌨ 10 rooms, 1 suite.*

$$$$ ▣ **The Governor's House Inn.** *B&B/Inn.* The stately architecture of this quintessential Charleston lodging radiates the grandeur, romance, and civility of the city's bountiful colonial era. **Pros:** pets are allowed in some rooms; free bicycles make exploring the city a breeze; free off-street parking in an elegant courtyard. **Cons:** kids not allowed in the main-building rooms. $ *Rooms from: $265 ⊠ 117 Broad St., South of Broad ☎ 843/720–2070, 800/720–9812 ⊕ www.governorshouse.com ⌨ 11 rooms ⦿ Breakfast.*

$$$$ 🏨 **John Rutledge House Inn.** *B&B/Inn.* In 1791, George Washington visited this elegant mansion, then residence of one of South Carolina's most influential politicians, John Rutledge; you can follow in his footsteps by booking one of the spacious accommodations within this National Historic Landmark. **Pros:** at night, when you pour a sherry, it's like being a blue-blood Charlestonian; quiet back courtyard; friendly staff; pets allowed in some rooms. **Cons:** you can hear some street and kitchen noise in the first-floor rooms; the two carriage houses are not as grand as the main house. $ *Rooms from: $300* ✉ *116 Broad St., South of Broad* ☎ *843/723–7999, 800/476–9741* 🌐 *www.johnrutledgehouseinn.com* 🛏 *16 rooms, 3 suites* 🍴 *Breakfast.*

$$$ 🏨 **Two Meeting Street Inn.** *B&B/Inn.* As pretty as a wedding cake, this 1892 Queen Anne–style mansion wears overhanging bays, colonnades, balustrades, and a turret; two original Tiffany stained-glass windows (worth as much as the house itself), carved-oak paneling, and a crystal chandelier dress up the public spaces. **Pros:** free on-street parking; community refrigerator on each floor; ringside seat for a Battery view and horse-drawn carriages clipping by. **Cons:** no credit cards accepted; not equipped for handicapped guests; children under 12 not allowed; the decor is on the grandmotherly side. $ *Rooms from: $225* ✉ *2 Meeting St., South of Broad* ☎ *843/723–7322* 🌐 *www.twomeetingstreet.com* 🛏 *9 rooms* 💳 *No credit cards* 🍴 *Breakfast.*

MOUNT PLEASANT

$$$ 🏨 **Charleston Harbor Resort & Marina.** *Resort.* Mount Pleasant's
FAMILY finest hotel sits on Charleston Harbor, so you can gaze at the city's skyline with your feet on this resort's sandy beach or from the waterfront pool. **Pros:** the most accessible hotel to downtown that's not in downtown (approximately 6 miles away); large pool and extensive grounds are perfect for enjoying a sunset glass of wine; on-site gym opened in 2013. **Cons:** a bit removed from the action; not pet-friendly; no complimentary breakfast. $ *Rooms from: $223* ✉ *20 Patriots Point Rd., Mount Pleasant* ☎ *843/856–0028, 888/856–0028* 🌐 *www.charlestonharborresort.com* 🛏 *119 rooms, 6 suites.*

$ 🏨 **Holiday Inn Mt. Pleasant.** *Hotel.* Just a five-minute drive over the scenic Arthur Ravenel Jr. **Pros:** some resort amenities, including a pool; good business center; pets are allowed with a fee. **Cons:** not downtown; no historic atmosphere; a condo complex blocks the bridge view. $ *Rooms from: $129* ✉ *250 Johnnie Dodds Blvd., Mount Pleasant,*

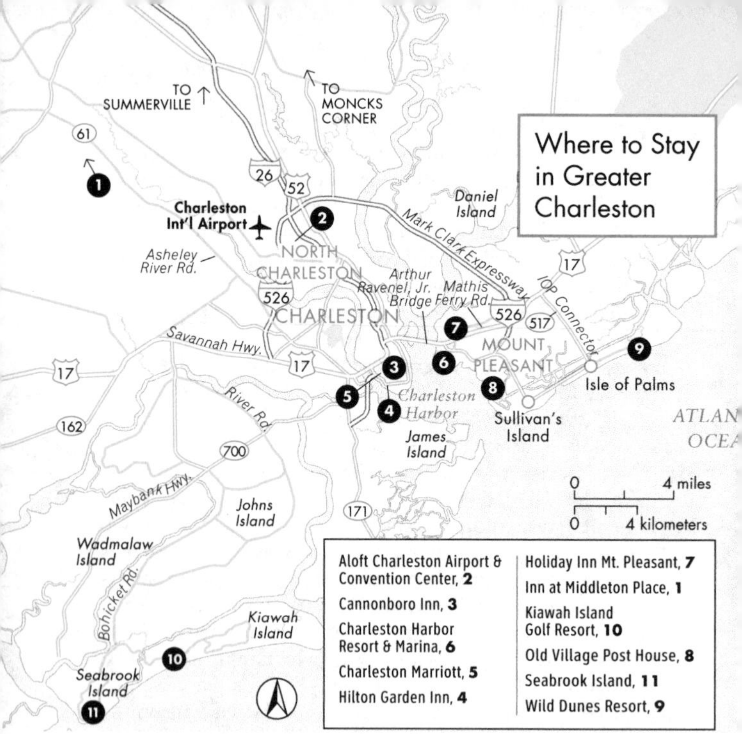
Where to Stay in Greater Charleston
TO SUMMERVILLE
TO MONCKS CORNER
61
26
52
Charleston Int'l Airport
Daniel Island
Mark Clark Expressway
Asheley River Rd.
NORTH CHARLESTON
526
Arthur Ravenel, Jr. Bridge
Mathis Ferry Rd.
17
IOP Connector
CHARLESTON
517
Savannah Hwy.
MOUNT PLEASANT
Isle of Palms
Charleston Harbor
Sullivan's Island
River Rd.
162
James Island
ATLAN
OCEA
700
Maybank Hwy.
Johns Island
171
4 miles
4 kilometers
Wadmalaw Island
Bohicket Rd.
Kiawah Island
Seabrook Island
Aloft Charleston Airport & Convention Center, 2
Cannonboro Inn, 3
Charleston Harbor Resort & Marina, 6
Charleston Marriott, 5
Hilton Garden Inn, 4
Holiday Inn Mt. Pleasant, 7
Inn at Middleton Place, 1
Kiawah Island Golf Resort, 10
Old Village Post House, 8
Seabrook Island, 11
Wild Dunes Resort, 9

Mount Pleasant ☎ *843/884–6000, 800/972–2513* 🌐 *www.himtpleasant.com* 🛏 *158 rooms* 🍴 *No meals.*

$ 🏨 **Old Village Post House.** *B&B/Inn.* This white wooden building anchoring Mount Pleasant's Historic District is three-in-one—an excellent restaurant, a neighborly tavern, and a cozy inn set at the top of a high staircase. **Pros:** prices are as affordable as some chain motels on the highway; in the most picturesque and walkable neighborhood in Mount Pleasant; close to Sullivan's Island and Isle of Palms. **Cons:** shares some public spaces with the downstairs restaurant; some minor old-building woes, including creaky wood floors; not a traditional hotel, so service can be quirky. [$] *Rooms from: $135* ✉ *101 Pitt St., Mount Pleasant* ☎ *843/388–8935* 🌐 *www.oldvillageposthouse.com* 🛏 *6 rooms* 🍴 *Breakfast.*

ELSEWHERE IN AND AROUND CHARLESTON

$ 🏨 **Aloft Charleston Airport & Convention Center.** *Hotel.* Designed with the young, hip, and high-tech traveler in mind, this chain hotel has everything from touch-screen check-in kiosks to a stylish bar with a pool table. **Pros:** high concept design; convenient for airport, convention center, and outlet shopping; pet-friendly vibe. **Cons:** noise from planes taking off; somewhat cramped rooms; no complimentary breakfast. [$] *Rooms from: $139* ✉ *4875 Tanger Outlet Blvd., North Charleston* ☎ *843/566–7300* 🌐 *www.aloftcharlestonairport.com* 🛏 *136 rooms.*

$$$ 🏨 **Cannonboro Inn.** *B&B/Inn.* On the edge of the Historic District, this B&B serves a full breakfast on a wide porch overlooking a garden, pours tea in the afternoon, and offers free use of bicycles for exploring the area. **Pros:** free off-street parking; tasty fudge at the afternoon receptions; laid-back atmosphere. **Cons:** not so convenient to the tourist area; children under 10 not allowed; refrigerator and phone are shared. [$] *Rooms from: $205* ✉ *184 Ashley Ave., Medical University of South Carolina* ☎ *843/723–8572, 800/235–8035* 🌐 *www.charleston-sc-inns.com* 🛏 *7 rooms, 1 suite* 🍴 *Breakfast.*

$ 🏨 **Charleston Marriott.** *Hotel.* The sunset views from the balconies of this river-view hotel get better the higher you go—they're wonderful from the seasonal rooftop Aqua Terrace bar and lounge, where drinks and tapas are served. **Pros:** inexpensive shuttle to downtown; great views of the Ashley River; classy location for conference and business travelers. **Cons:** not in the Historic District; fee for Wi-Fi access; no complimentary breakfast. [$] *Rooms from: $149* ✉ *170 Lockwood Dr., Medical University of South Carolina* ☎ *843/723–3000* 🌐 *www.marriott.com* 🛏 *335 rooms, 6 suites* 🍴 *No meals.*

$$ 🏨 **Hilton Garden Inn Charleston Waterfront.** *Hotel.* A sunny swimming pool and breezy patios overlooking the Ashley River are among the main attractions at the Hilton Garden Inn Charleston Waterfront, an addition to the local lodging scene in 2014. **Pros:** complimentary shuttle service to downtown; free parking; near the marinas. **Cons:** too far to walk to King Street; no complimentary breakfast; lacks the character of a historic hotel. [$] *Rooms from: $169* ✉ *45 Lockwood Dr., Medical University of South Carolina* ☎ *843/637–4074* 🌐 *hiltongardeninn3.hilton.com* 🛏 *132 rooms, 9 suites.*

$$ 🏨 **Inn at Middleton Place.** *B&B/Inn.* On the banks of the Ashley River, this country inn offers a peaceful respite from the city—there are even shady hammocks outside for afternoon naps. **Pros:** beautiful setting; free kayak tours and bike rentals; pet-friendly. **Cons:** a half-hour drive from downtown Charleston. [$] *Rooms from: $159* ✉ *4290 Ashley River Rd., West Ashley* ☎ *843/556–0500, 800/543–4774* 🌐 *www.theinnatmiddletonplace.com* 🛏 *54 rooms, 1 suite* 🍴 *Breakfast.*

★ $$$ Fodor's Choice **Kiawah Island Golf Resort.** *Resort.* Choose from one- to four-bedroom villas, three- to eight-bedroom private homes, or the Sanctuary at Kiawah Island, an amazing 255-room luxury waterfront hotel and spa that is one of the most prestigious resorts in the country and yet is still kid-friendly. **Pros:** smaller villas are more affordable; restaurant is an ideal venue for an anniversary or a proposal; the golf courses and tennis programs are ranked among the country's best. **Cons:** not all rooms ocean views; it is pricey and a long drive from town. [$] *Rooms from: $225* ✉ *1 Sanctuary Beach Dr., Kiawah Island* ☎ *843/768–2121, 800/576–1570* 🌐 *www.kiawahresort.com* 🛏 *242 rooms, 13 suites, 400 villas, 90 homes* 🍴 *No meals.*

$ FAMILY **Seabrook Island.** *Resort.* About 350 fully equipped one- to six-bedroom villas, cottages, townhomes, and homes are available on Seabrook, one of the most private of the area's island resorts, on a physically beautiful, relatively unspoiled island. **Pros:** safe haven for kids to play; the only place in the area where you can ride horses on the beach; nearby upscale shopping and restaurants. **Cons:** a 45-minute drive from Charleston; security can be stringent—don't drive over the posted 25 mph speed limit. [$] *Rooms from: $140* ✉ *3772 Seabrook Island Rd., Seabrook Island* ☎ *800/247–5050* 🌐 *www.wyndhamvacationrentals.com* 🛏 *350 units* 🍴 *No meals.*

WORD OF MOUTH. **"I love, love, love Kiawah for family vacations, golfing, and bike rides on the beach. Top it all off with a nice trip into Charleston for some seafood or barbecue and you are in heaven." —BradleyK**

★ $$$ Fodor's Choice **Wild Dunes Resort.** *Resort.* Guests at this 1,600-acre island beachfront resort can choose from a long list of recreational options, including Tom Fazio–designed golf courses and nationally ranked tennis programs. **Pros:** golf courses are first-class; free shuttle runs from 7 am to 11 pm to wherever you need to go within the complex; it's rarely crowded on the beach. **Cons:** in summer, kids dominate the pool areas and the boardwalk. [$] *Rooms from: $229* ✉ *5757 Palm Blvd., Isle of Palms* ☎ *888/778–1876, 843/886–6000* 🌐 *www.wilddunes.com* 🛏 *396 units, 93 rooms* 🍴 *No meals.*

NIGHTLIFE AND PERFORMING ARTS

By Stratton Lawrence

FOR A MIDSIZE CITY, CHARLESTON HAS A SURPRISINGLY VARIED AND SOPHISTICATED ARTS SCENE, though the city really shines during its major annual arts festival, Spoleto Festival USA. Still, throughout the year, there are ample opportunities to explore higher culture, from productions by the Footlight Players and PURE Theatre, to the concert schedule at the historic Charleston Music Hall.

The nightlife scene is similarly comprehensive, with nocturnal venues for all ages and tastes. If your image of Charleston is a buttoned-down town with men in seersucker suits and bow ties, think again. That may have been an image of Charlestonians in decades past—and light blue seersucker still makes frequent summer appearances—but that oldster can probably still out-dance his fraternity son and knock down his share of bourbon along the way.

Although some of the nightlife can be rowdy and more youth-oriented, there are options from jazz lounges to dance clubs. And here the nightlife begins at happy hour, which can start as early as 4 pm. Several bars and restaurants have incredible happy-hour deals, and a night of barhopping generally includes grazing on small plates. ■TIP→ **If you see long lines outside a place, you can usually assume that the crowd is young.** Long lines can also mean that there is a popular band playing, like at the Music Farm.

PERFORMING ARTS

ANNUAL FESTIVALS AND EVENTS

Spoleto USA is only the beginning—there are dozens of festivals held throughout the city each year. Some focus on food and wine, whereas others are concerned with gardens and architecture. Charleston is one of the few American cities that can claim a distinctive regional cuisine.

BB&T Charleston Food + Wine Festival. Since 2005, the BB&T Charleston Wine + Food Festival has been the city's marquee event for foodies. Spread over four days, it brings together the nation's leading chefs (including local James Beard award winners), food writers, and, of course, regular diners who love to eat and drink. Held the first full weekend of March, it emphasizes the Lowcountry's culinary heritage. Marion Square serves as the hub with its Culinary Village, but savvy attendees grab up tickets quickly for the numerous dinners and special events held around the city. ☎ 843/727–9998 ⊕ www.charlestonwineandfood.com.

Brewvival. What began as an annual gathering of local beer lovers on the lawn outside Coast Brewery has grown into one of the Southeast's premier beer festivals, with brewers from Oregon to New York bringing one-off specialties to share. The February event attracts big names in the business, including the founders of Sierra Nevada and Dogfish Head breweries. ⊠ 1250 2nd St. N, Old Charleston Naval Base, North Charleston ☎ 843/343–4727 ⊕ www.brewvival.com.

Charleston Fashion Week. Toasting emerging designers and models with runway shows, competitions, and exhibitions, the main events at this five-night festival in March are held beneath tents in Marion Square. Smaller shows are hosted by downtown boutiques. The festival has helped several designers launch their fashion careers. But even more impressive than the festival? Maybe the tony after-parties. ⊠ Marion Square, King and Calhoun Sts., Upper King ☎ 843/971–9811 ⊕ www.charlestonfashionweek.com.

Fall Tour of Homes. Sponsored every October by the Preservation Society of Charleston, the Fall Tour of Homes provides an inside look at Charleston's private buildings and gardens, from stately mansions on the Battery to intact Revolutionary-era houses. ⊠ 147 King St. ☎ 843/722–4630 ⊕ www.thefalltours.org.

Festival of Houses & Gardens. More than 100 private homes, gardens, and historic churches are open to the public for tours during the Festival of Houses & Gardens, held annually during March and April. There are also symphony galas in stately drawing rooms, plantation oyster roasts, and candlelight tours. ⊠ 108 Meeting St. ☎ 843/722–3405 ⊕ www.historiccharleston.org.

MOJA Arts Festival. Held each year in late September and early October, this festival celebrates the region's African heritage and Caribbean influences on local culture. It includes theater, dance, and music performances, art shows, films, lectures, and tours of the Historic District. ⊠ 180 Meeting St., Suite 200 ☎ 843/724–7305 ⊕ www. mojafestival.com.

FAMILY **Piccolo Spoleto Festival.** The spirited companion festival of Spoleto Festival USA showcases the best in local and regional talent from every artistic discipline. There are as many as 700 events—from jazz performances to puppet shows, military band concerts, and expansive art shows in Marion Square—from mid-May through early June. Many of the performances are free or inexpensive, and hundreds of these cultural experiences are kid-friendly. ✉ *180 Meeting St.* ☎ *843/724–7305* ⊕ *www.piccolospoleto.com.*

★ FodorsChoice **Spoleto Festival USA.** For 17 glorious days in late May and early June, Charleston gets a dose of culture from the Spoleto Festival USA. This internationally acclaimed performing-arts festival features a mix of distinguished artists and emerging talent from around the world. Performances take place in magical settings, such as the College of Charleston's Cistern beneath a canopy of ancient oaks or inside a centuries-old cathedral.

A mix of formal concerts and casual performances is what Pulitzer Prize–winning composer Gian Carlo Menotti had in mind when, in 1977, he initiated the festival as a complement to his opera-heavy Italian festival. He chose Charleston because of its European look and because its residents love the arts—not to mention any cause for celebration. He wanted the festival to be a "fertile ground for the young" as well as a "dignified home for the masters."

The finale is a must-do, particularly for the younger crowd. Staged outdoors at Middleton Place, the plantation house and lush landscaped gardens provide a dramatic backdrop. The inexpensive seating is unreserved and unlimited. The lawn is covered with blankets and chairs, and many families bring lavish spreads to munch and sip on. Recent performances have included bluegrass legend Del McCoury and the Carolina Chocolate Drops, an African American string band, followed by spectacular fireworks exploding over the Ashley River.

Some 45 events—with most tickets averaging between $25 and $50—include everything from improv to Shakespeare, from rap to chamber music, from ballet to salsa. Because events sell out quickly, insiders say you should buy tickets several weeks in advance. Tickets to midweek performances are a bit easier to secure. Hotels fill up quickly, so book a room at the same time and reserve your tables for the trendy downtown restaurants. ☎ *843/722–2764* ⊕ *www.spoletousa.org.*

FAMILY **Southeastern Wildlife Exposition.** One of Charleston's biggest annual events, this celebration of the region's flora and fauna takes place in mid-February, offering fine art by renowned wildlife artists, bird of prey demonstrations, dog competitions, an oyster roast, and a gala. Spread across three days, the expo generally attracts more than 500 artists and 40,000 participants to various venues around the city. ☎ 843/723–1748 ⊕ www.sewe.com.

CLASSICAL MUSIC

Charleston Symphony Orchestra. With a season that runs from late September through March, the Charleston Symphony Orchestra hosts full-scale symphonic performances, chamber ensembles, a pops series, family-oriented events, and holiday concerts. This symphony is nationally renowned and serves as the Spoleto Festival Orchestra. The orchestra's newly renovated home court—Gaillard Performance Hall—is slated to reopen in 2015. ☎ 843/723–7528 ⊕ www. charlestonsymphony.com.

DANCE

Charleston Ballet Theatre. Performances of everything from classical to contemporary dance take place in venues scattered around town, including the North Charleston Performing Arts Center, the Sottile Theatre, and Charleston Music Hall. Annual performances of *The Nutcracker* are a holiday treat. ✉ 709B Hwy. 17 N, Mount Pleasant ☎ 843/469–2080 ⊕ www.charlestonballet.com.

Charleston City Ballet. This semiprofessional company, which includes College of Charleston students, puts on a fall and spring program of jazz, classical, and modern dance at venues like the Sottile Theatre and the Charleston Music Hall. ✉ 1910 Savannah Hwy. ☎ 843/556–1343 ⊕ www. charlestoncityballet.org.

FILM

Regal Palmetto Grande Stadium 16. This grand art-deco-style multiplex is Charleston's most modern cinema, with comfortable stadium-style seats and the usual popcorn and treats. ✉ 1319 Theater Dr., Mount Pleasant ☎ 843/216–8150 ⊕ www.regmovies.com.

Terrace Theater. About 10 minutes from downtown, this local favorite hosts its own film festival every March. Its carpeted halls and theaters have the feel of an old-school cinema, screening a mix of new releases and indie films. Concessions include beer and wine. ✉ 1956 Maybank Hwy., James Island ☎ 843/762–4247 ⊕ www.terracetheater.com.

THEATER

Footlight Players. In a charming theater tucked into the French Quarter, this troupe produces original plays, musicals, and other events throughout the year. ✉ *20 Queen St., Market area* ☎ *843/722–4487* ⊕ *www.footlightplayers.net.*

PURE Theatre. In a cozy space facing Upper King Street, this local troupe produces comedies and classics throughout the year, as well as special holiday performances. ✉ *477 King St., Upper King* ☎ *843/723–4444* ⊕ *www.puretheatre.org.*

VENUES

Charleston Music Hall. Regularly hosting big-name bluegrass, blues, and country acts, the beautiful 928-seat Charleston Music Hall shines after an extensive renovation. Home to the Charleston Jazz Orchestra, it's in the heart of Upper King and within easy walking distance of numerous popular bars and restaurants for pre- and postshow refreshments. ✉ *37 John St., Upper King* ☎ *843/853–2252* ⊕ *www.charlestonmusichall.com.*

North Charleston Performing Art Center. Touring Broadway productions and big-name bands frequent the 2,300-seat North Charleston Performing Art Center. In recent years, performers such as Frankie Valli, Tony Bennett, and Willie Nelson have taken the stage. ■ TIP→ **It's worth paying extra for seats in the front half of the venue.** ✉ *5001 Coliseum Dr., North Charleston* ☎ *843/529–5000* ⊕ *www.northcharlestoncoliseumpac.com.*

NIGHTLIFE

Charleston loves a good party, and the city boasts an ever-growing array of choices for a night on the town. The more mature crowd goes to the sophisticated spots, and there are many wine bars, clubs featuring jazz groups, and trendy lounges with craft cocktail menus. Rooftop bars are a particular Charleston tradition, and the city has several good ones. Many restaurants offer live entertainment on at least one weekend night, catering to crowds of all ages. The Upper King area has grown exponentially in recent years, overtaking the Market area in terms of popularity and variety of bars and lounges. ⚠ **A city ordinance mandates that bars must close by 2 am, so last call is usually 1:30.**

NORTH OF BROAD

LOWER KING

BARS AND PUBS

Bin 152. Husband-and-wife Patrick and Fanny Panella ply their guests with selections from more than 130 bottles of wine and 40 varieties of cheeses and charcuterie, freshly baked breads, contemporary art, and antique furniture. All of it is imminently available, too, from the Sauvignon Blanc and Shiraz to the tables and chairs. Cast in low lighting, the wine bar serves as a comfortable backdrop for a pre- or post-dinner drink, or an entire evening. ✉ *152 King St., Lower King* ☎ *843/577–7359* ⊕ *www.bin152.com.*

MARKET AREA

BARS AND PUBS

Gin Joint. The cocktails here—frothy fizzes, slings, smashes, and juleps—are retro, some dating back to before Prohibition. The bartenders don bowties and suspenders, but the atmosphere is utterly contemporary, with slick gray walls and subtle lighting. The bar is named after Humphrey Bogart's famous line in *Casablanca*: "Of all the gin joints, in all the towns, in all the world, she walks into mine." The kitchen serves up small plates like cheeses, pork buns, and buttermilk fried chicken hearts. ✉ *182 East Bay St., Market area* ☎ *843/577–6111* ⊕ *www.theginjoint.com.*

The Griffon. Dollar bills cover just about every square inch of the Griffon, helping the bar achieve nearly legendary status around the city. It's wood interior is dark, dusty, and well worn, yet somehow still seems charming. A rotating selection of draft beers comes from local breweries like Westbrook, Coast, and Holy City. It's a popular lunchtime and happy-hour watering hole, and hosts live music on weekend nights. ✉ *18 Vendue Range, Market area* ☎ *843/723–1700* ⊕ *www.griffoncharleston.com.*

Henry's House. The longest continuously operating restaurant and bar in South Carolina, Henry's House has evolved since it opened in 1930. On the first floor is a large horseshoe bar with floor-to-ceiling windows looking out to the Market. The second floor, recently converted into a whiskey bar, has exposed brick, black-and-white photos of jazz musicians, and rugs scattered across hardwood floors. A few steps up is a deck and the enclosed NV Dance Lounge, which is open Thursday through Saturday and attracts a young crowd. ✉ *54 N. Market, Market area* ☎ *843/723–4363.*

5

UP ON THE ROOF. Locals head to the city's rooftop bars on summer evenings where cool breezes offer relief from the heat. Establishments like the Pavilion, Rooftop at Vendue, and Henry's House have made rooftop terraces into bars and lounges. At sunset, you can watch the horizon change colors and view the boats in the harbor.

★ Fodor'sChoice **Pavilion Bar.** Atop the Market Pavilion Hotel, the swanky outdoor Pavilion Bar offers panoramic views of the city and harbor, set around the hotel's posh swimming pool. Enjoy appetizers like lobster and duck with one of the specialty mojitos or martinis. The dress code dictates no flip-flops, baseball caps, visors, or tank tops. ⊠ *Market Pavilion Hotel, 225 E. Bay St., Market area* ☎ *843/266–4218* ⊕ *www.marketpavilion.com.*

Pearlz Oyster Bar. People come here from far and wide for the raw or steamed oysters—fat, juicy, and plucked from the Louisiana Gulf, Nova Scotia, and various points in between. Try the oyster shooters: one oyster in a shot glass, topped with Absolut Peppar vodka and a few squirts of spicy cocktail sauce. Consider it an opening sortie, providing apt energy for pop-ins at the other East Bay Street–area hot spots in downtown Charleston. ⊠ *153 East Bay St., Market area* ☎ *843/577–5755* ⊕ *www.pearlzoysterbar.com.*

The Rooftop. Have a cocktail and appetizer as you watch the colorful sunset behind the church steeples. There are actually two bars at this venue atop the recently renovated Vendue Inn; the lower Deck Bar has tables and chairs shaded by umbrellas, but the view of the water is partially obscured by condo towers. Keep going to the higher-level bar, which offers a 360-degree panorama and an open-air atmosphere. You'll find live music by local and regional bands on weekends. Get here early, as it closes at midnight. ⊠ *Vendue Inn, 19 Vendue Range, Market area* ☎ *843/577–7970* ⊕ *www.thevendue.com.*

Social Wine Bar & Restaurant. If you need help choosing from the city's most extensive wine list—with everything from full-bodied Tempranillos to light Proseccos available by glass, bottle, and flight—knowledgeable sommelier and owner Brad Ball is your man. The restaurant features entrées with flight pairings and terrific hand-spun pizzas from the wood-fired oven. ⊠ *188 E. Bay St., Market area* ☎ *843/577–5665* ⊕ *www.socialwinebar.com.*

Southend Brewery & Smokehouse. Towering over a bustling corner in prime tourist territory, this three-story brick restaurant has a lively bar serving beer brewed on the premises. Try a seasonal ale or porter with a wood-oven pizza before shooting a round of pool at the championship-sized tables on the top floor. ✉ *161 E. Bay St., Market area* ☎ *843/853–4677.*

JAZZ CLUBS

★ Fodor'sChoice **Charleston Grill.** The elegant Charleston Grill hosts live jazz seven nights a week, drawing from the city's most renowned musicians. Performers range from the internationally acclaimed Brazilian guitarist Duda Lucena to the Bob Williams Duo, a father and son who play classical guitar and violin. The place draws an urbane thirtysomething crowd. Down the hall, the neighboring Thoroughbred Club offers nightly live music and an impressive selection of bourbons. ✉ *Charleston Place Hotel, 224 King St., Market area* ☎ *843/577–4522* ⊕ *www.charlestongrill.com.*

LIVE MUSIC

Salty Mike's. This bar offers fine service to sailors, college kids, and out-of-towners alike, with cheap domestic beer and old-fashioned cocktails. Situated beneath the Marina Variety Store Restaurant—itself a Charleston landmark dating back to 1963—Salty Mike's provides a crusty, no-frills ambience and a dreamy seaside view of the Ashley River and Charleston City Marina. ✉ *17 Lockwood Dr., North of Broad* ☎ *843/937–0208* ⊕ *www.varietystorerestaurant.com.*

Tommy Condon's. Enjoy Irish music by local group the Bograts Thursday through Saturday at this rollicking pub. If you're hungry, dig into the Irish nachos—cubed potatoes, cheddar cheese, jalapeños, tomatoes, and ranch dressing—with a Guinness or Harp. ✉ *160 Church St., Market area* ☎ *843/577–3818* ⊕ *www.tommycondons.com.*

UPPER KING

BARS AND PUBS

★ Fodor'sChoice **The Belmont.** This place doesn't seek attention—heck, it won't even list its phone number. But with a soaring tin ceiling, exposed-brick walls, and a penchant for projecting black-and-white films onto the wall, the charisma comes naturally. An inventive cocktail menu served up by sharply dressed mixologists helps, too. Try their take on the spicy-sweet Brown Derby, a bourbon drink made with jalapeño-infused honey, or the Bells of Jalisco, featuring *reposado* tequila, more jalapeño honey, and lime juice. ✉ *511 King St., Upper King* ⊕ *www.thebelmontcharleston.com.*

Burns Alley. You'll do well just to find this place. Attached to La Hacienda Mexican restaurant off King Street (just keep on truckin' past the bathrooms at the rear), Burns Alley offers cozy quarters for sports fans in need of cheap beers and a giant projection screen. A small upstairs area overlooks the action, offering a premium vantage point during crowded evenings. ✉ *354B King St., Upper King* ☎ *843/723–6735* ⊕ *www.burnsalley.com.*

Charleston Beer Works. This friendly watering hole with 30 draft beers on tap offers a late-night menu of wings and pub grub. Live music on weekends and ample screens for sports events make this a popular hangout for the college crowd. ✉ *468 King St., Upper King* ☎ *843/577–5885* ⊕ *www.charlestonbeerworks.com.*

Closed for Business. This "draught emporium" offers more than 40 taps pouring pints and liters of local and seasonal brews. With pale wood paneling, leather club chairs, and lightbulbs flickering in a fireplace, the place has plenty of charm. CFB also features a tasty menu of upscale pub fare, including Chicago-style hot dogs and a fried pork cutlet sandwich called the Pork Slap. ✉ *453 King St., Upper King* ☎ *843/853–8466* ⊕ *www.closed4business.com.*

The Cocktail Club. This establishment characterizes the craft cocktail movement with its "farm-to-shaker" seasonal selection of creative concoctions. The bar showcases exposed-brick walls and wooden beams inside its lounge areas, though warm evenings are best spent outside on the rooftop patio. Inside, some of Charleston's best (and best-looking) bartenders muddle and shake clever mixtures like Safety Word, made from habañero-spiked tequila, muddled kiwi, and lime juice, and the Double Standard, a serrano-pepper-infused gin and cucumber vodka blend. ✉ *479 King St., #200, Upper King* ☎ *843/724–9411* ⊕ *www. thecocktailclubcharleston.com.*

Dudley's on Ann. A local landmark, the city's oldest gay bar hosts lively karaoke parties, DJs and dancing on weekends, and rollicking drag shows. ✉ *42 Ann St., Upper King* ☎ *843/577–6779* ⊕ *www.dudleysonann.com.*

O-Ku. Done up in black and white, this edgy Japanese establishment serves exquisite small plates like ceviche with mango, pear, and mint-*yuzu* vinaigrette that pair perfectly with a sake flight. You can lounge on the couches during happy hour—which runs from 5 to 7 Monday, Wednesday, and Friday—and enjoy half-priced sake and signature sushi rolls. On Saturday night, a high-energy DJ cranks out tunes while the place becomes a velvet rope club. ⊠ *463 King St., Upper King* ☎ *843/737–0112* ⊕ *www.o-kusushi.com.*

Prohibition. A new addition to the bustling Upper King scene, this throwback speakeasy mixes signature craft cocktails and offers a small but respectable beer and wine selection to accompany Southern-inspired burgers, pork chops, and duck dishes. A ragtime jazz band plays in the early evening on weekends, then the tables are removed and a DJ instantaneously transforms the place into a full-on dance club. ⊠ *547 King St., Upper King* ☎ *843/793–2964* ⊕ *prohibitioncharleston.com.*

Proof. These cozy quarters on King Street, complete with communal tables surrounded by barstools, bustle at happy hour and on weekend evenings. The upscale bar offers seasonal signature cocktails, as well as a respectable selection of wines and craft beers. ⊠ *437 King St., Upper King* ☎ *843/793–1422.*

DANCE CLUBS

Club Pantheon. Charleston's biggest gay dance club is a vast, unadorned space with a stage where drag shows draw big crowds on Friday to Sunday nights. Male go-go dancers shake their stuff on the bar, and there's a DJ on weekends. Although the crowd is primarily gay, straight folks and bachelorette parties come here, too, and are made welcome. The cover charge is typically $5. ⊠ *28 Ann St., Upper King* ☎ *843/557–2582* ⊕ *www.clubpantheon.net.*

Trio Club. Funky sounds from the '70s and '80s mix with the latest club anthems at this perennially popular dance club. Listen to the cover bands at the downstairs bar, mingle on the outdoor patio, or head upstairs for the DJ-led dance party. It's open only Friday and Saturday nights. ⊠ *139 Calhoun St., Upper King* ⊕ *www.triocharleston.com.*

LIVE MUSIC

Music Farm. Once a train depot, this massive space is filled to the max when popular bands like Galactic, the North Mississippi Allstars, and Passion Pit play. Tickets typically range from \$15 to \$25. The bar is open only on nights when a concert is scheduled. ✉ *32 Ann St., Upper King* ☎ *843/577–6989* ⊕ *www.musicfarm.com.*

MOUNT PLEASANT

Spirit of Carolina. Dine and dance the night away aboard the wide-beamed, motor yacht *Spirit of Carolina.* Dinner is three or more courses and includes a choice of five entrees, from shrimp and grits to New York strip. Live musicians perform blues and beach music during the cruise. This three-hour excursion appeals to an older crowd, but everyone enjoys seeing the twinkling lights of the harbor. The ship departs from Patriots Point in Mount Pleasant. Reservations are essential for evening cruises. ✉ *40 Patriots Point Rd., Mount Pleasant* ☎ *843/722–2628* ⊕ *www. spiritlinecruises.com.*

GREATER CHARLESTON

ISLE OF PALMS

LIVE MUSIC
The Windjammer. An oceanfront bar with well-known rock bands performing on the raised stage, the Windjammer attracts a mix of young people just out of college, salty locals, and visiting tourists. Expect to pay \$10 admission when there's a live band, but if you sit on the back deck there's generally no cover charge. The place hosts bikini contests throughout the summer. ✉ *1008 Ocean Blvd., Isle of Palms* ☎ *843/886–8948* ⊕ *www.jammercam.com.*

SULLIVAN'S ISLAND

BARS AND PUBS
Dunleavy's Pub. Just a block from the beach, this friendly pub is a local favorite, often featuring Irish, folk, and blues music throughout the week. St. Patrick's Day weekend is a treat, as the main drag on Sullivan's Island is closed, allowing pedestrians to sally forth from bar to bar. ✉ *2213 Middle St., Sullivan's Island* ☎ *843/883–9646* ⊕ *www.dunleavysonsullivans.com.*

6

SPORTS AND THE OUTDOORS

By Kinsey
Gidick

CHARLESTON IS A GREAT PLACE TO GET OUTDOORS.
Called the Lowcountry because it's at sea level—and sometimes even below—the city is surrounded by an array of
tidal creeks, estuaries, and rivers that flow out to the deep
blue Atlantic Ocean. The region's beaches are taupe sand,
and the Carolina sun warms them nine months out of the
year. Many are uncrowded, especially in the spring and
fall, when it's not hard to find the perfect spot.

Several barrier islands within easy driving distance of the
city are studded with lacy palm trees and live oaks hung
with Spanish moss. The islands are fairly extensively developed, but still shelter plenty of wildlife. Charlestonians
will tell you (without bragging) that this is one of the most
beautiful regions on this planet. Here you can commune
with nature, perhaps like you haven't in years.

Sailing is an increasingly popular activity in this port city.
If you already know how to sail, you can rent a small sailboat. If you don't, you can take sailing lessons or head out
on a charter boat. Among the annual sailing events are the
Keel Boat Regatta and Charleston Race Week both held
in April, and the much-televised Charleston-to-Bermuda
Race in late May. Charleston's Harbor Fest, traditionally
held during the third week in June, draws visitors from
far and wide. The parade of Tall Ships is always a delight.

Many of the region's best outdoor activities can be expensive, and this may give pause to families on a budget. But
regularly scheduled dolphin-watching tours make for inexpensive outings, and crabbing at low tide is free. You'll also
find an amazing number of low-cost options, from biking to
kayaking to nature walks. In the warm weather, the beach
is the thing. Those looking for more of an adrenaline rush
can rent surfboards and ride the waves.

The area's golf courses are reasonably priced compared
with, say, Hilton Head. The championship courses on the
nearby islands are the most beautiful, though they can be
costly. There are plenty of public courses where you can
enjoy the region's scenery without emptying your wallet.

SPORTS AND ACTIVITIES

BASEBALL

Fans who like to hear the crack of the bat and the cheers of the crowd can plan on attending a game at "the Joe" (Joseph P. Riley Jr. Stadium).

Charleston Riverdogs. The local minor-league baseball team plays at "the Joe," on the banks of the Ashley River near the Citadel. Kids love the mascot, Charlie T. Riverdog. After games, fireworks often illuminate the summer sky in honor of this all-American pastime. The season runs from April through September. Tickets cost a reasonable $7 to $12. ⊠ *Joseph P. Riley Jr. Stadium, 360 Fishburne St., Hampton Park Terrace* ☎ *843/577–3647* ⊕ *www.riverdogs.com.*

BEACHES

There are glorious beaches just outside the Charleston city limits. You and your kids can build sand castles, gather seashells after high tide, or bring a kite and let it loose on a long lead. The Charleston area's mild climate means you can swim from March through October. Public beaches generally have lifeguards in season, snack bars, restrooms and dressing areas, outdoor showers, umbrella and chair rentals, and large parking lots.

FAMILY **Edisto Beach.** Edisto's south side has 4 miles of public beach. At its western end, the beach faces St. Helena Sound and has smaller waves. There is beach access at each intersection along Palmetto Boulevard and free public parking along the road. The beach itself has narrowed because of erosion, so it's best to time your visit for low tide. These clean coastal waters teem with both fish and shellfish, and it's common to see people throwing cast nets for shrimp. It's a great beach for beachcombing. Alcohol is allowed as long as it is not in glass containers. There's little shade and no food stands, so be sure to pack an umbrella and snacks. **Amenities:** none. **Best for:** solitude; sunset; swimming. ⊠ *Palmetto Blvd., from Coral St. to Yacht Club Rd., Edisto Beach* ⊕ *www.townofedistobeach.com.*

Folly Beach. Folly Beach is the Lowcountry's most iconic summer playground, featuring strong waves, a narrower beach, and the Folly Beach Pier. However, as of summer 2012, alcohol of any kind is no longer allowed on the beach at any time. To the left of the stairway to the pier is a good seafood restaurant called Blu, with a bar, deck, and incredible ocean views. Street parking is free, but to avoid a ticket, all four wheels have to be on the grass, not the pavement. Small parking lots right next to beach access cost $1 per hour from 10 to 5. If you are a surfer, keep driving until you reach Folly's Washout. Regulations about littering and parking are strictly enforced. **Amenities:** food and drink; lifeguards; parking (fee). **Best for:** swimming, surfing. ⊠ *East Ashley Ave., off U.S. 17, which becomes Center St.; turn left at the Holiday Inn, Folly Island, Folly Beach* ⊕ *www.cityoffollybeach.com.*

Front Beach. If you want a singles scene and beach bars like the Windjammer, with bands and bikini contests, then the commercial Front Beach section of the Isle of Palms is for you. For generations it has been a big draw for beach lovers. Bicyclists are welcome, as are leashed pets, but no alcohol or beer is allowed. Check out *iop.net/visitors/beachaccessandparking. aspx* for the rules on beach parking outside the Isle of Palms County Park. Parking regulations are strictly enforced. **Amenities:** food and drink; parking (fee). **Best for:** partiers; sunset; sunrise; windsurfing. ⊠ *10th Ave.–14th Ave., U.S. 17 north to I–517, the Isle of Palms connector; once on the island look for 10th Ave., Isle of Palms.*

NO SWIMMING. The No Swimming signs by the Isle of Palms Bridge over Breach Inlet are there because the current is treacherous and, sadly, every year people drown.

FAMILY **Isle of Palms County Park.** Play beach volleyball or quietly sunbathe in a lounge chair at this 600-foot-long beach. This beach is as good as the island's idyllic name. The sands are golden, the water is temperate, and the waves are gentle. It's great for little children, seniors with limited mobility, or those who seek peace. It is also the only lifeguard-protected area on the Isle of Palms. **Amenities:** lifeguards; toilets; food and drink; showers (seasonal). **Best for:** surfing; walking; swimming. ⊠ *1 14th Ave., U.S. 17 north to I–517, the Isle of Palms connector; once on the island go through the traffic light and then straight ahead; the parking lot is on the left, Isle of Palms* ☎ *843/886–3863, 843/768–4386* ⊕ *www. ccprc.com* ☜ *$8 per car* ☉ *Nov.–Feb., daily 10–5; Mar.–Apr. and Sept.– Oct., daily 10–6; May–Labor Day, daily 9–7.*

BEACH SAFETY. It may seem inviting to walk out to a sandbar at low tide, but the tide sweeps in fast and the sandbars disappear, leaving people stranded far from shore.

TOP OUTDOOR EXPERIENCES

Beaches: Charleston's palm-studded coastline and the beaches of its barrier islands rival those of the Caribbean—and are often cleaner, safer, and less congested. The shoulder seasons of spring and fall are good for beachcombing, and summer is the time for swimming and water sports.

Biking: Charleston's Historic District is particularly bike-friendly, and setting off on two wheels is a wonderful way to avoid traffic and parking hassles. You can ride through the various in-town parks, like Marion Square, Waterfront Park, and Hampton Park, or take the bike path on the colossal Arthur Ravenel Jr. Bridge. On the island resorts, a bike is the ideal way to get around, especially for families with older kids.

Boating: Charleston's waters offer something for both the blue-water sailor and those who just want to take a waterborne tour. Fishing is a popular pastime, and a charter is an excellent way to spend the day in search of a trophy-size catch.

Golf: The weather is ideal for golf in the spring and fall, or even during the region's relatively mild winter. Summer's strong rays make morning and late afternoon the most popular tee times. Though some are not quite up to par with the courses of Hilton Head, golf on the nearby island resorts, especially at Kiawah Island Golf Resort, is exceptional.

Kayaking: This relatively inexpensive activity is one of the best ways to explore the Lowcountry's many waterways. Try paddling to keep up with the schools of dolphins you'll encounter while gliding silently along the Intracoastal Waterway. You can rent kayaks at Middleton Place, offering you the opportunity to push your paddle through former rice fields with views of the famous Butterfly Gardens. In Mount Pleasant, you can kayak in Shem Creek, the center of its shrimping industry, and if you are fit, you can paddle all the way to Sullivan's Island.

★ Fodor'sChoice **Kiawah Beachwalker Park.** The public park about 28 miles southwest of Charleston has an ample 500-foot-wide beach. Stunningly beautiful Kiawah is one of the Southeast's largest barrier islands, with 10 miles of wide, immaculate ocean beaches. You can walk safely for miles, shelling and beachcombing to your heart's content. The beach is complemented by the Kiawah River, with lagoons filled with birds and wildlife, and golden marshes that make the sunsets even more glorious. **Amenities:** food and drink; lifeguards; showers; toilets. **Best for:** solitude; sunset; swimming; walking. ✉ *1 Beachwalker Dr., Kiawah Island* ☎ *843/768–2395* ⊕ *www.ccprc.com* 🚗 *$8 per car* ⊙ *Jan. and Feb., daily 10–5; Mar. and Apr., daily 10–6; May–Labor Day, daily 9–7; Sept., daily 10–6; Oct., weekdays 9–5, weekends 10–6; Nov. and Dec., daily 10–5.*

WORD OF MOUTH. **"I prefer the flatter, wider beaches with calmer surf of the southern S.C. coast (Isle of Palms, Hilton Head). The N.C. beaches tend to be shelly-er, with rougher surf and often steeper drop offs into the water." —Brian_in_Charlotte**

Sullivan's Island Beach. This is one of the most pristine beaches in the Charleston area. The beachfront is owned by the town—some 190 acres of maritime forest overseen by the Lowcountry Open Land Trust. The downside is that there are no amenities like public toilets and showers. There are, however, a number of good small restaurants on nearby Middle Street, the island's main drag. There are approximately 30 public-access paths (four are wheelchair accessible) that lead to the beach. "Sully's" is a delightful island with plenty to see, including Fort Moultrie National Monument. The island is home to some 2,000 people, whose numbers swell in summer with vacationers occupying the many beach houses. **Amenities:** none. **Best for:** swimming; sunrise; walking; windsurfing. ✉ *Atlantic Ave., Sullivan's Island* ⊕ *www.sullivansisland-sc.com.*

BIKING

As long as you stay off the busier roads, the historic district is ideal for bicycling. Many of the city's green spaces, including Colonial Lake and Palmetto Islands County Park, have bike trails. If you want to rent a bike, expect to pay about $25 a day.

Cycling at your own pace is one of the best ways to see Charleston. Those staying at the nearby island resorts, particularly families with children, almost always rent bikes, especially if they are there for a week.

Affordabike. This shop sells and rents bikes. Rentals are a mere $20 for a 24-hour day ($45 a week), which includes a helmet, lock, and basket. Conveniently located in the Upper King area, it is also open on Sunday from noon to 5—the best day for riding in downtown Charleston and/

or across the Ravenel Bridge. ⊠ *534 King St., Upper King* ☎ *843/789–3281* ⊕ *www.affordabike.com.*

Bicycle Shoppe. Open seven days a week, this shop rents simple beach cruisers for $7 an hour or $28 a day, and that includes a helmet. For those wanting to tackle the Ravenel Bridge, the store offers hybrids for $10 an hour or $40 a day. There's a second branch at 1539 Johnnie Dodds Boulevard in Mount Pleasant. ⊠ *281 Meeting St., Market area* ☎ *843/722–8168* ⊕ *www.thebicycleshoppecharleston.com.*

Charleston Bicycle Tours. You'll see the quiet streets and hidden secrets of Charleston when you take a multiday tour with Charleston Bicycle Tours. You'll ride past plantations as well as over the Ravenel Bridge, exploring the nearby islands and quaint surrounding towns. Tours include bikes, accommodations, and dining in the area's best restaurants. There's a van shuttle, licensed guide, and even a mechanic. Prices range from $1,295 for a three-day trip visiting the area's plantations to $2,790 for a six-day tour to Savannah. ⊠ *1321 Bellview Dr., Mount Pleasant* ☎ *843/881–9878* ⊕ *charlestonbicycletours.com.*

Island Bike and Surf Shop. Rent beach bikes for very moderate weekly rates, or check out hybrids, mountain bikes, bicycles built for two, and a wide range of equipment for everyone in the family. The shop will even deliver to Kiawah and Seabrook islands. ⊠ *3665 Bohicket Rd., Johns Island* ☎ *843/768–1158, 800/323–0579* ⊕ *www. islandbikeandsurf.com.*

BOATING

Kayak through isolated marshes and estuaries to outlying islands, or explore Cape Romain National Wildlife Refuge. Rates vary depending on your departure point and whether you go it alone or join a guided tour. Rentals are about $20 per hour, and a two-hour guided tour will run you about $40. The nearby resort islands, especially Kiawah and Wild Dunes, tend to have higher rates.

The boating options are incredibly varied, from a small johnboat with an outboard motor to a chartered sailboat. If you're a newcomer to sailing, arranging lessons is no problem.

AquaSafaris. If you want a sailboat or yacht charter, a cruise to a private beach barbecue, or just a day of offshore fishing, contact AquaSafaris. Captain John Borden takes seaworthy sailors out daily, leaving from Shem Creek and Isle of Palms. A sunset cruise on the *Palmetto Breeze* catamaran offers panoramic views of Charleston Harbor set to a soundtrack of Jimmy Buffett tunes. Enjoy beer and cocktails as you cruise in one of the smoothest sails in the Lowcountry. ⊠ *24 Patriots Point Rd., Mount Pleasant* ☎ *843/886–8133* ⊕ *www.aqua-safaris.com.*

Charleston Kayak Company. Guided kayak tours with Charleston Kayak Company depart from the grounds of the Inn at Middleton Place or Folly Beach. From Middleton, you'll glide down the Ashley River and through brackish creeks in the Lowcountry's only State Scenic River Corridor. Naturalists tell you about the wetlands and the river's cultural history. It's not uncommon to spot an alligator, but thankfully they take no interest in kayakers. Tours last two hours (reservations essential) and cost $45 per person. Both single and tandem kayaks are available starting at $30, including all safety gear. ⊠ *Middleton Place Plantation, 4290 Ashley River Rd., West Ashley* ☎ *843/556–6020, 843/628–2879* ⊕ *www.charlestonkayakcompany.com.*

Coastal Expeditions. Outings for individuals, families, and large groups are arranged by Coastal Expeditions. A kayak tour with a naturalist guide costs $58 per person, and kayak rentals start at $38 for a half day. The company provides exclusive access to Cape Romain National Wilderness Area on Bull Island via the Bull Island Ferry. The ferry departs from Garris Landing and runs Tuesday and Thursday to Saturday from April through November. It costs $30 round-trip. Bull Island has rare natural beauty, a "boneyard beach," shells galore, and 277 species of migrating birds. Coastal Expeditions has additional outlets at Crosby's Seafood on Folly Beach and at Isle of Palms Marina. ⊠ *Shem Creek Maritime Center, 514B Mill St., Mount Pleasant* ☎ *843/884–7684* ⊕ *www.coastalexpeditions.com.*

Ondeck Charleston. Learn how to command your own 26-foot sailboat on Charleston's beautiful harbor with the guidance of an instructor at Ondeck Charleston. This academy can teach you and your family how to sail comfortably on any size sailboat, and can take you from coastal navigation to ocean proficiency. Instructors are fun and experienced, and are U.S. Sailing–certified professionals. Skippered charters are also available and start at $285. ⊠ *24 Patriots Point Rd., Mount Pleasant* ☎ *843/971–0700* ⊕ *www.ondecksailing.us.*

St. John's Kayaks. Just minutes from the entrance to Kiawah and Seabrook islands, St. John's Kayaks offers guided ecotours by kayak, fishing expeditions, and powerboat excursions. Safe and stable, easy-boarding kayaks are ideal for everyone from kids to seniors. Local owners share their love and passion for the barrier sea islands. They welcome groups and offer discounted rates. ⊠ *4460 Betsy Kerrison Pkwy., Johns Island* ☎ *843/330–9777* ⊕ *www. stjohnskayaks.com.*

FISHING

Fishing can be a real adventure in and around Charleston. If you travel offshore with an experienced guide, you'll probably come back with enough fish stories to last until your next trip. This is a pricey adventure best shared with as many of your fishing buddies as possible. Expect to pay about $120 an hour, including bait and tackle. For inshore fly-fishing, guides generally charge $350 for two people for a half day. Deep-sea fishing charters cost about $1,400 for 12 hours for a boatload of anglers.

Bohicket Marina. If you want to catch the big one, Bohicket Marina has half- and full-day charters on 24- to 48-foot boats. Small boat rentals are also available, as well as sunset dolphin-watching cruises. This marina is the closest to Kiawah and Seabrook islands, and this company has a long-standing reputation. For three hours of inshore fishing, expect to pay about $375 for one to three people and $400 to $550 for four or more people, including bait, tackle, and licenses. ⊠ *1880 Andell Bluff Blvd., Johns Island* ☎ *843/768–1280* ⊕ *www.bohicket.com.*

Captain Richard Stuhr. Saltwater fly-fishers looking for an Orvis-endorsed guide do best by calling Captain Richard Stuhr, who has been fishing the waters of Charleston, Kiawah, and Isle of Palms since 1991. He'll haul his 19-foot Action Craft to you and take you on a half-day tour through Charleston's harbor and tributaries for $350. ☎ *843/881–3179* ⊕ *www.captstuhr.com.*

GOLF

With fewer golfers than in Hilton Head, the courses in the Charleston area have more prime tee times available. Even if you're not a guest, you can arrange play at private island resorts, such as Kiawah Island, Seabrook Island, and Wild Dunes. There you will find breathtaking ocean views within a pristine setting. Don't be surprised to find a white-tailed deer grazing a green or an alligator floating in a water hole. For top courses like Kiawah's Ocean Course, expect to pay in the $200 to $300 range during peak season in spring and early fall.

Municipal golf courses are a bargain, often costing less than $25 for 18 holes. Somewhere in between are well-regarded courses at Shadowmoss Plantation Golf Club, west of the Ashley River, and the Links at Stono Ferry in Hollywood.

Charleston Area Golf Guide. For everything from green fees to course statistics and vacation packages in the area, contact the Charleston Area Golf Guide. ☎ *800/774–4444* ⊕ *www. charlestongolfguide.com.*

Charleston Municipal Golf Course. This walker-friendly public course isn't as gorgeous as the resort courses—a highway bisects it—but it does have a lot of shade trees, and the price is right. About 6 miles from downtown and 20 miles from the resort islands of Kiawah and Seabrook, the course has a simple snack bar serving breakfast and lunch, as well as beer and wine. ✉ *2110 Maybank Hwy., James Island* ☎ *843/795–6517* ⊕ *www.charleston-sc.gov* ⚑ *18 holes, 6450 yds, par 72. Green Fee: $17–$24* ☞ *Facilities: Driving range, putting green, pitching area, golf carts, pull carts, rental clubs, lessons, restaurant, bar.*

Charleston National Golf Club. The best nonresort golf course in Charleston tends to be quiet on weekdays, which translates into lower prices. The setting is captivating, carved along the intracoastal waterway and traversing wetlands, lagoons, and pine and oak forests. Finishing holes are set along golden marshland. Diminutive wooden bridges and a handsome clubhouse that looks like an antebellum mirage add to the natural beauty of this well-maintained course. ✉ *1360 National Dr., Mount Pleasant* ☎ *843/884–7799, 843/884–4653* ⊕ *www. charlestonnationalgolf.com* ⚑ *18 holes, 6412 yds, par 72. Green Fee: $56–$66* ☞ *Facilities: Driving range, putting green, pitching area, golf carts, pull carts, rental clubs, pro shop, golf academy/lessons, restaurant, bar.*

WORD OF MOUTH. "Downtown Charleston, obviously, will not have golf courses, but my husband loves to play golf and there is plenty of golf within an easy drive of town. . . . We usually have Fall Break the second week of October and there is nothing I love better than renting a house on Isle of Palms or Sullivan's

Island, spending my days on the very pleasant beaches and then spending the afternoons and/or evenings downtown. . . . I would rent a house on IOP or Sullivan's Island, let my husband play golf in the mornings while I was at the beach, go shop myself silly in the afternoons, and then save the evenings for those romantic dinners!" —BetsyinKY

Dunes West Golf & River Club. Designed by Arthur Hill, this championship course has great marsh and river views and lots of modulation on the Bermuda-covered greens shaded by centuries-old oaks. The generous fairways have greens that may be considered small by today's standards, making approach shots very important. Located about 15 miles from downtown Charleston, it's in a gated residential community with an attractive antebellum-style clubhouse. ✉ *3535 Wando Plantation Way, Mount Pleasant* ☎ *843/856– 9000* ⊕ *www.duneswestgolfclub.com* ⅄ *18 holes, 6871 yds, par 72. Green Fee: $52–$86* ☞ *Facilities: Driving range, putting green, pitching area, golf carts, rental clubs, pro shop, golf academy/lessons, restaurant, bar.*

Links at Stono Ferry. Built atop a Revolutionary War battle-field, the reasonably priced Links at Stono Ferry is the closest course to Kiawah and Seabrook islands. It's 30 minutes from downtown Charleston, however. It's been ranked among the top 100 courses in the Carolinas. Set in a rural area, the course is an upscale residential community with a focus on golf and horses. Its clubhouse has Southern style. ✉ *4812 Stono Links Dr., Hollywood* ☎ *843/763–1817* ⊕ *www.stonoferrygolf.com* ⅄ *18 holes, 6814 yds, par 72. Green Fee: $53–$89* ☞ *Facilities: Driving range, putting green, pitching area, golf carts, rental clubs, pro shop, golf academy/lessons, restaurant, bar.*

Patriots Point Links. A partly covered driving range and spectacular harbor views make this golf course feel special. It's just across the spectacular Ravenel Bridge, and if you drive here you can take advantage of the free public parking. You could also take the water taxi from downtown and arrange for a staffer to pick you up. Four pros offer one-on-one instruction, as well as lessons and clinics. There's a junior camp during the summer. ✉ *1 Patriots Point Rd., Mount Pleasant* ☎ *843/881–0042* ⊕ *www.patriotspointlinks.com* ⅄ *18 holes, 6900 yds, par 72. Green Fee: $52–$74* ☞ *Facilities: Driving range, putting green, pitching area, golf carts, rental clubs, pro shop, golf academy/lessons, restaurant, bar.*

6

Seabrook Island Resort. On this island with acres of untamed maritime forests you'll find two championship courses: Crooked Oaks, designed by Robert Trent Jones Sr., and Ocean Winds, by Willard Byrd. Crooked Oaks, which follows an inland path, is the more player friendly of the two. Ocean Winds is aptly named for three holes that run along the Atlantic; when the wind is up, those ocean breezes make it challenging. Both courses are run out of the same pro shop and have the same green fee. This is a private island, but guest privileges at the resort are extended to anyone who has a golf club membership. Your hometown golf pro must call for a reservation. ✉ *3772 Seabrook Island Rd., Seabrook Island* ☎ *843/768–2529* ⊕ *www.discoverseabrook.com* ⚑ *36 holes, 6800 yds, par 72. Green Fee: $115–$170* ☞ *Facilities: Driving range, putting green, pitching area, golf carts, pull carts, rental clubs, pro shop, golf academy/lessons, restaurant, bar.*

Shadowmoss Plantation Golf Club. This forgiving course has one of the best finishing holes in the area. It's just off Highway 61, about 17 miles from downtown and 20 miles from the resort islands of Kiawah and Seabrook. A seasoned, well-conditioned course, it meanders through the residential enclave that grew up around it. It's a good value for the money. ✉ *20 Dunvegan Dr.* ☎ *843/556–8251* ⊕ *www.shadowmossgolf.com* ⚑ *18 holes, 6701 yds, par 72. Green Fee: $36–$55* ☞ *Facilities: Driving range, putting green, pitching area, golf carts, pull carts, rental clubs, pro shop, golf academy/lessons, restaurant, bar.*

ISLE OF PALMS

Wild Dunes Resort is a 1,600-acre oceanfront resort on the tip of the Isle of Palms some 30 minutes from downtown Charleston. It has two nationally renowned, Tom Fazio–designed courses, the **Links** and the **Harbor** courses.

Harbor Course. Tom Fazio designed this course, shaping a million dollars' worth of dirt into an unforgettable landscape. The dunes are adorned with greens, and hazards can be found around every bend. Nine holes are situated along the Intracoastal Waterway and require shots across the water. ✉ *Wild Dunes Resort, 5757 Palm Blvd., Isle of Palms* ☎ *843/886–2004* ⊕ *www.wilddunes.com* ⚑ *18 holes, 6446 yds, par 70. Green Fee: $65–$110* ☞ *Facilities: Driving range, putting green, pitching area, golf carts, rental clubs, pro-shop, golf academy/lessons, restaurant, bar.*

Links Course. With prevailing ocean breezes, undulating dunes, and natural water hazards, this course has been called a seaside masterpiece. Considered one of architect Tom Fazio's best Lowcountry layouts, the Links Course is challenging enough for the most avid golfer. It's consistently ranked among the top 100 courses in the country. Players are permitted to walk the length of the course, regardless of time or day. ⊠ *Wild Dunes Resort, 10001 Back Bay Dr., Isle of Palms* ☎ *843/886–2002* ⊕ *www.wilddunes. com* ⚑ *18 holes, 6396 yds, par 70. Green Fee: $115–$165* ☞ *Facilities: Driving range, putting green, pitching area, golf carts, caddies, rental clubs, pro shop, golf academy/ lessons, restaurant, bar.*

KIAWAH ISLAND

Kiawah Island Golf Resort is home to five championship courses: the world-famous **Ocean Course,** designed by Pete Dye; the Jack Nicklaus–designed **Turtle Point; Osprey Point,** designed by Tom Fazio; **Cougar Point,** designed by Gary Player; and **Oak Point,** redesigned by Clyde Johnston.

Cougar Point Golf Course. This is Kiawah's Gary Player design, which features holes playing along tidal marshes and offering panoramic views of the Kiawah River and golden spans of spartina grass. Reservations essential. ⊠ *Kiawah Island Golf Resort, 1 Sanctuary Beach Dr., Kiawah Island* ☎ *843/266–4020* ⊕ *www.kiawahresort.com* ⚑ *18 holes, 6503 yds, par 72. Green Fee: $215 nonguests/$183 resort guests* ☞ *Facilities: Driving range, putting green, pitching area, golf carts, caddies, rental clubs, pro shop, golf academy/lessons, restaurant, bar.*

Oak Point Golf Course. Outside the Kiawah gate, in the center of Hope Plantation, a residential enclave that was an indigo plantation, lies this Scottish-American-style course and its $1 million clubhouse. Reservations essential. ⊠ *Kiawah Island Golf Resort, 4394 Hope Plantation Dr., Kiawah Island* ☎ *843/266–4100* ⊕ *www.kiawahresort.com* ⚑ *18 holes, 6450 yds, par 72. Green Fee: $66–$215 depending on season* ☞ *Facilities: Driving range, putting green, pitching area, golf carts, caddies, rental clubs, pro-shop, golf academy/lessons, restaurant, bar.*

★ Fodor'sChoice **Ocean Course.** Considered one of Pete Dye's most superb designs, this seaside course is famous for hosting every major PGA event in the country. The course, which offers spectacular views along 2½ miles of beachfront, starred in Robert Redford's film *The Legend of Bagger*

Vance. The superbly manicured fairways and greens challenge amateurs and professionals alike. Carts are included in the green fee, as are caddies (but not their gratuities). In the morning, this is a walking course. The stellar clubhouse, with its seafood restaurant and full-service bar, are exceptional. Reservations are essential. ⊠ *Kiawah Island Golf Resort, 1000 Ocean Course Dr., Kiawah Island* ☎ *843/266–4670* ⊕ *www.kiawahresort.com* ⸙ *18 holes, 7873 yds, par 72. Green Fee: $222–$338* ☞ *Facilities: Driving range, putting green, pitching area, golf carts, caddies, rental clubs, pro shop, golf academy, restaurant, bar.*

Osprey Point Golf Course. This Tom Fazio course offers the utmost in views that the Lowcountry has to offer: maritime forests, pristine lagoons, natural lakes, and saltwater marshes. Every hole has picturesque vistas. It's a favorite of residents and resort guests. The impressive clubhouse with 14,000 square feet of pro shop selling attractive, high-quality apparel; attended locker rooms; and a semiprivate dining room certainly add points. ⊠ *Kiawah Island Golf Resort, 1000 Governors Dr., Kiawah Island* ☎ *843/266–4640* ⊕ *www.kiawahresort.com* ⸙ *18 holes, 6932 yds, par 72. Green Fee: $114/$212* ☞ *Facilities: Driving range, putting green, pitching area, golf carts, caddies, rental clubs, pro shop, golf academy/lessons, restaurant, bar.*

Turtle Point Golf Course. This famed Jack Nicklaus course has hosted many amateur and professional tournaments, including the 1990 PGA Cup Matches and the Carolinas Amateur Championship. It features three spectacular oceanfront holes. The undulating course flows seamlessly through interior forests of hardwoods and palmettos and along backwater lagoons, and boasts a $7.5 million clubhouse built in a classic Lowcountry style. Reservations essential. ⊠ *Kiawah Island Golf Resort, 1 Turtle Point Dr., Kiawah Island* ☎ *843/266–4050* ⊕ *www.kiawahresort.com* ⸙ *18 holes, 7061 yds, par 72. Green Fee: $99–$215* ☞ *Facilities: Driving range, putting green, pitching area, golf carts, caddies (on request), rental clubs, pro shop, golf academy/lessons, restaurant, bar.*

HORSEBACK RIDING

Put your foot in the stirrup and get a leg up! You can tour the beaches, maritime forests, marshlands, and former rice fields all from horseback. Several good stables in the area offer trail rides. Expect to pay $40 for rides through wooded terrain and $85 for those along the beach.

Middleton Equestrian Center. This long-established stable specializes in English riding lessons. It offers trail rides along wooded and open terrain and through former rice fields. All experience levels are welcome, and headgear is provided. Kids ages 8 and older can ride. ⊠ *Middleton Place, 4280 Ashley River Rd., West Ashley* ☎ *843/556–8137* ⊕ *www.middletonplace.org.*

Seabrook Island Equestrian Center. This classy equestrian center 24 miles south of Charleston has walking trails for beginning and advanced riders. Beach rides are only for advanced riders who can handle a horse competently at a walk, trot, and canter. Parent-led pony rides are $45 for a half hour, and as many as three kids can take a turn. Private instructions are $55 for a half hour. The center hosts annual equestrian events and notable hunter and jumper shows. ⊠ *3772 Seabrook Island Rd., Seabrook Island* ☎ *843/768–7541* ⊕ *www.discoverseabrook.com.*

SCUBA DIVING

Experienced divers can explore the Cooper River Underwater Heritage Diving Trail, upriver from Charleston. The 2-mile-long trail has six submerged sites, including ships that date to the Revolutionary War. Expect to pay $100 to $150 a trip. Equipment rentals average $10 for a tank.

Charleston Scuba. Whether you're just learning or an old pro, this dive outfitter offers everything from introductory classes to open-water drives. The company frequents a total of eight sites, and prices range from $130 to $175 for two-tank dives. ⊠ *335 Savannah Hwy., West Ashley* ☎ *843/763–3483* ⊕ *www.charlestonscuba.com.*

SOCCER

Charleston Battery. Charleston's soccer team plays at Blackbaud Stadium, the first privately funded soccer facility in the country. Games are played from April through September and feature fun-filled giveaways and promotions. The stadium seats 5,100, and tickets range from $10 to

$18. ✉ *Blackbaud Stadium, 1990 Daniel Island Dr., Daniel Island* ☎ *843/971–4625* ⊕ *www.charlestonbattery.com.*

TENNIS

The Charleston area offers tennis options for every skill level. Spring and fall are ideal for play at the area's inexpensive municipal courses. The resort islands have tennis that can be extremely costly, depending on whether or not you are a guest.

Charleston is the home of the world-class Family Circle Cup, a professional women's tournament. Held over nine days every April at the Family Circle Tennis Center, it attracts some 90,000 fans from around the globe and boasts a roster of former champions, including Chris Evert, Martina Navratilova, Jennifer Capriati, and Venus and Serena Williams.

Charleston Tennis Center. With 15 outdoor courts lighted for nighttime matches, this tennis center is among the city's most popular. (The $8 admission fee certainly doesn't hurt.) There are restrooms on the premises, and balls and racquets are for sale. ✉ *19 Farmfield Ave., West Ashley* ☎ *843/769–8258* ⊕ *www.charleston-sc.gov.*

★ **Fodor's Choice** **Family Circle Tennis Center.** This world-class facility is, without question, one of the top places to play tennis in the Southeast. Open to the public, the 17 courts (13 clay, 4 hard) are lighted for night play. Rates are $10 for the hard courts, $15 for clay. Four miniature courts for kids four to eight make this a destination for the whole family. With one of the best-qualified teaching staffs in the country, the Instinctive Tennis Academy offers private lessons and clinics for players of all ages. The Family Circle Cup, a signature event for women's tennis, is hosted here each April. Not coincidentally, this is also the city's top venue for concerts under the stars. ✉ *161 Seven Farms Dr., Daniel Island* ☎ *843/856–7900* ⊕ *www.familycirclecup.com.*

Maybank Tennis Center. Talk about a bargain: the Maybank Tennis Center's eight hard courts are $4 an hour, and its three clay courts are $9 an hour. Balls and racquets are available for purchase, and there are restrooms on the premises. ✉ *1880 Houghton Dr., James Island* ☎ *843/406–8814* ⊕ *www.charleston-sc.gov.*

ISLE OF PALMS

Wild Dunes Tennis Center. This tennis center started out as a small, local tennis club, and it has never lost its love for the game. The tennis complex lies in the center of the Wild Dunes resort, where 17 Har-Tru courts include 1 stadium-style court and 5 lighted for night play. The pros in the ranked teaching program gear their lessons to each player, from novice to expert. Wild Dunes offers adult, junior, and Tiny Tot programs, professional instruction, and matchmaking for all levels. The full-service pro shop sells, rents, and repairs racquets. All Wild Dunes Resort guests can have one hour of complimentary court time per room, per day from noon to 6. For additional hours or court times reserved before noon, the cost is $15 per hour for guests renting accommodations. ⊠ *Wild Dunes Resort, 5757 Palm Blvd., Isle of Palms* 🕾 *843/886–2113, 843/886–6000* ⊕ *www.wilddunes.com.*

KIAWAH ISLAND

Roy Barth Tennis Center. In Kiawah Island Golf Resort's East Beach Village, the Roy Barth Tennis Center is a short walk from the resort's luxurious oceanfront hotel and spa. Open year-round, it has 10 Har-Tru courts (one lighted), three hard courts (one lighted), and a practice court with a ball machine and an automated ball retrieval system. Court time is $34 an hour for guests and $43 for everyone else. ⊠ *Kiawah Island Golf Resort, East Beach Village, 1 Sanctuary Dr., Kiawah Island* 🕾 *843/768–2838* ⊕ *www. kiawahresort.com.*

West Beach Tennis Club. Open early March to early September, the West Beach Tennis Club features 10 Har-Tru courts and two lighted hard courts. Private instruction ranges from $30 an hour for group classes with a pro to $80 an hour for private lessons with a center's director. ⊠ *Kiawah Island Golf Resort, West Beach Village, 1000 Kiawah Beach Dr., Kiawah Island* 🕾 *843/768–2820* ⊕ *www.kiawahresort.com.*

WATER SPORTS

When it comes to water sports, Charleston is a great place to get our feet wet. Surfboards can be rented for as little as $5 an hour. An hour of surf lessons will run you about $40, and includes use of a board.

Island Bike and Surf Shop. Rent surfboards and kayaks from this shop and the staff will happily deliver them to your resort on Kiawah or Seabrook island. Boards cost $20 a day. ✉ *3665 Bohicket Rd., Johns Island* ☎ *843/768–1158* ⊕ *www.kiawahislandbikerental.com.*

McKevlin's Surf Shop. The pros at McKevlin's Surf Shop can teach you what you need to know about riding the waves at Folly Beach. Surfboards start at $7 per hour, and an hour of instruction is an additional $40. ✉ *8 Center St., Folly Beach* ☎ *843/588–2247* ⊕ *www.mckevlins.com.*

Sun & Ski. Rent Jet Skis at this shop next to the fishing pier in Folly Beach. You can also rent a double-chair setup and an umbrella for the day for $23. ✉ *1 Center St., Folly Beach* ☎ *843/588–0033* ⊕ *www.sunandski.com.*

7

SHOPPING

Visit Fodors.com for advice, updates, and bookings

By Kinsey
Gidick

ONE-OF-A-KIND BOUTIQUES, WHERE THE HOTTEST TRENDS in fashion hang on the racks, make up an important part of the contemporary Charleston shopping experience. Long-established, Christian Michi anchors the corner of Market and King across from the former Saks Fifth Avenue; its window displays are like artworks, and its innovative and European designs are treasured by well-heeled, sophisticated clients. Forever 21 has replaced Saks, which is indicative of Charleston's demographics. More mature shoppers are pleased to find such high-end shops that sell either their own designer fashions or carry names that are found in Paris, New York, and South Beach, like Kate Spade in the Shops at Charleston Place.

High-end shoe stores make up a category that tends to draw repeat visitors. The number and quality of shoe stores on King Street is surprising for the city's size. Family-owned shops like Berlin's are city institutions. Newer shops like Sugar Snap Peas cater to the growing family demographic.

The Upper King District has furniture shops interspersed between the clothing boutiques and restaurants. These locally owned shops give the personal service that has always been a hallmark of existing King Street merchants in this area. The revival of this neighborhood has sparked a new wave of home-fashion stores; long-term antiques hunters, accustomed to buying on Lower King, have been lured uptown as well. Haute Design is one of the most tasteful of these shops, offering a wide selection of antiques, particularly lighting, imported from France and Italy. Charleston has more than 25 fine-art galleries, making it one of the top art towns in America. Local Low-country art, which includes both traditional landscapes of the region as well as more contemporary takes, is among the most prevalent styles here. Such innovative artists as Betty Smith and Fred Jamar, a Belgian known for his whimsical cityscapes, can give you a piece of Charleston to keep close until your next visit. Collectors will find high-end nationally and internationally renowned work in such exquisite galleries as Ann Long Fine Art and the more contemporary Martin Gallery.

SHOPPING DISTRICTS

City Market. A cluster of shops and restaurants surrounds the old City Market. Sweetgrass basket weavers work here and you can buy their wares, although these crafts have become expensive. There are T-shirt shops as well as upscale clothing boutiques. In the covered market, vendors have stalls selling everything from jewelry to dresses and purses. You can peruse the middle section of the market in air-conditioned comfort. ⊠ *E. Bay and Market Sts., Market area* ⊕ *www.thecharlestoncitymarket.com.*

★ ~~Fodor's~~Choice **King Street.** The city's main shopping strip, King Street is divided into informal districts: Lower King (from Broad Street to Market Street) is the Antiques District, lined with high-end dealers; Middle King (from Market Street to Calhoun Street) is the Fashion District, a mix of national chains like Banana Republic and Pottery Barn and locally owned boutiques; and Upper King (from Calhoun Street to Spring Street) has been dubbed the Design District, an up-and-coming area becoming known for its furniture and interior-design stores. Check out Second Sundays on King, when the street closes to cars from Calhoun Street to Queen Street. Make sure to visit the farmers' market in Marion Square throughout the spring and summer months.

7

SHOPPING REVIEWS

NORTH OF BROAD

LOWER KING

ANTIQUES AND COLLECTIBLES

George C. Birlant & Co. You'll find mostly 18th- and 19th-century English antiques here, but keep your eye out for a Charleston Battery bench (which you can spot at White Point Garden), for which they are famous. Founded in 1922, Birlant's is fourth-generation family-owned. ⊠ *191 King St., Lower King* ☎ *843/722–3842* ⊕ *www.birlant.com* ⊗ *Mon.–Sat. 9–5:30.*

Jacques' Antiques. As the name suggests, most of the antiques here are imported from France, and the rest are either European or English from the 17th to the 20th centuries. Decorative arts include ceramics, porcelains, and crystal. From the candlesticks to the armoires, all are in exquisite taste. ⊠ *160 King St., Lower King* ☎ *843/577–0104* ⊕ *www. jacantiques.com* ⊗ *Mon.–Sat. 10–5.*

Sweetgrass Baskets

The purchase of a handwoven Charleston sweetgrass basket is proof to your friends that you've been here. For centuries, Gullah artisans have been weaving and selling these baskets in the City Market, where they sit busily in their chairs and place their wares on the sidewalk around them. Other places where they are known to set up are beside the downtown post office on Meeting and Broad streets, and on the right side of Highway 17 North, past Mount Pleasant (where you'll find the best prices). Prices range from about $60 for a small basket up into the hundreds for the larger sizes. Many buyers display these treasures in their homes like artworks. Note: Be respectful of the renowned presence of the "basket ladies" in this city. Before taking their photograph, ask permission and offer a tip to show your appreciation.

CLOTHING

Ben Silver. Charleston's own Ben Silver, premier purveyor of blazer buttons, has more than 800 designs, including college and British regimental motifs. The shop also sells British neckties, embroidered polo shirts, and blazers. This Charleston institution was founded in the 1960s. ⊠ *149 King St., Lower King* ☎ *843/577–4556* ⊕ *www.bensilver. com* ☉ *Weekdays 9–6, Sat. 10–6.*

Berlin's Clothing Store. Family-owned for four generations, this Charleston institution has a reputation as a destination for special-occasion clothing. The store, which for generations sold the preppy styles, has now added European designers. There is a complimentary parking lot across the street. ⊠ *114–116 King St., Lower King* ☎ *843/722–1665* ⊕ *www.berlinsclothing.com* ☉ *Mon.–Sat. 9:30–6.*

Billy Reid. The darling of Southern tailors offers fashion-forward shoppers the best in aristocratic men's and women's clothing. Be sure to check out the basement sale racks, where prices are slashed as much as 50%. ⊠ *150 King St., Lower King* ☎ *843/577–3004* ⊕ *www.billyreid.com* ☉ *Mon.–Sat. 10–6, Sun. noon–6.*

Christian Michi. This shop carries tony women's clothing and accessories. Designers from Italy, such as Piazza Sempione, are represented, as is Hoss Intropia from Spain. Known for its evening wear, the shop has pricey but gorgeous gowns and a fine selection of cocktail dresses. High-end fragrances add to the luxurious air. ⊠ *220 King St., Lower King* ☎ *843/723–0575* ⊕ *www.christianmichi.com* ⊘ *Mon.– Sat. 10–6, Sun. noon–6.*

Forever 21. The big city has come to Charleston with the arrival of this chain. Housed in the former Saks Fifth Avenue building, it offers a variety of inexpensive, trendy clothing. ⊠ *211 King St., Lower King* ☎ *843/937–5087* ⊕ *forever21.com.*

Sugar Snap Pea. This sweet shop stocks the ultimate in kiddie wear, from Petit Bateau to Jellycat and Tea brand. Owner Zhenya Kuhne keeps the clothing options fresh and new. There's also a Mount Pleasant branch at 712 S. Shelmore Boulevard. ⊠ *161½ King St., Lower King* ☎ *843/793–2621* ⊕ *www.sugarsnappea.com* ⊘ *Mon.–Sat. 10–6.*

JEWELRY AND ACCESSORIES

Buckar Jewelry Architects. This shop has been crafting custom-design jewelry in Charleston for decades. Their friendly staff will take the time to visit as well as find the perfect gem for you. ⊠ *17 Princess Street, Lower King* ☎ *843/937–8400* ⊕ *www.buckar.com.*

Croghan's Jewel Box. Ring the doorbell for fine new jewelry as well as antiques at this shop, a Charleston institution for more than 100 years. Inside you'll find wonderful wedding gift items. Should the need arise, Croghan's does excellent repair work. ⊠ *308 King St., Lower King* ☎ *843/723–3594* ⊕ *www.croghansjewelbox.com* ⊘ *Weekdays 9:30–5:30, Sat. 10–5.*

Dixie Dunbar Studio. Dealing in one-of-a-kind pieces, this contemporary jewelry shop has been here for decades. The handmade items can be delightfully unpredictable. ⊠ *192 King St., Lower King* ☎ *843/722–0006* ⊕ *www.dixiedunbar. com* ⊘ *Mon.–Sat. 10–5:30.*

SHOES, HANDBAGS, AND LEATHER GOODS

Bob Ellis. In business for more than 60 years, this Charleston landmark sells some gorgeous shoes from Prada, Manolo Blahnik, YSL, Jimmy Choo, and Christian Louboutin, among other high-end designers. ⊠ *332 King St., King St., Fashion District* ☎ *843/722–2515* ⊕ *www.bobellisshoes. com* ⊘ *Mon.–Sat.10–6.*

SPAS

Stella Nova. In a historic Charleston house, Stella Nova sits just off King Street. It's serious about all of its treatments, from body wraps to salt scrubs. If looking great is a priority, the collagen mask and massage can erase years. For couples, there are romantic aromatherapy massages. Enjoy refreshments on the breezy verandas. Stella Nova has a top-of-the-line salon with specially trained stylists and makeup artists. The VIP Spa Suite, with butler service, is a good bet for bridal parties and girlfriend getaways. Known for its excellent service, the spa is open daily. ✉ *78 Society St., Lower King* ☎ *843/723–0909* ⊕ *www.stella-nova.com.*

MARKET AREA

ART

Corrigan Gallery. Owner Lese Corrigan displays her own paintings and the works of some 16 other painters and photographers. Most pieces fit the genre of contemporary Southern art. Prices start at $50 and go up from there. ✉ *62 Queen St., Market area* ☎ *843/722–9868* ⊕ *www. corrigangallery.com* ⊘ *Mon.–Sat. 10–5.*

CHARLESTON'S FRENCH QUARTER. The downtown neighborhood known as the French Quarter, named after the founding French Huguenots, has become a destination for art lovers. The French Quarter Gallery Association (⊕ *www.frenchquarterarts.com*) consists of roughly 30 art galleries within the original walled city. Galleries here host a delightful art walk, with wine and some refreshments, from 5 to 8 pm on the first Friday in March, May, October, and December. The Charleston Fine Art Dealers' Association has a list of member galleries as well as art events on its website, ⊕ *www.cfada.com.*

Horton Hayes Fine Art. This gallery carries the sought-after Lowcountry paintings depicting coastal life by Mark Kelvin Horton, who also paints architectural and figurative works. Shannon Rundquist is among the other Lowcountry artists shown; she has a fun, whimsical way of painting local life and is known for her blue-crab art. ✉ *30 State St., Market area* ☎ *843/958–0014* ⊕ *www.hortonhayes.com* ⊘ *Mon.– Sat. 10:30–5:30, Sun. 12:30–5.*

Robert Lange Studio. The most *avant* of the contemporary galleries, this striking, minimalist space is a working studio for Robert Lange and other exceptionally talented young artists. Most of the work has a hyper-realistic style with surreal overtones. Belgian Fred Jamar is the senior anchorman here, and his "bubble tree" Charleston cityscapes are whimsical, even cartoonlike. ⌂ *2 Queen St., Market area* ☎ *843/805–8052* ⊕ *www.robertlangestudios.com* ⊙ *Daily 11–5.*

Smith-Killian Fine Art. This gallery exhibits contemporary paintings by Betty Smith and her talented triplets, Jennifer, Shannon, and Tripp. Her son, Tripp, is a nature photographer specializing in black-and-white images. The bronze wildlife sculptures are by nationally recognized Darrell Davis; the acclaimed oil paintings by Kim English are attention-getters. ⌂ *9 Queen St., Market area* ☎ *843/853–0708* ⊕ *www.smithkillian.com* ⊙ *Mon.–Sat. 10–5, Sun. noon–4.*

★ Fodor$Choice **Wells Gallery.** Showcasing the talents of many fine artists, Wells Gallery shows still-life paintings, black-and-white photographs, bronze sculptures, and hand-blown glass. Everything here is done in excellent taste, from the contemporary decor to the meet-the-artist receptions. There's another branch at 1 Sanctuary Beach Drive on Kiawah Island. ⌂ *125 Meeting St., Market area* ☎ *843/853– 3233* ⊕ *www.wellsgallery.com* ⊙ *Mon.–Sat. 10–5.*

CLOTHING
The Trunk Show. This upscale consignment shop sells designer dresses, handbags, and shoes. The back room has been converted into a men's department, with mostly new clothes but some vintage items as well. The shop has become known for its estate jewelry and custom-made jewelry from semiprecious stones. There's an excellent selection of gowns and evening wear. ⌂ *281 Meeting St., Market area* ☎ *843/722–0442* ⊕ *www.charlestontrunkshow.com* ⊙ *Mon.–Sat. 11–6.*

FOOD AND WINE
Market Street Sweets. Make time to stop at Market Street Sweets for the melt-in-your-mouth pralines, bear claws, fudge, and especially the famous glazed pecans—cinnamon and sugar is the favorite. ⌂ *100 N. Market St., Market area* ☎ *843/722–1397* ⊕ *www.riverstreetsweets.com* ⊙ *Tues.– Sun. 9 am–11 pm.*

O'Hara & Flynn. One of Charleston's best-known wine shops also has a wine bar, open Monday through Saturday. If you buy a bottle of wine at retail price, you can drink it at the tables or right at the wine bar for just a $10 corkage fee. Meats (including imported sausage and salami), cheeses, and fresh olive oil are sold here, and you can order some

Charleston's Sweet Tooth

Pralines, glazed pecans, bear claws, and benne wafers—Charlestonians have a sweet tooth.

Stroll the sidewalks of the Market area and breathe in the come-hither aroma of pralines. Employees of candy shops like **Market Street Sweets** (⊠ 100 N. Market St.) stand outside offering samples of their wares, including pralines and cinnamon-and-sugar-glazed pecans.

Benne wafers, which are sweet cookies rather than sesame crackers as the name might suggest, are a Charleston original. Benne is the African word for sesame seeds, which were brought over on slave ships. Once in Charleston, all it took was a little brown sugar and a confection was born. A traditional recipe for benne wafers can be found in the classic cookbook *Charleston Receipts*. These diminutive cookies, the size of a quarter, can be sampled at Charleston's Farmers' Market, downtown in Marion Square on Saturday. They are also found at **Harris Teeter** (⊠ 290 E. Bay St.),

packaged appropriately for gift giving by Charleston Favorites. If you develop an addiction to them, they can be ordered online at ⊕ www. foodforthesouthernsoul.com, along with benne candy, praline pecans, and more.

And, so y'all don't think we're behind the sweet times, the cupcake invasion made it down to Charleston a while back. **Cupcake** (⊠ 433 King St.) sells the latest flavors popularized in Manhattan, like dark chocolate with caramel frosting sprinkled with sea salt. The adorably quaint **Sugar Bake Shop** (⊠ 59½ Cannon St.) specializes in cupcakes such as grapefruit and chocolate raspberry, homemade ice cream, and cookies. And on a final sweet note, we have been invaded once again, this time by macaroons. The French-influenced confection can be bought at the **Macaroon Boutique** (⊠ 45 John St. ⊕ www.macaroonboutique. com). Raspberry is proving to be the flavor of choice, but then, it is one of Charleston's favorite colors—pink.

as small appetizer plates. There's live jazz and acoustic music on Friday and Saturday evenings. ⊠ 225 Meeting St., Market area ☎ 843/534–1916 ☾ Mon.–Thurs. 11–11, Fri. and Sat. 11 am–midnight.

Ted's Butcherblock. In addition to gourmet meals to go, Ted's Butcherblock offers wines, cheeses, cold meats, and olive oils. Attend one of the frequent wine tastings, or stop by to see what's cooking on Ted's Big Green Egg grill.

✉ *334 E. Bay St., Ansonborough* ☎ *843/577–0094* ⊕ *www. tedsbutcherblock.com* ⊘ *Tues.–Sat. 11–7.*

GIFTS AND SOUVENIRS

Charleston Cooks/Maverick Kitchen Store. Here you'll find just about every gourmet kitchen tool and accessory you can imagine. Regional cookbooks abound, and you can also enjoy cooking classes and demonstrations. ✉ *194 E. Bay St., Market area* ☎ *843/722–1212* ⊕ *www.charlestoncooks. com* ⊘ *Mon.–Sat. 10–9, Sun. noon–6.*

The Smoking Lamp. Charleston's oldest smoke shop sells cigars, pipes, and accessories. ✉ *401 B King St., King Street* ☎ *843/577–7339* ⊕ *www.smokinglamp.com* ⊘ *Mon.–Thurs. 10–10, Fri–Sat. 10–midnight, Sun. 10–6.*

HOME DECOR

Historic Charleston Foundation. Bring home superb replicas of Charleston furniture, china, and decorative accessories. These Charleston mementos, including bags of Carolina Rice, make treasured gifts. ✉ *108 Meeting St., Market area* ☎ *843/723–1623* ⊕ *www.historiccharleston.org* ⊘ *Mon.– Sat. 9–6, Sun. noon–5.*

SPAS

Charleston Place Spa. This truly deluxe day spa has nine treatment rooms and a wet room where exotic body wraps like their signature Magnolia Moments treatment and other treatments, like the Moroccan oil scalp, neck, and shoulder massage with hot stones, are administered. Four-handed massages for couples are a popular option. Locker rooms for men and women have showers and saunas; men also have a steam room. Adjacent is a fitness room, an indoor/outdoor pool with retractable roof, and a spacious hot tub available for hotel guests or clients who purchase a spa package. Also any purchase of their signature bracelets funds the spa's I Will Reflect campaign to help melanoma research. ✉ *130 Market St., Market area* ☎ *843/722–4900* ⊕ *www.charlestonplacespa.com.*

Earthling Day Spa. Charleston's first global spa continues to grow. Decorated in a soothing, Southeast Asian design, the spa has an extensive menu that includes two-hour treatments from $200 to $250: Javanese beauty rituals, a Thai detox ritual (in which you're wrapped in banana leaves), and the Hammam Turkish cleansing with a red-flower scrub. The latter is based on Turkish bath rituals with exotic spices like cardamom and olive stones to invigorate the circulation and lymph systems. Facials are Earthling's specialty, and the Alpha Effect with algae mineral mask will leave you glowing. There is also a Pilates studio, and a well-being boutique offers spa products, jewelry, and gifts. ⊠ *245 East Bay St., Market area* ☎ *843/722–4737* ⊕ *www. earthlingdayspa.com.*

MIDDLE KING

BOOKS

Heirloom Book Co. Thanks to Charleston's booming culinary scene, Heirloom Book Co. is a thriving cookbook shop. From hard-to-find vintage cookbooks to the latest best sellers, chef Sean Brock's favorite bookstore keeps acclaimed toques and wannabe Julia Childs up to date. Check their website for frequent events. ⊠ *123 King St., Middle King* ☎ *843/722–6377* ⊕ *www.heirloombookcompany.com.*

CLOTHING

Bits of Lace. When this exclusive lingerie shop opened in 1977, no one thought it would make it in such a conservative town. It's still here and now also stocks beautiful sleepwear and swimsuits. It has become known for its bra-fitting service, especially for bigger cup sizes. There's a second location at 453 West Coleman Boulevard in Mount Pleasant. ⊠ *302 King St., Middle King* ☎ *843/266–6985* ⊕ *www.bitsoflace.com* ☉ *Mon.–Sat. 10–6.*

Copper Penny. Shop Copper Penny for trendy dresses and names like Trina Turk, Millie, Tibi, and Diane von Furstenberg. ⊠ *311 King St., Middle King* ☎ *843/723–2999* ⊕ *www. shopcopperpenny.com* ☉ *Mon.–Sat. 10–6, Sun. noon–6.*

Everything But Water. In the Shops at Charleston Place, this store has one of the town's largest and finest collections of swimwear for all ages. ⊠ *Shops at Charleston Place, 130 Market St., Middle King* ☎ *843/722–5884* ⊕ *www. everythingbutwater.com* ☉ *Mon.–Wed. 10–6, Thurs.–Sat. 10–8, Sun. noon–5.*

Finicky Filly. This boutique carries exceptional women's apparel and accessories by such designers as Lela Rose, Schumacher, All Dressed Up, and Etro. It appeals to women from college age to seniors. ⊠ *303 King St., Middle King* ☎ *843/534–0203* ⊕ *www.thefinickyfilly.com* ☉ *Mon.–Sat. 10–5:30, Sun. 1–5.*

Hampden Clothing. One of the city's trendiest boutiques attracts the young and well heeled, who come here for an edgier style. Hot new designers like Yigal Azrouël, Vena Cava, Alexander Wang, and Jenni Kayne help make it a premier destination for the latest in fashion. ✉ *314 King St., Middle King* ☎ *843/724–6373* ⊕ *www.hampdenclothing. com* ☉ *Mon.–Sat. 10–6, Sun. noon–5.*

FOOD AND WINE

Caviar and Bananas. This upscale specialty market and café features out-of-the-ordinary items like duck confit, pâté, and truffles. Note the locally produced items such as Callie's Pimento Cheese and Jack Rudy Cocktail Co. Small Batch Tonic Water. ✉ *51 George St., Middle King* ☎ *843/577–7757* ⊕ *www.caviarandbananas.com* ☉ *Weekdays 7 am–8:30 pm, Sat. 8:30–8:30, Sun. 8–8.*

GIFTS AND SOUVENIRS

Vieuxtemps. This is where Charlestonians go to pick out wedding china. The only Charleston store to offer Herend, Royal Crown Derby, Haviland, and Spode, the store is a discerning bride's dream. Linens and antiques are also great reasons to pop by. ✉ *180 King St., Middle King* ☎ *843/723–7309* ⊕ *www.vieuxtemps.net* ☉ *Mon.–Sat.10–5:30.*

7

Worthwhile. Designer women's clothing, shoes, and jewelry make it fun to shop at Worthwhile. You can also find artsy and hip baby gear. ✉ *268 King St., Middle King* ☎ *843/723–4418* ⊕ *www.shopworthwhile.com* ☉ *Mon.–Sat. 10–6, Sun. noon–5.*

SHOES AND ACCESSORIES

Gucci of Charleston. In the Shops at Charleston Place, this branch of the fashion powerhouse carries a full line of handbags, luggage, jewelry, and even a dress or two. ✉ *Shops at Charleston Place, 132 Market St., Middle King* ☎ *843/722–3788* ⊕ *www.gucci.com* ☉ *Mon.–Wed. 10–6, Thurs.–Sat. 10–7, Sun. noon–5.*

UPPER KING

ANTIQUES AND COLLECTIBLES

Haute Design. This shop sells French and Italian furniture, crystal chandeliers, and other antiques, as well as custom-designed pieces like tables and mirrors. Belgian linens and hand-printed fabrics are a specialty. ✉ *489 King St., Upper King* ☎ *843/577–9886* ⊕ *www.hautedesign.com.*

ART

Gallery Chuma. This gallery showcases Gullah art, with your choices ranging from inexpensive prints to original works by artists like Jonathan Green. The vibrantly colored paintings of this highly successful South Carolina artist have helped to make Gullah extremely popular. ⊠ *188 Meeting St., Upper King* ☎ *843/722–1702* ⊕ *www.gallerychuma. com* ⊙ *Daily 9:30–6.*

BOOKS

Blue Bicycle Books. Look for out-of-print and rare books, including hardcover classics, at the recently remodeled Blue Bicycle Books. It has a large selection of everything from military history and cookbooks. There are frequent book signings by the likes of Pat Conroy and Dorothea Benton Frank. ⊠ *420 King St., Upper King* ☎ *843/722–2666* ⊕ *www. bluebicyclebooks.com* ⊙ *Mon.–Sat. 10–7:30, Sun. 1–6.*

CLOTHING

Ellington. Chic and classy, this shop is known for its washable, packable clothing made of feel-good fabrics like silk, linen, and cashmere. Its fashions have classic lines but always feel up to date. ⊠ *473 King St., Upper King* ☎ *843/722–7999* ⊙ *Mon.–Sat. 10:30–5:30.*

Kids on King. Having traveled the world, the owners of Kids on King bring you the finest in children's apparel and accessories from just about everywhere. You'll be transported to other lands with handcrafted designs. ⊠ *195 King St., Upper King* ☎ *843/720–8647* ⊕ *www.kidsonking.com* ⊙ *Mon.–Sat. 10–6, Sun. noon–5.*

HOME DECOR

Old Charleston Joggling Board Co. As the name suggests, this shop sells joggling boards, historic Lowcountry oddities on which young, courting couples once bounced toward each other. Nowadays, they are simply used for sitting, usually on front verandas. ⊠ *652 King St., Upper King* ☎ *843/723–4331* ⊕ *www.oldcharlestonjogglingboard.com* ⊙ *Mon.–Thurs. 8:30–4, Fri. 8:30–noon.*

JEWELRY AND ACCESSORIES

Felice Designs. Owner Felice Killian forms Italian Murano glass into beads to create her mesmerizing jewelry. She also pairs the beads with crystals and pearls to create unique looks. Many designs mirror sea life such as anemones and jellyfish. ⊠ *424 King St., Upper King* ☎ *843/853–3354* ⊕ *www.felicedesigns.com* ⊙ *Weekdays 10–5:30, Sat. 10–5.*

SPAS

★ Fodor'sChoice **Seeking Indigo.** This 6,000-square-foot spa provides a delightful, delicious sensory overload. Behind the carved wooden Indonesian doors, a tranquil day spa, a Pilates studio, and a holistic wellness center await. Here, ancient healing meets modern technology with everything from detox footbaths to Ayurvedic treatments to Thai massage. Stressed professionals stop by for a 20-minute thermal massage. Book ahead for the Ayurvedic treatment that features a warm ginger compress and cloth soaked with aromatic oils. Among the state-of-the-art equipment here is a hyperbaric oxygen chamber. ✉ *445 King St., Upper King* ☎ *843/725–0217* ⊕ *www.seekingindigo.com.*

SOUTH OF BROAD

ART

Ann Long Fine Art. Serious art collectors head to Ann Long Fine Art for neoclassical and modern works. This world-class gallery has some outstanding, albeit pricey, works by both gifted American and European artists. Many are painted with Old Master techniques. In addition, the gallery manages the estate of Otto Neumann. ✉ *54 Broad St., South of Broad* ☎ *843/577–0447* ⊕ *www.annlongfineart. com* ☽ *Weekdays 10–5; summer hrs vary.*

Charleston Renaissance Gallery. This gallery carries museum-quality art—in fact, more than half of the beautifully framed works are sold to museums. Visit, nonetheless—these are paintings of rare beauty. ✉ *103 Church St., South of Broad* ☎ *843/723–0025* ⊕ *www.charlestonrenaissancegallery.com* ☽ *Weekdays 9:30–5:30.*

Ellis-Nicholson Gallery. Showcasing painters and sculptors ranging from those just starting their careers to veterans with international reputations, this gallery has a top-of-the-line selection of works. This is also a great place to go for handcrafted jewelry. ✉ *1½ Broad St., South of Broad* ☎ *843/722–5353* ⊕ *www.ellis-nicholsongallery.com* ☽ *Mon.–Sat. 10–6, Sun. by appt.*

★ Fodor'sChoice **Martin Gallery.** In a former bank building, this grand space is the city's most impressive gallery. It sells works by nationally and internationally acclaimed artists, sculptors, and photographers, and is especially well known for its bronzes and large wooden sculptures, as well as glass pieces and custom-designed jewelry. ✉ *18 Broad St., South of Broad* ☎ *843/723–7378* ⊕ *www.martingallerycharleston. com* ☽ *Mon.–Sat. 10–6, Sun. 11–5.*

MOUNT PLEASANT AND VICINITY

ANTIQUES AND COLLECTIBLES

Page's Thieves Market. Specializing in furniture—especially tables, desks, and chests—this market frequently hosts auctions on weekends. Drop by on your way to the beach at Sullivan's Island or Isle of Palms. ✉ *1460 Ben Sawyer Blvd., Mount Pleasant* ☎ *843/884–9672* ⊕ *www.pagesthievesmarket.com* ☉ *Weekdays 9–5, Sat. 9–4.*

HOME DECOR

Carolina Lanterns. Stop in for copper gas and electric lanterns based on designs from downtown's Historic District, as well as a host of other lights and accessories. ✉ *1362 Chuck Dawley Blvd., Mount Pleasant* ☎ *843/881–4170, 877/881–4173* ⊕ *www.carolinalanterns.com* ☉ *Mon.–Thurs. 9–5:30, Fri. 9–5, Sat. 11–3.*

MALLS AND SHOPPING CENTERS

Mount Pleasant Towne Centre. Across the Ravenel Bridge from Charleston, this mall has 60 stores, including Old Navy, White House/Black Market, Loft, Barnes & Noble, and more. The mall has the area's best movie theater, the wide-screen Palmetto Grande. ✉ *1600 Palmetto Grande Drive, Mount Pleasant* ☎ *843/216–9900* ⊕ *www.mtpleasanttownecentre.com* ☉ *Daily 10–6.*

GREATER CHARLESTON

CANNONBOROUGH

CLOTHING

Indigo & Cotton. This men's store is the go-to boutique for the latest in gentlemen's tailoring featuring brands such as Gitman Vintage, Filson Red Label bags, and Raleigh Denim. The Cannonborough shop is also brimming with bow ties, handkerchiefs, and other accessories. ✉ *79 Cannon St., Cannonborough* ☎ *843/718–2980* ⊕ *www.indigoandcotton.com* ☉ *Weekdays 11–6, Sat. 11–5.*

GIFTS AND SOUVENIRS

Mac & Murphy. This hole-in-the-wall is for anyone who favors old-fashioned methods of communication, with the trendiest in notepads, pens, wrapping paper, and stationery, including Cheree Berry, Crane & Co., Dude and Chick. ✉ *74 Cannon St., Cannonborough* ☎ *843/576–4394* ⊕ *www.macandmurphy.com* ☉ *Weekdays 10:30–6, Sat. 10:30–5.*

JOHNS ISLAND
MALLS AND SHOPPING CENTERS
Freshfields Village. At the crossroads of Kiawah and Seabrook islands, this shopping area includes a variety of homegrown stores. There are French and Italian restaurants, an ice-cream shop, a sports outfitter, and stores selling upscale apparel. More than just a shopping destination, Freshfields has become a major social center, offering everything from wine and beer tastings to movie and concerts on the green. ✉ *Kiawah Island Pkwy., Johns Island* ☎ *843/768–6491* ⊕ *www.freshfieldsvillage.com* ⊗ *Mon.–Sat. 10–6, Sun. 1–6.*

NORTH CHARLESTON
MALLS AND SHOPPING CENTERS
Tanger Outlet. If you are a dedicated outlet shopper, head to Tanger Outlet in North Charleston. This spiffy, contemporary mall houses 80 name-brand outlets like Loft, Kenneth Cole, J.Crew, Timberland, and Saks Fifth Avenue OFF 5TH. ✉ *Centre Pointe Dr., off I–26, North Charleston* ☎ *843/529–3095* ⊕ *www.tangeroutlet.com* ⊗ *Mon.–Sat. 10–9, Sun. 11–6.*

WEST ASHLEY
ANTIQUES AND COLLECTIBLES
Livingston Antiques. This shop deals in 18th- and 19th-century English and Continental furnishings, clocks, and bric-a-brac. It's in a suburb south of the city, and the prices are often quite reasonable. ✉ *2137 Savannah Hwy., West Ashley* ☎ *843/556–6162* ⊕ *www.livingstonantiques.com* ⊗ *Tues.–Sat. 10–4.*

7

8

HILTON HEAD
AND THE
LOWCOUNTRY

Visit Fodors.com for advice, updates, and bookings

Updated
by Sally
Mahan

HILTON HEAD ISLAND IS A UNIQUE AND INCREDIBLY BEAUTIFUL RESORT town that anchors the southern tip of South Carolina's coastline. What makes this semitropical island so unique? At the top of the list is the fact that visitors won't see large, splashy billboards or neon signs. What they will see is an island where the environment takes center stage, a place where development is strictly regulated.

There are 12 miles of sparkling white-sand beaches, amazing world-class restaurants, top-rated golf courses—Harbour Town Golf Links annually hosts the Heritage Golf Tournament, a PGA Tour event—and a thriving tennis community. Wildlife abounds, including loggerhead sea turtles, alligators, snowy egrets, wood storks, great blue heron, and, in the waters, dolphins, manatees, and various species of fish. There are lots of activities offered on the island, including parasailing, charter fishing, kayaking, and many other water sports.

The island is home to several private gated communities, including Sea Pines, Hilton Head Plantation, Shipyard, Wexford, Long Cove, Port Royal, Indigo Run, Palmetto Hall, and Palmetto Dunes. Within these you'll find upscale housing (some of it doubling as vacation rentals), golf courses, shopping, and restaurants. Sea Pines is one of the most famous of these communities, as it is known for the iconic candy-cane-striped Hilton Head Lighthouse. There are also many areas on the island that are not behind security gates.

ORIENTATION AND PLANNING

GETTING ORIENTED

Hilton Head is just north of South Carolina's border with Georgia. The 42-square-mile island is shaped like a foot, hence the reason locals often describe places as being at the "toe" or "heel" of Hilton Head. This part of South Carolina is best explored by car, as its points of interest are spread across a flat coastal plain that is a mix of wooded areas, marshes, and sea islands. The more remote areas are accessible only by boat or ferry.

Hilton Head's neighbor, Bluffton, is an artsy town rich with history. In the last several years the tiny community has grown to cover about 50 square miles. South of Hilton Head is the city of Savannah, which is about a 45-minute

TOP REASONS TO GO

Beachcombing: Hilton Head Island has 12 miles of beaches. You can swim, soak up the sun, or walk along the sand.

Beaufort: This small antebellum town offers large doses of heritage and culture; nearly everything you might want to see is within its downtown historic district.

Challenging Golf: Hilton Head's nickname is "Golf Island," and its many challenging courses have an international reputation.

Serving Up Tennis: Home to hundreds of tennis courts, Hilton Head is one of the nation's top tennis destinations.

Staying Put: This semitropical island has been a resort destination for decades, and it has all the desired amenities for visitors: a vast array of lodgings, an endless supply of restaurants, and excellent shopping.

drive from the island. North of Hilton Head is Beaufort, a cultural treasure and a graceful antebellum town. Beaufort is also about 45 minutes from Hilton Head.

Hilton Head Island. One of the Southeast coast's most popular tourist destinations, Hilton Head is known for its golf courses and tennis courts. It's a magnet for time-share owners and retirees. Bluffton is Hilton Head's quirky neighbor to the west. The old-town area is laden with history and charm.

Beaufort. This charming town just inland from Hilton Head is a destination in its own right, with a lively dining scene and cute bed-and-breakfasts.

Daufuskie Island. A scenic ferry ride from Hilton Head, Daufuskie is now much more developed than it was during the days when Pat Conroy wrote *The Water Is Wide*, but it's still a beautiful island to explore, even on a day trip. You can stay for a few days at a variety of fine rental properties, tool down shady dirt roads in a golf cart, and delight in the glorious, nearly deserted beaches.

PLANNING

WHEN TO GO

The high season follows typical beach-town cycles, with June through August and holidays year-round being the busiest and most costly. Mid-April, during the annual RBC Heritage Golf Tournament, is when rates tend to be highest.

Thanks to the Lowcountry's mostly moderate year-round temperatures, tourists are ever-present. Spring is the best time to visit, when the weather is ideal for tennis and golf. Autumn is almost as active for the same reason.

WILL IT RAIN? Don't be discouraged when you see a weather forecast during the summer months saying there's a 30% chance of rain for Hilton Head. It can be an absolutely gorgeous day and suddenly a storm will pop up late in the afternoon. That's because on hot sunny days, the hot air rises up into the atmosphere and mixes with the cool air, causing the atmosphere to become unstable, thereby creating thunderstorms. Not to worry, though: these storms move in and out fairly quickly.

To get a good deal, it's imperative that you plan ahead. The choicest locations can be booked six months to a year in advance, but booking agencies can help you make room reservations and get good deals during the winter season, when the crowds fall off. Villa-rental companies often offer snowbird rates for monthly stays during the winter season. Parking is always free at the major hotels, but valet parking can cost from $17 to $25; the smaller properties have free parking, too, but no valet service.

PLANNING YOUR TIME
No matter where you stay, spend your first day relaxing on the beach or hitting the links. After that, you'll have time to visit some of the area's attractions, including the Coastal Discovery Museum or the Sea Pines Resort. You can also visit the Tanger outlet malls on U.S. 278 in Bluffton. Old-town Bluffton is a quaint area with many locally owned shops and art galleries. If you have a few more days, visit Beaufort on a day trip or even spend the night there. This historic antebellum town is rich with history. Savannah is also a short drive away.

GETTING HERE AND AROUND

AIR TRAVEL
Most travelers use the Savannah/Hilton Head International Airport, less than an hour from Hilton Head, which is served by American Eagle, Delta, JetBlue, United, and US Airways. Hilton Head Island Airport is served by US Airways.

Air Contacts **Hilton Head Island Airport** ✉ *120 Beach City Rd.,
North end, Hilton Head* ☎ *843/255–2950* ⊕ *www.hiltonheadairport.
com.* **Savannah/Hilton Head International Airport** ✉ *400 Airways Ave., Northwest, Savannah, Georgia* ☎ *912/964–0514* ⊕ *www.
savannahairport.com.*

BOAT AND FERRY TRAVEL

Hilton Head is accessible via boat, with docking available
at Harbour Town Yacht Basin, Skull Creek Marina, and
Shelter Cove Harbor.

Boat Docking Information **Harbour Town Yacht Basin** ✉ *Sea
Pines, 149 Lighthouse Rd., South end, Hilton Head* ☎ *843/363–8335*
⊕ *www.seapines.com.* **Shelter Cove Marina** ✉ *Shelter Cove, 1
Shelter Cove La., Mid-island, Hilton Head* ☎ *843/842–7001* ⊕ *www.
palmettodunes.com.* **Skull Creek Marina** ✉ *1 Waterway La., North
end, Hilton Head* ☎ *843/681–8436* ⊕ *www.theskullcreekmarina.com.*

BUS TRAVEL

The Lowcountry Regional Transportation Authority,
known as the Palmetto Breeze, has buses that leave Bluffton in the morning for Hilton Head, Beaufort, and some
of the islands. The fare is $2, and exact change is required.

Bus Contacts **Lowcountry Regional Transportation Authority**
☎ *843/757–5782* ⊕ *www.palmettobreezetransit.com.*

CAR TRAVEL

Driving is the best way to get onto Hilton Head Island. Off
Interstate 95, take Exit 8 onto U.S. 278 East, which leads
you through Bluffton (where it's known as Fording Island
Road) and then to Hilton Head. Once on Hilton Head,
U.S. 278 forks: on the right is William Hilton Parkway,
and on the left is the Cross Island Parkway (a toll road
that costs $1.25 each way). If you take the Cross Island
(as the locals call it) to the south side where Sea Pines and
many other resorts are located, the trip will take about 10
to 15 minutes. If you take William Hilton Parkway the trip
will take about 30 minutes. Be aware that at check-in and
checkout times on Friday, Saturday, and Sunday, traffic on
U.S. 278 can slow to a crawl. ∎TIP➔ **Be careful of putting the
pedal to the metal, particularly on the Cross Island Parkway. It's
patrolled regularly.**

Once on Hilton Head Island, signs are small and blend in
with the trees and landscaping, and nighttime lighting is
kept to a minimum. The lack of streetlights makes it difficult
to find your way at night, so be sure to get good directions.

TAXI TRAVEL

There are several taxi services available on Hilton Head, including Hilton Head Taxi and Limousine, Yellow Cab HHI, and Diamond Transportation, which has SUVs and passenger vans available for pickup at Savannah/Hilton Head International Airport and Hilton Head Airport. Prices range from $20 to $120, depending on where you're headed.

Taxi Contacts **Diamond Transportation** ☎ 843/247–2156 ⊕ hilton-headrides.com. **Hilton Head Taxi and Limousine** ☎ 843/785–8294. **Yellow Cab HHI** ☎ 843/686–6666 ⊕ www.yellowcabhhi.com.

TRAIN TRAVEL

Amtrak gets you as close as Savannah or Yemassee.

Train Contacts **Savannah Amtrak Station** ✉ 2611 Seaboard Coastline Dr., Savannah, Georgia ☎ 800/872–7245 ⊕ www.amtrak.com.

RESTAURANTS

The number of fine-dining restaurants on Hilton Head is extraordinary, given the size of the island. Because of the proximity to the ocean and the small farms on the mainland, most locally owned restaurants are still heavily influenced by the catch of the day and seasonal harvests. Most upscale restaurants open at 11 and don't close until 9 or 10, but some take a break between 2 and 4. Many advertise early-bird menus, and sometimes getting a table before 6 can be a challenge. During the height of the summer season, reservations are a good idea, though in the off-season you may need them only on weekends. There are several locally owned breakfast joints and plenty of great delis where you can pick up lunch or the fixings for a picnic. Smoking is prohibited in restaurants and bars in Bluffton, Beaufort, and on Hilton Head. Beaufort's restaurant scene has certainly evolved, with more trendy restaurants serving contemporary cuisine moving into the downtown area.

HOTELS

Hilton Head is known as one of the best vacation spots on the East Coast, and its hotels are a testimony to its reputation. The island is awash in regular hotels and resorts, not to mention beachfront or golf-course-view villas, cottages, and luxury private homes. You can expect the most modern conveniences and world-class service at the priciest places. Clean, updated rooms and friendly staff are everywhere, even at lower-cost hotels—this is the South, after all. Staying in cooler months, for extended periods of time, or commuting from nearby Bluffton can save money.

WHAT IT COSTS				
	$	$$	$$$	$$$$
Restaurants	under $15	$15–$19	$20–$24	over $24
Hotels	under $150	$150–$200	$201–$250	over $250

Restaurant prices are for a main course at dinner, excluding sales tax. Hotel prices are for two people in a standard double room in high season, excluding service charges and tax.

TOURS

Hilton Head's Adventure Cruises hosts dolphin-watching cruises, sport crabbing, and more. Several companies, including H20 Sports, Live Oac, Outside Hilton Head, and Low Country Nature Tours run dolphin-watching, shark-fishing, kayak, sunset, and delightful environmental trips. Low Country Nature Tours offers a family-friendly fireworks tour during the summer, as well as educational and fun bird-watching tours that children are sure to enjoy.

Gullah Heritage Trail Tours gives a wealth of history about slavery and the Union takeover of the island during the Civil War; tours leave from the Coastal Discovery Museum at Honey Horn Plantation. Tickets are $32.

There's a wide variety of tours available at Harbour Town Yacht Basin, including sunset cruises, fireworks, and dolphin tours. Pau Hana & Flying Circus Sailing Charters offers tours on a catamaran sailboat, and fireworks and sunset cruises. The captains provide an interactive, educational adventure, and the catamaran makes for smooth sailing.

8

Tour Contacts Adventure Cruises ⊠ *Shelter Cove Marina, 9 Harbourside La., Mid-Island, Hilton Head Island* ☎ *843/785–4558* ⊕ *www.cruisehiltonhead.com.* **Gullah Heritage Trail Tours** ⊠ *Coastal Discovery Museum, 70 Honey Horn Dr., North end, Hilton Head* ☎ *843/681–7066* ⊕ *www.gullaheritage.com.* **H2O Sports** ⊠ *Harbour Town Marina, 149 Lighthouse Rd., South End, Hilton Head Island* ☎ *843/671–4386, 877/290–4386* ⊕ *www.h2osports.com.* **Harbour Town Yacht Basin** ⊠ *Sea Pines, 149 Lighthouse Rd., South End, Hilton Head Island* ☎ *843/363–2628* ⊕ *harbourtownyachtbasin.com.* **Live Oac** ⊠ *Hilton Head Harbor, 43A Jenkins Rd., North End, Hilton Head Island* ☎ *843/384–4141* ⊕ *www.liveoac.com.* **Low Country Nature Tours** ⊠ *Shelter Cove Marina, 1 Shelter Cove La., Mid-Island, Hilton Head Island* ☎ *843/683–0187* ⊕ *www.lowcountrynaturetours.*

com. **Outside Hilton Head** ✉ *Shelter Cove Marina, 1 Shelter Cove La., Mid-Island, Hilton Head Island* ☎ *843/686–6996* ⊕ *www.outsidehiltonhead.com.* **Pau Hana & Flying Circus Sailing Charters** ✉ *Palmetto Bay Marina, 86 Helmsman Way, South End, Hilton Head Island* ☎ *843/686–2582* ⊕ *www.hiltonheadislandsailing.com.*

VISITOR INFORMATION

As you're driving into town, you can pick up brochures and maps at the Hilton Head Island-Bluffton Chamber of Commerce and Visitor and Convention Bureau.

Visitor Information **Hilton Head Island-Bluffton Chamber of Commerce and Visitor and Convention Bureau** ✉ *1 Chamber of Commerce Dr., Mid-Island, Hilton Head Island* ☎ *843/785–3673* ⊕ *www.hiltonheadisland.org.*

HILTON HEAD ISLAND

Hilton Head Island is known far and wide as a vacation destination that prides itself on its top-notch golf courses and tennis programs, world-class resorts, and beautiful beaches. But the island is also part of the storied American South, steeped in a rich, colorful history. It has seen Native Americans and explorers, battles from the Revolutionary War to the Civil War, plantations and slaves, and development and environmentally focused growth.

More than 10,000 years ago, the island was inhabited by Paleo-Indians. From 8000 to 2000 BC, Woodland Indians lived on the island. A shell ring made from their discarded oyster shells and animal bones from that period can be found in the Sea Pines Nature Preserve.

The recorded history of the island goes back to the early 1500s, when Spanish explorers sailing coastal waters came upon the island and found Native American settlements. Over the next 200 years, the island was claimed at various times by the Spanish, the French, and the British. In 1663, Captain William Hilton claimed the island for the British crown (and named it for himself), and the island became home to indigo, rice, and cotton plantations.

During the Revolutionary War, the British harassed islanders and burned plantations. During the War of 1812, British troops again burned plantations, but the island recovered from both wars. During the Civil War, Union troops took Hilton Head in 1861 and freed the more than 1,000 slaves on the island. Mitchelville, one of the first settlements for

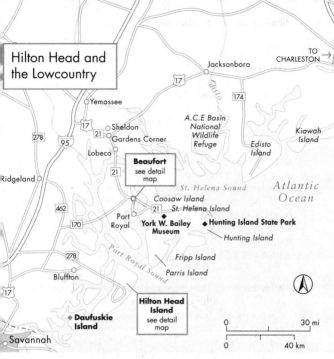

TO CHARLESTON →

Jacksonboro

Yemassee

Sheldon

Gardens Corner

Lobeco

Ridgeland

Beaufort
see detail map

Coosaw Island

St. Helena Island

Port Royal

York W. Bailey Museum

A.C.E Basin National Wildlife Refuge

Edisto Island

Kiawah Island

St. Helena Sound

Atlantic Ocean

Hunting Island State Park

Hunting Island

Fripp Island

Parris Island

Port Royal Sound

Bluffton

Daufuskie Island

Hilton Head Island
see detail map

Savannah

0   30 mi

0   40 km

freed blacks, was created. There was no bridge to the island, so its freed slaves, called "Gullah," subsisted on agriculture and the seafood-laden waters.

Over the years, much of the plantation land was sold at auction. Then, in 1949, General Joseph Fraser purchased 17,000 acres, much of which would eventually become various communities, including Hilton Head Plantation, Palmetto Dunes, and Spanish Wells. The general bought another 1,200 acres, which his son, Charles, used to develop Sea Pines. The first bridge to the island was built in 1956, and modern-day Hilton Head was born.

What makes Hilton Head so special now? Charles Fraser and his business associates focused on development while preserving the environment. And that is what tourists will see today: an island that values its history and its natural beauty.

GETTING HERE AND AROUND

Hilton Head Island is 19 miles east of Interstate 95. Take Exit 8 off Interstate 95 and then U.S. 278 east, directly to the bridges. If you're heading to the southern end of the island, your best bet to save time and avoid traffic is the Cross Island Parkway toll road. The cost is $1.25 each way.

EXPLORING

TOP ATTRACTIONS

★ Fodor'sChoice **Coastal Discovery Museum.** This wonderful
FAMILY museum tells about the history of the Lowcountry. For
instance, you'll learn about the early development of Hilton
Head as an island resort from the Civil War to the 1930s.
There is also a butterfly enclosure, various hands-on programs for children, guided walks, and much more. Take a
walk around the grounds to see marshes, open fields, live
oaks dripping with Spanish moss, as well as South Carolina's largest southern red cedar tree, which dates back to
1595. Admission is free, but lectures and tours on various
subjects cost $10. Although the museum is just off the
Cross Island Parkway, the peaceful grounds make it feel
miles away. ✉ *70 Honey Horn Dr., off Hwy. 278, North
End* ☎ *843/689–6767* ⊕ *www.coastaldiscovery.org* ✉ *Free*
⊙ *Mon.–Sat. 9–4:30.*

Old Town Bluffton. Tucked away from the resort areas, charming Old Town Bluffton has several historic homes and
churches on oak-lined streets. At the end of Wharf Street in
this artsy community is the Bluffton Oyster Company (63
Wharf Street), a place to buy fresh raw local shrimp, fish,
and oysters. Grab some picnic fixings from the Downtown
Deli (27 Mellichamp Drive) and head to the boat dock at
the end of Pritchard Street for a meal with a view. Another
incredibly beautiful spot for a picnic is the grounds of the
Church of the Cross. ✉ *May River Rd. and Calhoun St.,
Old Town, Bluffton* ⊕ *www.oldtownbluffton.com.*

Sea Pines Forest Preserve. Walking and biking trails take
you past a stocked fishing pond, a waterfowl pond, and
a 3,400-year-old Native American shell ring at this 605-
acre public wilderness tract. Pick up the extensive activity
guide at the Sea Pines Welcome Center to take advantage
of goings-on—moonlight hayrides, storytelling around
campfires, and alligator- and bird-watching boat tours. The
preserve is part of the grounds at Sea Pines Resort. Overlooking a small alke, the outdoor chapel has five wooden
pews and a wooden lectern engraved with the Prayer of
St. Francis. ✉ *Sea Pines Resort, 32 Greenwood Dr., South
End* ☎ *843/363–4530, 866/561–8802* ⊕ *www.seapines.com*
✉ *$5 per car* ⊙ *Daily dawn–dusk.*

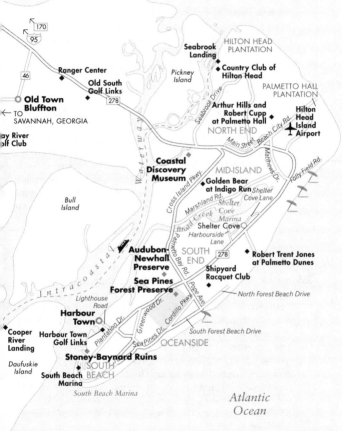

Hilton Head Island

Port Royal Sound

↑ 170
↑ 95

46

Ranger Center

Old Town Bluffton

← TO SAVANNAH, GEORGIA

ay River olf Club

278

HILTON HEAD PLANTATION

Seabrook Landing

Pickney Island

Country Club of Hilton Head

PALMETTO HALL PLANTATION

Old South Golf Links

Seabrook Drive

Arthur Hills and Robert Cupp at Palmetto Hall

NORTH END

Main Street

Beach City Rd.

Hilton Head Island Airport

Matthews Dr.

Folly Field Rd.

Coastal Discovery Museum

Cross Island Pkwy.

Bull Island

MID-ISLAND

Golden Bear at Indigo Run

Marshland Rd.

Shelter Cove Lane

Shelter Cove Marina

Shelter Cove

Broad Creek

Harbourside Lane

SOUTH END

278

Robert Trent Jones at Palmetto Dunes

Palmetto Bay Rd.

Audubon-Newhall Preserve

Shipyard Racquet Club

Intracoastal

Sea Pines Forest Preserve

Lighthouse Road

Pope Ave.

North Forest Beach Drive

Harbour Town

Plantation Dr.

Greenwood Dr.

Cordillo Pkwy.

South Forest Beach Drive

Cooper River Landing

Harbour Town Golf Links

Sea Pines Dr.

OCEANSIDE

Daufuskie Island

Stoney-Baynard Ruins

SOUTH BEACH

South Beach Marina

South Beach Marina

Atlantic Ocean

0   1/2 mi
0   1/2 km

WORTH NOTING

Audubon-Newhall Preserve. There are hiking trails, a self-guided tour, and seasonal walks on this 50-acre preserve. Native plant life is tagged and identified in this pristine forest. ✉ *Palmetto Bay Rd., off the Cross Island Pkwy., South End* ☎ *843/842–9246* 🌐 *www.hiltonheadaudubon.org.*

Harbour Town. The closest thing the Sea Pines development has to a downtown is Harbour Town, a charming area centered on a circular marina that's filled with interesting shops and restaurants. Rising above it all is the landmark candy-cane-stripe Hilton Head Lighthouse, which you can climb to enjoy a view of Calibogue Sound. ✉ *Lighthouse Rd., South End.*

Stoney-Baynard Ruins. Check out the Stoney-Baynard Ruins, the remnants of a plantation home and slave quarters built in the 1700s by Captain John "Saucy Jack" Stoney. A cotton planter named William Edings Baynard bought the place in 1840. On the National Register of Historic Sites, only parts of the walls are still standing. The ruins are not easy to find, so ask for directions at the Sea Pines Welcome Center at the Greenwood Drive gate. ✉ *Plantation Dr., near Baynard Cove Rd., South End* 🌐 *www.exploreseapines.com/historical-sites.asp* 🎟 *Free* 🕒 *Open 24 hrs.*

WHERE TO EAT

$$$ 🍴 **Black Marlin Bayside Grill.** *Seafood.* If you want to dine with a view of the "blue," then head to this seafood eatery in Palmetto Bay Marina. Attracting local boaters, the place draws a steady stream of customers most days, but Saturday and Sunday brunch are the highlights for eggs Benedict and live entertainment. For lunch, the best bets include the fish tacos. The outdoor Hurricane Bar has a Key West vibe and hops during happy hour. There's an early dining menu from 4 to 5:30, and the kitchen cranks out entrées until 10 every night. [$] *Average main: $23* ✉ *Palmetto Bay Marina, 86 Helmsman Way, South End* ☎ *843/785–4950* 🌐 *www.blackmarlinhhi.com.*

$$$ 🍴 **Captain Woody's.** *Seafood.* If you're looking for a fun, casual, kid-friendly seafood restaurant, the reasonably priced Captain Woody's is the place to go. Start with the creamy and delicious crab bisque, a dozen oysters on the half shell or the sampler platter, which includes crab legs, shrimp, and oysters. The grouper sandwiches—the buffalo grouper, grouper melt, and grouper Reuben—are staples

FAMILY

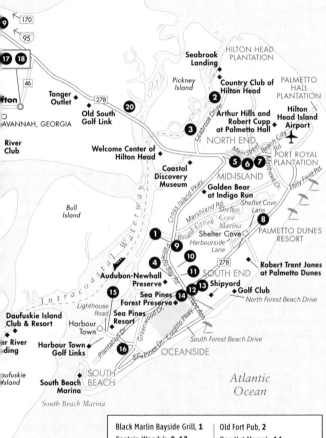

Where to Eat on Hilton Head Island

KEY
- Beach
- Ferry

Port Royal Sound

170
95
17 18
lton
46
Tanger
Outlet
278
20
AVANNAH, GEORGIA
Old South
Golf Link
River
Club

Seabrook Landing

HILTON HEAD PLANTATION

Pickney Island

Country Club of Hilton Head 2

PALMETTO HALL PLANTATION

Arthur Hills and Robert Cupp at Palmetto Hall

Hilton Head Island Airport

Welcome Center of Hilton Head

3

NORTH END

Seabrook Drive

Beach City Rd.
Main Street

5 6 7

Matthews Dr.
PORT ROYAL PLANTATION

Folly Field Rd.

Coastal Discovery Museum

MID-ISLAND

Bull Island

Cross Island Pkwy.

Golden Bear at Indigo Run

Marshland Rd.
Shelter Cove Lane

Shelter Cove Marina

8

1

Palmetto Bay Rd.
Broad Creek

Shelter Cove

9
Harbourside Lane

10

PALMETTO DUNES RESORT

4

Audubon-Newhall Preserve

11
278
SOUTH END

Robert Trent Jones at Palmetto Dunes

15

Sea Pines Forest Preserve

12 13
14

Shipyard
Golf Club
North Forest Beach Drive

Intracoastal Waterway

Lighthouse Road

Sea Pines Resort

Greenwood Dr.

Daufuskie Island Club & Resort

Harbour Town

er River ding

Harbour Town Golf Links

Plantation Dr.

16

Sea Pines Dr.
Cordillo Pkwy.

South Forest Beach Drive

aufuskie sland

SOUTH BEACH

South Beach Marina

South Beach Marina

OCEANSIDE

Atlantic Ocean

0   1/2 mi
0   1/2 km

Black Marlin Bayside Grill, **1**	Old Fort Pub, **2**
Captain Woody's, **9, 17**	One Hot Mama's, **14**
Claude & Uli's Bistro, **20**	Red Fish, **11**
CQs, **15**	Santa Fe Cafe, **8**
Dye's Gullah Fixin's, **7**	Signe's Heaven Bound Bakery &Café, **10**
Frankie Bones, **5**	Skull Creek Boathouse, **3**
Hinoki, **12**	Truffles Cafe, **16, 19**
Michael Anthony's, **13**	WiseGuy's, **6**
Mi Tierra, **4, 18**	

here. The restaurant has a second location in Bluffton. [$] *Average main: $22* ✉ *6 Target Rd., South End* ☎ *843/785–2400* 🌐 *www.captainwoodys.com* ✍ *Reservations not accepted.*

★ Fodor's Choice ✕ **CQs.** *Eclectic.* If you've heard that all of Hilton

$$$$ Head's restaurants lack atmosphere and are tucked away in shopping centers, then you need to experience CQs. Its rustic ambience—heart-pine floors, sepia-tone photos, and a lovely second-story dining room—coupled with its stellar cuisine, personable staff, and feel-good spirit, put most of the island's other eateries to shame. Start with the mussels with lemon butter broth or the oven-roasted beets with pecan-crusted goat cheese to start, and then the ahi tuna for your main course. The staff can suggest just the right wine from an impeccable list. In Harbour Town, the restaurant will reimburse you for the gate pass fee. [$] *Average main: $29* ✉ *140 Lighthouse Rd., Harbour Town, South End* ☎ *843/671–2779* 🌐 *www.cqsrestaurant.com* ✍ *Reservations essential* ⏲ *No lunch.*

$$ ✕ **Dye's Gullah Fixin's.** *Southern.* It's often hard to find the real thing, but this is true Gullah food: decadent, delicious, and comforting. Owner Dye Scott-Rhodan uses recipes handed down by generations of her Gullah family: fried chicken, shrimp and grits, collard greens, and Lowcountry boil (shrimp, smoked sausage, potatoes, corn, and seasonings). Wash it down with the South's most popular beverage, sweet tea. There is also a full bar, and a Sunday buffet from noon to 3. [$] *Average main: $19* ✉ *840 William Hilton Pkwy., Mid-Island* ☎ *843/681–8106* 🌐 *www.dyesgullahfixins.com* ✍ *Reservations essential* 💳 *No credit cards* ⏲ *No lunch Sat.*

$$$ ✕ **Frankie Bones.** *Italian.* This restaurant is dedicated to the loving memory of Frank Sinatra, so you might assume that its name is also one of the handles of "Ole Blue Eyes. You'd be wrong, because Bones was a Chicago gangster before Prohibition. This dining room appeals to an older crowd that likes the traditional parmesanas and marsalas on the early dining menu. But during happy hour, the bar and the surrounding cocktail tables are populated with younger patrons who order flat-bread pizzas and small plates of pasta. Some dishes have innovative twists, including the 16-ounce rib eye with a sweetened coffee rub. Consider drinking your dessert, something Amaretto-based such as a Godfather or a Burnt Almond. [$] *Average main: $22* ✉ *1301 Main St., North end, Hilton Head* ☎ *843/682–4455* 🌐 *www.frankiebonesshhi.com* ✍ *Reservations essential.*

CLOSE UP

Shrimp Boats Forever

Watching shrimp trawlers coming into their home port at sunset, with mighty nets raised and an entourage of hungry seagulls, is a cherished Lowcountry tradition. The shrimping industry has been an integral staple of the South Carolina economy for nearly a century. (Remember Bubba Gump?) It was booming in the 1980s. But alas, cheap, farm-raised shrimp from foreign markets and now the cost of diesel fuel are decimating the shrimpers' numbers.

The season for fresh-caught shrimp is May to December. Lowcountry residents support the freelance fishermen by buying only certified, local wild shrimp in restaurants and in area fish markets and supermarkets. Visitors can follow suit by patronizing local restaurants and markets that display the logo that reads "Certified Wild American Shrimp." Or you can simply ask before you eat.

★ Fodor'sChoice ✕ **Hinoki.** *Japanese.* A peaceful oasis awaits you
$$$ at Hinoki, which has some of the best sushi on Hilton Head. As you make your way into the dining room, fishponds and Japanese flora flank the boardwalk. The interior has an intimate feel, with bamboo touches throughout. Try the Hilton Head roll, which is white fish tempura and avocado, or the Hinoki roll with asparagus and spicy fish roe topped with tuna and avocado. One of the specialties of the house is a to-die-for tuna sashimi salad with spicy mayo, cucumbers, onions, salmon roe, and crabmeat. There are more than 50 sushi and sashimi choices on the menu, along with udon noodle dishes and bento boxes. There's also an extensive sake menu. [$] *Average main: $23* ✉ *Orleans Plaza, 37 New Orleans Rd., South End* ☎ *843/785–9800* 🌐 *hinokihhi.com* ⏲ *Closed Sun.*

MODERN TAKEOUT. **When you just don't feel like going out for a bite, a local delivery service is here to help. Hiltonheaddelivers.com delivers restaurant food to homes, condos, and hotels from 5 to 9:45 pm seven days a week for a $5.50 delivery charge. A variety of restaurants take part, including One Hot Mama's, WiseGuys, and more. Visit 🌐 *hiltonheaddelivers.com* for more details.**

★ Fodor'sChoice ✕ **Michael Anthony's.** *Italian.* Owned by a tal-
$$$$ ented, charismatic Philadelphia family, this restaurant has a convivial spirit, and its innovative pairings and plate presentations are au courant. You can expect fresh, top-quality ingredients, simple yet elegant sauces, and waiters who

know and care about the food they serve. An added bonus: The restaurant offers cooking demonstrations/classes and wine tastings in the upstairs dining room, which has a Tuscan farmhouse feel. $ *Average main: $30* ✉ *Orleans Plaza, 37 New Orleans Rd., Suite L, South End* ☎ *843/785–6272* 🌐 *www.michael-anthonys.com* ✍ *Reservations essential* 🕒 *Closed Sun. No lunch.*

COOKING CLASS. **Learn to prepare Italian cuisine in a hands-on cooking class at Michael Anthony's. Classes include samples of the dishes and wine. Demonstration classes, wine tastings, and programs for visiting corporate groups are also available. There is a high demand for these classes, so reserve your place as far in advance as possible on Michael Anthony's website (🌐 *www.michael-anthonys.com*).**

$ ✕ **Mi Tierra.** *Mexican.* There's nothing fancy here, just great Mexican food. The decor has a Southwestern feel, with tile floors, colorful sombreros, and paintings of chili peppers hanging on the walls. Start with a margarita and the chips and salsa, and don't forget to order the guacamole and bean dip as well. For your main course, try the *enchiladas suizas*, tortillas filled with chicken and topped with green tomatillo sauce, sour cream, and avocado. Another local favorite is the *arroz con camarones*, butterfly shrimp sautéed with garlic butter and vegetables. The menu is extensive and includes a kid's section. There's a second location in Bluffton. $ *Average main: $14* ✉ *130 Arrow Rd., South End* ☎ *843/342–3409* 🌐 *www.mitierrabluffton.com* 🕒 *No lunch weekends.*

$$$$ ✕ **Old Fort Pub.** *European.* Overlooking the sweeping marshlands of Skull Creek, this romantic restaurant has almost panoramic views. It offers one of the island's best overall dining experiences: the building is old enough to have some personality, and the professional staffers diligently do their duty. More important, the kitchen serves flavorful food, including a great starter of roasted calamari with sundried tomatoes and olives. Entrées like the bouillabaisse and filet mignon with chanterelles hit the spot. The wine list is extensive, and there's outdoor seating on a third-floor porch for toasting the sunset. Sunday brunch is celebratory and includes a mimosa. $ *Average main: $33* ✉ *65 Skull Creek Dr., Hilton Head Plantation, North End* ☎ *843/681–2386* 🌐 *www.oldfortpub.com* 🕒 *No lunch.*

$$ ✕ **One Hot Mama's.** *Barbecue.* This heavenly barbecue joint
FAMILY is a Hilton Head institution because of its upbeat atmosphere, graffiti-strewn walls, and melt-in-the-mouth pulled

pork and fall-off-the-bone ribs. But the place also offers some unusual choices: the wings, which have won multiple awards at Hilton Head's Rib Burnoff and Wing Fest, come with tasty sauces ranging from strawberry-jalapeño to teriyaki to the Holy Hula Hula with pineapple, ginger, and ghost peppers. The delectable rib sampler includes hot Asian, chocolate barbecue, and "Mama's Perfect 10." In addition to food that will wake up your taste buds, there are also 15 beers on tap, about a dozen flat-screen TVs, and an outdoor patio with a big brick fireplace for the cooler months. [$] *Average main: $17* ✉ *7A Greenwood Dr., South End* ☎ *843/682–6262* 🌐 *onehotmamas.com.*

★ $$$$ FodorsChoice ✕ **Red Fish.** *American.* This seafood eatery's "naked" catch of the day—seafood grilled with olive oil, lime, and garlic—is a heart-healthy specialty that many diners say is the best thing on the menu. Caribbean and Cuban flavors permeate the rest of the menu in dishes such as Latin ribs and a Cajun shrimp-and-lobster burger. The restaurant's wine cellar is filled with some 1,000 bottles, and there's also a retail wine shop so you can take a bottle home. Although the commercial-strip location isn't inspired, the lively crowd, the soft candlelight, and the subdued artwork more than make up for it. [$] *Average main: $28* ✉ *8 Archer Rd., South End* ☎ *843/686–3388* 🌐 *www.redfishofhiltonhead.com* ⏲ *No lunch Sun.*

$$$$ ✕ **Santa Fe Cafe.** *Southwestern.* Walk through the doors of the Santa Fe Cafe and you're greeted by the sights, sounds, and aromas of New Mexico: Native American rugs, Mexican ballads, steer skulls and horns, and the pungent smells of chilies and mesquite on the grill. The restaurant is perhaps best experienced on a rainy, chilly night when the adobe fireplaces are cranked up. Go for the rush of spicy food chased with an icy Mexican *cerveza* (beer) or one of the island's best margaritas (order one up, with top-shelf tequila, and let the fiesta begin). This place is a party for the senses: after the fiery and artistic Painted Desert soup (a thick puree of red pepper and chilies in chicken stock), you can chill with the tortilla-crusted salmon. Forgo burritos and other Tex-Mex standards and opt for dishes like mesquite lamb with cranberry-chipotle sauce. There are also several gluten-free dishes available. Plan on listening to *guitarra* music in the rooftop cantina Wednesday to Saturday night. [$] *Average main: $28* ✉ *807 William Hilton Pkwy., Mid-Island* ☎ *843/785–3838* 🌐 *santafecafehiltonhead.com* ✍ *Reservations essential* ⏲ *No lunch weekends.*

★ $ Fodor's Choice ✕ **Signe's Heaven Bound Bakery & Café.** *American.* Every morning locals roll in for the deep-dish French toast, crispy polenta, and whole-wheat waffles. Since 1972, European-born Signe has been feeding islanders her delicious soups and quiches, curried chicken salad, and loaded hot and cold sandwiches. The beach bag ($12 for a cold sandwich, pasta or fresh fruit, chips, and cookie) is a great deal, especially because they also throw in a beverage. The melt-in-your-mouth cakes and the rave-worthy breads are amazing. [$] *Average main: $8* ✉ *93 Arrow Rd., South End* ☎ *843/785–9118* 🌐 *www.signesbakery.com* ⊗ *Closed Sun. Dec.–Feb. No dinner.*

★ $$ Fodor's Choice ✕ **Skull Creek Boathouse.** *American.* Soak up the salty atmosphere in this pair of dining areas where almost every table has a view of the water. Outside is a third dining area and a bar called the Buoy Bar at Marker 13. Adirondack chairs invite you to sit back, relax, and catch the sunset. The Dive Bar features raw seafood served as sushi, ceviche, or carpaccio. Options for lunch include chilled seafood dishes, salads, sandwiches, po'boys, burgers, and hot dogs. For dinner there's a wide variety of seafood dishes that are perfect for sharing, or you can also bring in your freshly caught fish and the chef will prepare it however you like. You may have trouble deciding what to order, but you can take your time and enjoy the beautiful view. [$] *Average main: $17* ✉ *397 Squire Pope Rd., North End* ☎ *843/681–3663* 🌐 *www.skullcreekboathouse.com.*

$$ ✕ **Truffles Cafe.** *American.* When a restaurant keeps its customers happy for decades, there's a reason. You won't find any of the namesake truffles on the menu; instead there's grilled salmon with a mango-barbecue glaze and barbecued baby-back ribs. The Oriental Napa salad with tuna is big enough to be a main course. If you're on a budget, choose a specialty like the Kobe burger with pimento cheese. Or, for a splurge, opt for the juicy, center-cut steaks. There's a second Hilton Head location on Pope Avenue, and a Bluffton branch that has a lovely outdoor seating area. [$] *Average main: $17* ✉ *Sea Pines Center, 71 Lighthouse Rd., South End* ☎ *843/671–6136* 🌐 *www.trufflescafe.com* ✍ *Reservations essential* ⊗ *Closed Sun. No lunch.*

$$$$ ✕ **WiseGuys.** *Steakhouse.* The red-and-black decor is modern and sophisticated at this restaurant—it's a little art deco, a little contemporary. The food is a spin on the classics, starting with seared tuna sliders and an incredible beef tenderloin carpaccio topped with baby arugula and horseradish cream. The go-to entrée is definitely the charred rib-eye

steak, which comes with a choice of butters that include brandied mushroom, fois gras, and truffle. The attentive waitstaff is well trained and can recommend what to sip from the extensive wine list. To-die-for desserts include the delightful crème brûlée flight and deep-fried bread pudding so good you may feel like you just died and went to heaven. There's also a variety of gluten-free dishes. $ *Average main: $30* ✉ *1513 Main St., North End* ☎ *843/842–8866* 🌐 *wiseguyshhi.com* 🕓 *No lunch.*

BLUFFTON

$$$$ ✕ **Claude & Uli's Bistro.** *European.* It's hard to go wrong with a chef who has cooked at Maxim's in Paris, the Connaught Hotel in London, and Ernie's in San Francisco. Chef Claude Melchiorri, who grew up in Normandy, France, and his wife, Uli, offer divine food at this atmospheric restaurant tucked away in a strip mall right before the bridges to Hilton Head. Candles and fresh flowers top the white linen–covered tables. Parisian art lines the walls; a large painting of dogs at a French bar adds a touch of humor. The French-European cuisine is simply irresistible. Before ordering appetizers and dinner, order the Soufflé Grand Marnier with chocolate sauce ahead for dessert, then start with the seafood crepe with white-wine sauce. For the entrée, try the veal Normandy with brandied mushroom cream sauce. All the seafood is fresh, and all the sauces are handmade. $ *Average main: $25* ✉ *Moss Creek Village, 1533 Fording Island Rd., Bluffton* ☎ *843/837–3336* 🌐 *claudebistro.com* 🕓 *No lunch Sun.–Tues. No lunch in summer.*

8

WHERE TO STAY

$$$ 🏨 **Beach House Hilton Head Island.** *Resort.* On one of the island's most popular stretches of sand, the Beach House Hilton Head Island is within walking distance of lots of shops and restaurants. **Pros:** the location cannot be beat; renovations have made this a very desirable destination; professional staff. **Cons:** in summer the number of kids raises the noise volume; small front desk can get backed up. $ *Rooms from: $249* ✉ *1 S. Forest Beach Dr., South End* ☎ *843/785–5126* 🌐 *www.hihiltonhead.com* 🛏 *202 rooms* 🍴 *No meals.*

$$$$ FAMILY 🏨 **Disney's Hilton Head Island Resort.** *Resort.* The typical cheery colors and whimsical designs at Disney's Hilton Head Island Resort create a look that's part Southern beach resort, part Adirondack hideaway. **Pros:** family-friendly vibe; young and friendly staffers; plenty of space to spread out. **Cons:**

Where to Stay on Hilton Head Island

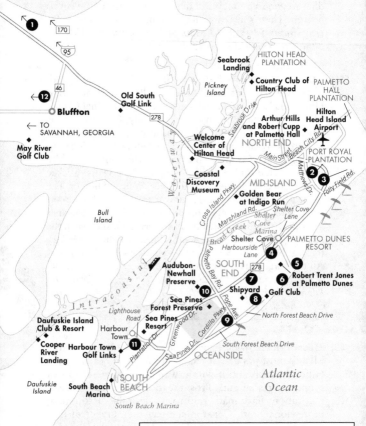

KEY

⚓ Beach
🚢 Ferry

Port Royal Sound

HILTON HEAD PLANTATION

Pickney Island

Seabrook Landing

Country Club of Hilton Head

PALMETTO HALL PLANTATION

Old South Golf Link

278

Arthur Hills and Robert Cupp at Palmetto Hall

Hilton Head Island Airport

❶

170

95

46

❷ Bluffton

← TO SAVANNAH, GEORGIA

May River Golf Club

Welcome Center of Hilton Head

NORTH END

Main Street

Beach City Rd.

Matthews Dr.

Folly Field Rd.

PORT ROYAL PLANTATION

❷ ❸

Coastal Discovery Museum

MID-ISLAND

Golden Bear at Indigo Run

Cross Island Pkwy.

Marshland Rd.

Shelter Cove Lane

Shelter Cove Marina

Bull Island

Broad Creek

Shelter Cove

Harbourside Lane

PALMETTO DUNES RESORT

❹

❺

Audubon-Newhall Preserve

SOUTH END

278

Robert Trent Jones at Palmetto Dunes

❼

❻

Golf Club

Shipyard

❿

Palmetto Bay Rd.

Pope Ave.

❽

Intracoastal

Sea Pines Forest Preserve

Lighthouse Road

Sea Pines Resort

Greenwood Dr.

Cordillo Pkwy.

❾

North Forest Beach Drive

Daufuskie Island Club & Resort

Harbour Town

⓫

Sea Pines Dr.

South Forest Beach Drive

OCEANSIDE

Cooper River Landing

Harbour Town Golf Links

Plantation Dr.

Daufuskie Island

South Beach Marina

SOUTH BEACH

Atlantic Ocean

South Beach Marina

| 0 | 1/2 mi |
| 0 | 1/2 km |

Beach House Hilton Head Island, **9**

Candlewood Suites, **1**

Disney's Hilton Head Island Resort, **4**

Hampton Inn on Hilton Head Island, **2**

Hilton Head Marriott Resort & Spa, **5**

The Inn at Harbour Town, **11**

The Inn at Palmetto Bluff, **12**

Omni Hilton Head Oceanfront Resort, **6**

Park Lane Hotel & Suites, **7**

The Sea Pines Resort, **10**

Sonesta Resort Hilton Head Island, **8**

Westin Hilton Head Island Resort & Spa, **3**

it's a time-share property; expensive rates. $ *Rooms from: $375* ✉ *22 Harbourside La., Mid-Island* ☎ *843/341–4100* 🌐 *www.disneybeachresorts.com/hilton-head-resort* 🛏 *102 villas, 21 deluxe studios* 🍴 *No meals.*

$$$ FAMILY 🏨 **Hampton Inn on Hilton Head Island.** *Hotel.* Although it's not on the beach, this attractive hotel is a good choice for budget travelers. **Pros:** good customer service; moderate prices; more amenities than you might expect. **Cons:** not on a beach; parking lot views. $ *Rooms from: $209* ✉ *1 Dillon Rd., Mid-Island* ☎ *843/681–7900* 🌐 *www.hamptoninn.com* 🛏 *95 rooms, 8 suites, 12 studios* 🍴 *Breakfast.*

$$$$ 🏨 **Hilton Head Marriott Resort & Spa.** *Hotel.* Private balconies with views of the palm-shaded grounds are the best reason to stay at this resort facing the Atlantic Ocean. **Pros:** steps from the beach; lots of amenities; one of the best-run operations on the island. **Cons:** rooms could be larger; in summer kids are everywhere. $ *Rooms from: $339* ✉ *1 Hotel Circle, Palmetto Dunes, Mid-Island* ☎ *843/686–8400* 🌐 *www.marriott.com/hotels/travel/hhhgr-hilton-head-marriott-resort-and-spa* 🛏 *476 rooms, 36 suites* 🍴 *No meals.*

★ $$$$ Fodor'sChoice 🏨 **The Inn at Harbour Town.** *Hotel.* The most buzzworthy of Hilton Head's properties, this European-style boutique hotel has a proper staff clad in kilts that pampers you with British service and a dose of Southern charm. **Pros:** a service-oriented property; central location; unique, one of the finest hotels on island; complimentary parking. **Cons:** no water views; two-day minimum on most weekends. $ *Rooms from: $293* ✉ *Sea Pines, 7 Lighthouse La., South End* ☎ *843/785–3333* 🌐 *www.seapines.com* 🛏 *60 rooms* 🍴 *No meals.*

8

★ $$$$ Fodor'sChoice 🏨 **The Inn at Palmetto Bluff.** *B&B/Inn.* About 15 minutes from Hilton Head, the Lowcountry's most luxurious resort sits on 20,000 acres that have been transformed into a perfect replica of a small island town, complete with its own clapboard church. **Pros:** member of the Preferred Small Hotels of the World; tennis/bocce/croquet complex has an impressive retail shop; the river adds both ambience and boat excursions. **Cons:** the mock Southern town is not the real thing; not that close to the amenities of Hilton Head. $ *Rooms from: $556* ✉ *1 Village Park Sq., Bluffton* ☎ *843/706–6500, 866/706–6565* 🌐 *www.palmettobluffresort.com* 🛏 *50 cottages* 🍴 *No meals.*

$$$$ 🏨 **Omni Hilton Head Oceanfront Resort.** *Resort.* At this beachfront hotel with a Caribbean sensibility, the spacious accommodations range from studios to two-bedroom suites. **Pros:** competes more with condos than hotels because of

the size of its accommodations; lots of outdoor dining options. **Cons:** wedding parties can be noisy; cell phone service is spotty. $ *Rooms from: $283* ✉ *23 Ocean La., Palmetto Dunes, Mid-Island* ☎ *843/842–8000* 🌐 *www.omnihiltonhead.com* 🛏 *303 studios, 20 suites* 🍴 *No meals.*

$$ 🏨 **Park Lane Hotel & Suites.** *Hotel.* The island's only all-suites property has a friendly feel, which is probably why many guests settle in for weeks. **Pros:** one of the island's most reasonably priced lodgings; parking and Wi-Fi are free; playground for the kids. **Cons:** doesn't have an upscale feel; more kids mean more noise, especially around the pool area. $ *Rooms from: $159* ✉ *12 Park La., South End* ☎ *843/686–5700* 🌐 *www.hiltonheadparklanehotel.com* 🛏 *156 suites.*

$$$$ 🏨 **Sonesta Resort Hilton Head Island.** *Resort.* Set in a luxuriant garden that always seems to be in full bloom, the Sonesta Resort is the centerpiece of Shipyard Plantation, which means you'll have access to all its various amenities, including golf and tennis. **Pros:** close to all the restaurants and nightlife in Coligny Plaza; spacious rooms; free parking. **Cons:** Wi-Fi and cell phone service can be a problem; service is sometimes impersonal. $ *Rooms from: $289* ✉ *Shipyard Plantation, 130 Shipyard Dr., South End, Hilton Head Island* ☎ *843/842–2400, 800/334–1881* 🌐 *www.sonesta.com/hiltonheadisland* 🛏 *331 rooms, 9 suites* 🍴 *No meals.*

$$$$ 🏨 **Westin Hilton Head Island Resort & Spa.** *Resort.* A circular drive winds around a sculpture of long-legged marsh birds as you approach this beachfront resort, whose lush landscape lies on the island's quietest stretch of sand. **Pros:** great for destination weddings; the beach here is absolutely gorgeous; pampering spa. **Cons:** lots of groups in the off-season. $ *Rooms from: $309* ✉ *2 Grass Lawn Ave., Port Royal Plantation, North End* ☎ *800/933–3102, 843/681–4000* 🌐 *www.westinhiltonheadisland.com* 🛏 *416 rooms* 🍴 *No meals.*

BLUFFTON

$ 🏨 **Candlewood Suites.** *Hotel.* At this suites-only hotel, the guest rooms are comfortable and tastefully decorated in muted browns and beiges. **Pros:** location makes it convenient to Hilton Head, Beaufort, and Savannah. **Cons:** cell phone service is hit-or-miss; set back from road, it can be difficult to find. $ *Rooms from: $129* ✉ *5 Young Clyde Court, Bluffton* ☎ *843/705–9600* 🌐 *www.candlewoodsuites.com/blufftonsc* 🛏 *124 suites* 🍴 *No meals.*

CLOSE UP

How to Talk to Locals

Hilton Head is known as a place where people come to start a new life, or to happily live out their golden years. It is politically incorrect to immediately ask someone you just met, "Where did you come from?" or "What brought you here?" or "What did you do in your former life?" Residents are asked these questions all the time, and it gets old, especially if they moved here decades ago. Their reluctance to tell all does not mean that they necessarily have skeletons in their closets.

Now, conversely, they are allowed to ask *you* where you are from—not to mention how long you are staying—or they may be considered unwelcoming. But do let them tell you about themselves in time, or over a cocktail. You may learn that your golfing partner was the CEO of a big national corporation, or the guy next to you at the bar is a best-selling author, or the friendly fellow in line at the store is a billionaire entrepreneur who might even be a household name.

PRIVATE VILLA RENTALS

Hilton Head has some 6,000 villas, condos, and private homes for rent, almost double the number of the island's hotel rooms. Villas and condos seem to work particularly well for families with children, especially if they want to avoid the extra costs of staying in a resort. Often these vacation homes cost less per diem than hotels of the same quality. Guests on a budget can further economize by cooking some of their own meals.

Villas and condos are primarily rented by the week, Saturday to Saturday. It pays to make sure you understand exactly what you're getting before making a deposit or signing a contract. For example, a property owner in the Hilton Head Beach & Tennis Club advertised that his villa sleeps six. That villa had one small bedroom, a foldout couch, and a hall closet with two very narrow bunk beds. That's a far cry from the three-bedroom villa you might have expected. ■TIP→ **Before calling a vacation rental company, make a list of the amenities you want.** Ask for pictures of each room and ask when the photos were taken. If you're looking for a beachfront property, ask exactly how far it is to the beach. Make sure to ask for a list of all fees, including those for parking, cleaning, pets, security deposits, and utility costs. Finally, get a written contract and a copy of the refund policy.

RENTAL AGENTS

Hilton Head Vacation Rentals. Representing more than 250 vacation rentals ranging in size from one to seven bedrooms, Hilton Head Vacation Rentals has villas, condos, and homes with oceanfront views. It offers various packages that include golf and other activities. Rentals are generally for three to seven days. ✉ *578 William Hilton Pkwy.* ☎ *843/785–8687* ⊕ *www.hiltonheadvacation.com.*

Resort Rentals of Hilton Head Island. This company represents some 275 homes and villas, including many located inside the gated communities of Sea Pines, Palmetto Dunes, and Shipyard Plantation. Others are in North and South Forest Beach and the Folly Field area. Stays are generally Saturday to Saturday during the peak summer season; three- or four-night stays may be possible off-season. Most of the properties are privately owned, so decor and amenities can vary. ✉ *32 Palmetto Bay Rd., Suite 1B, Mid-Island* ☎ *800/845–7017* ⊕ *www.hhivacations.com.*

Sea Pines Resort. The vast majority of the overnight guests at Sea Pines Resort rent one of the 500 suites, villas, and beach houses. One- and two-bedroom villas have a minimum stay of four nights. For stays of four or more nights, you must arrive on Saturday, Sunday, Monday, or Tuesday. Three- and four-bedrooms villas have a minimum stay of seven nights, and you've got to check in on Saturday. All houses have Internet access, and most have Wi-Fi. Housekeeping is usually an additional charge. ✉ *32 Greenwood Dr., South End* ☎ *843/785–3333, 866/561–8802* ⊕ *www.seapines.com/vacation-rentals.*

NIGHTLIFE AND PERFORMING ARTS

NIGHTLIFE

Bars, like everything else on Hilton Head, are often in gate communities or shopping centers. Some are hangouts frequented by locals, and others get a good mix of both locals and visitors. There are a fair number of clubs, many of them restaurants that crank up the music after diners depart.

Big Bamboo. Decked out like a World War II–era officers' club, this South Pacific–themed bar and restaurant features live music most nights of the week. ✉ *Coligny Plaza, 1 N. Forest Beach Dr., South End* ☎ *843/686–3443* ⊕ *www.bigbamboocafe.com.*

Comedy Magic Cabaret. Several nights a week this lounge brings top-flight comedic talent to Hilton Head. Start off with dinner and drinks downstairs at the Kingfisher, which serves some of the best crab in town, then head upstairs for the comedy. Tickets are $18 to $22 per person. ■TIP→ **Book ahead, because the shows sell out fairly quickly.** ✉ *Shelter Cove, 18 Harbourside La., South End* ☎ *843/681–7757* ⊕ *www.comedymagiccabaret.com.*

Hilton Head Plaza. Dubbed the "Barmuda Triangle" by locals, the bars at this plaza include One Hot Mama's, Reilley's, the Hilton Head Brewing Company, the Lodge Martini, and Jump & Phil's Bar & Grill. It's the closest thing Hilton Head Island has to a raging club scene. ✉ *Hilton Head Plaza, Greenwood Dr., right before gate to Sea Pines, South End.*

★ Fodor's Choice **The Jazz Corner.** The elegant supper-club atmosphere at this popular spot makes it a wonderful setting in which to enjoy an evening of jazz, swing, and blues. The owner, horn player Bob Masteller, sometimes takes the stage. There's a special martini menu, an extensive wine list, and a late-night menu. ■TIP→ **The club fills up quickly, so make reservations.** ✉ *The Village at Wexford, 1000 William Hilton Pkwy., Suite C-1, South End* ☎ *843/842–8620* ⊕ *www.thejazzcorner.com.*

★ Fodor's Choice **The Salty Dog Cafe.** If there's one thing you
FAMILY shouldn't miss on Hilton Head Island, it's the iconic Salty Dog Cafe. It's the ideal place to escape, sit back, and enjoy the warm nights and ocean breezes in a tropical setting at the outdoor bar. There's live music (think Jimmy Buffett) seven nights a week during high season. Bring the family along for kid-friendly entertainment, including music, magic, and face painting at 7 pm throughout the summer. ✉ *South Beach Marina, 224 S. Sea Pines Dr., South End* ☎ *843/671–5199* ⊕ *www.saltydog.com.*

Santa Fe Cafe. A sophisticated spot for cocktails in the early evening, the Santa Fe Cafe is also a great place to lounge in front of the fireplace or sip top-shelf margaritas at the rooftop cantina. ✉ *807 William Hilton Pkwy., Mid-Island* ☎ *843/785–3838* ⊕ *www.santafehhi.com.*

Turtle's Poolside Beach Bar & Grill. With an open-air deck where you can enjoy the cool breezes, this popular spot offers live entertainment nightly. If you're hungry, the kitchen serves Lowcountry food with a Caribbean twist. ✉ *2 Grasslawn Ave., Westin Resort & Spa, North End* ☎ *843/681–4000.*

8

CLOSE UP

Island Gators

The most famous photo of Hilton Head's brilliant developer, Charles Fraser, ran in the *Saturday Evening Post* in the late 1950s. It shows him dressed as a dandy, outfitted with a cane and straw hat, with an alligator on a leash.

These prehistoric creatures are indeed indigenous to this subtropical island. What you will learn if you visit the Coastal Discovery Museum, where the old photograph is blown up for an interpretive board on the island's early history, is that someone else had the gator by the tail (not shown) so that it would not harm Fraser or the photographer.

Nowadays, in Sea Pines Center, there is a life-size, metal sculpture of an alligator that all the tourists, and especially their kids, climb on to have their pictures taken. And should you happen to see a live gator while exploring the island or playing a round of golf, please don't feed it. Although, if you have the courage, you might want to take a snapshot.

PERFORMING ARTS

★ Fodor'sChoice **Arts Center of Coastal Carolina.** Locals love the exhibits at the Walter Greer Gallery and the theater productions at the Arts Center of Coastal Carolina. Programs for children are also popular. ✉ *14 Shelter Cove La., Mid-Island* ☎ *843/686–3945* ⊕ *www.artshhi.com.*

Hilton Head Island Gullah Celebration. This showcase of Gullah life through arts, music, and theater is held at a variety of sites throughout the Lowcountry in February. ☎ *843/255–7304* ⊕ *www.gullahcelebration.com.*

Hilton Head Symphony Orchestra. A selection of summer concerts—including the popular "Picnic and Pops"—are among the year-round performances by the symphony. Most events are at the First Presbyterian Church. ✉ *First Presbyterian Church, 540 William Hilton Pkwy., Mid-Island* ☎ *843/842–2055* ⊕ *www.hhso.org.*

FAMILY **Main Street Youth Theatre.** A variety of performances showcasing young local talent are presented by Main Street Youth Theatre. ✉ *25 New Orleans Rd., Mid-Island* ☎ *843/689–6246* ⊕ *www.msyt.org.*

SPORTS AND THE OUTDOORS

Hilton Head Island is a mecca for the sports enthusiast and for those who just want a relaxing walk or bike ride on the beach. There are 12 miles of beaches, 24 public golf courses, more than 50 miles of public bike paths, and more than 300 tennis courts. There's also tons of water sports, including kayaking and canoeing, parasailing, fishing, sailing, and much more.

BEACHES

A delightful stroll on the beach can end with an unpleasant surprise if you don't put your towels, shoes, and other earthly possessions way up on the sand. Tides here can fluctuate as much as 7 feet. Check the tide chart at your hotel.

Alder Lane Beach Park. A great place for solitude even during the busy summer season, this beach has hard-packed sand at low tide, making it great for walking. It's accessible from the Marriott Grand Ocean Resort. **Amenities:** lifeguards; showers; toilets. **Best for:** solitude; walking; swimming. ⊠ *Alder La., off South Forest Beach Rd, South End.*

BEACH RULES. Animals are not permitted on Hilton Head beaches between 10 and 5 from Memorial Day through Labor Day. Animals must be on leash. No alcohol, glass, littering, indecent exposure, unauthorized vehicles, fires and fireworks, shark fishing, removal of any live beach fauna, sleeping between midnight and 6 am, and kites not under manual control.

Burkes Beach. This beach is usually not crowded, mostly because it is a bit hard to find and there are no lifeguards on duty. **Amenities:** none. **Best for:** solitude, sunrise, swimming, windsurfing. ⊠ *60 Burkes Beach Rd., at William Hilton Pkwy., Mid-Island.*

FAMILY Fodor'sChoice **Coligny Beach.** The island's most popular beach is ★ a lot of fun, but during high season it can get very crowded. Accessible from the Beach House Hilton Head Island and several other hotels, it has choreographed fountains that delight little children, bench swings, and beach umbrellas and chaise longues for rent. If you have to go online, there's also Wi-Fi access. **Amenities:** lifeguards; food and drink; parking; showers; toilets. **Best for:** windsurfing; swimming. ⊠ *1 Coligny Circle, at Pope Ave. and South Forest Beach Dr., South End.*

8

FAMILY **Driessen Beach.** A good destination for families, Driessen Beach is peppered with people flying kites, making it colorful and fun. There's a long boardwalk to the beach. **Amenities:** parking; lifeguards; toilets; showers. **Best for:** walking; sunrise; swimming. ⊠ *43 Bradley Beach Rd., at William Hilton Pkwy., Mid-Island.*

SAND DOLLARS. Hilton Head Island's beaches hold many treasures, including starfish, sea sponges, and sand dollars. Note that it is strictly forbidden to pick up any live creatures on the beach, especially live sand dollars. How can you tell if they are alive? Live sand dollars are brown and fuzzy and will turn your fingers yellow and brown. You can take sand dollars home only if they're white. Soak them in a mixture of bleach and water to remove the scent once you get home.

Folly Field Beach Park. Next to Driessen Beach, Folly Field is a treat for families. It can get crowded in high season, but even so it's a wonderful spot for a day of sunbathing and swimming. The first beach cottages on Hilton Head Island were built here in the 1950s. **Amenities:** lifeguards; parking; toilets; outdoor showers. **Best for:** swimming; sunrise; walking. ⊠ *55 Starfish Dr., off Folly Field Rd., North End.*

Mitchelville Beach Park. Not ideal for swimming because of the many sharp shells on the sand and in the water, Mitchelville Beach Park is a terrific spot for a walk or beachcombing. It is not on the Atlantic Ocean, but rather on Port Royal Sound. **Amenities:** parking; toilets. **Best for:** solitude; walking. ⊠ *124 Mitchelville Rd., Hilton Head Plantation, North End.*

MAY RIVER SANDBAR. Known as the "Redneck Riviera," the May River Sandbar is pure party. Basically, the sandbar is just that: a small island of sand on the May River in Bluffton, which is the town that vacationers must go through on U.S. 278 to get to Hilton Head. The sandbar is accessible only by boat and only at low tide. Locals will plan their weekends around the time of low tide to head out to the sandbar. Boaters drop anchor and the party begins. Horseshoe and cornhole games are set up, picnic baskets unpacked, and cold drinks poured. To get there, go north by boat on Calibogue Sound and turn left west at the May River. The sandbar is at Red Marker 6.

BIKING

More than 50 miles of public paths crisscross Hilton Head Island, and pedaling is popular along the firmly packed beach. The island keeps adding more to the boardwalk network as visitors are using it and because it's such a safe alternative for kids. Bikes with wide tires are a must if you want to ride on the beach. They can save you a spill should you hit loose sand on the trails. Keep in mind when crossing streets that, in South Carolina, vehicles have the right-of-way. ■ TIP→ **For a map of trails, visit ⊕ www. hiltonheadislandsc.gov.**

Bicycles from beach cruisers to mountain bikes to tandem bikes can be rented either at bike stores or at most hotels and resorts. Many can be delivered to your hotel, along with helmets, baskets, locks, child carriers, and whatever else you might need.

Hilton Head Bicycle Company. You can rent bicycles, helmets and adult tricycles from the Hilton Head Bicycle Company. ⊠ *112 Arrow Rd., South End* ☎ *843/686–6888, 800/995–4319* ⊕ *www.hiltonheadbicycle.com.*

Pedals Bicycles. Rent beach bikes for adults and children, kiddy karts, jogging strollers, and mountain bikes at Pedals. ⊠ *71A Pope Ave., South End* ☎ *843/842–5522, 888/699–1039* ⊕ *www.pedalsbicycles.com.*

South Beach Cycles. Rent bikes, helmets, tandems, and adult tricycles at this spot in Sea Pines. ⊠ *230 South Sea Pines Dr., Sea Pines, South End* ☎ *843/671–2453* ⊕ *www.south-beach-cycles.com.*

CANOEING AND KAYAKING

This is one of the most delightful ways to commune with nature on this commercial but physically beautiful island. Paddle through the creeks and estuaries and try to keep up with the dolphins.

Outside Hilton Head. Boats, canoes, kayaks, and paddleboards are available for rent. The company also offers nature tours and dolphin-watching excursions. ⊠ *Shelter Cove Marina, 1 Shelter Cove La., Mid-Island* ☎ *843/686–6996, 800/686–6996* ⊕ *www.outsidehiltonhead.com.*

FISHING

Although anglers can fish in these waters year-round, in April things start to crank up and in May most boats are heavily booked. May is the season for cobia, especially in Port Royal Sound. In the Gulf Stream you can hook king mackerel, tuna, wahoo, and mahimahi. ■TIP→ **A fishing license is necessary if you are fishing from a beach, dock, or pier. They are $11 for 14 days.** Licenses aren't necessary on charter fishing boats because they already have their licenses.

Bay Runner Fishing Charters. With more than four decades of experience fishing these waters, Captain Miles Altman takes anglers out for trips lasting three to eight hours. Evening shark trips are offered May to August. ✉ *Shelter Cove Marina, 1 Shelter Cove La., Mid-Island* ☎ *843/290–6955* ⊕ *www.bayrunnerfishinghiltonhead.com.*

FAMILY **Capt. Hook Party Boat.** Deep-sea fishing tours are available on this large party boat, which sells concessions as well. The friendly crew teaches children how to bait hooks and reel in fish. ✉ *Shelter Cove Marina, 1 Shelter Cove La., Mid-Island* ☎ *843/785–1700* ⊕ *www.hiltonheadisland.com/captainhook.*

Fishin' Coach. Captain Dan Utley offers a variety of fishing tours on his 22-foot boat to catch redfish and other species year-round. ✉ *1640 Fording Island Rd., Mid-Island* ☎ *843/368–2126* ⊕ *www.fishincoach.com.*

Gullah Gal Sport Fishing. Fishing trips are available on a pair of 34-foot boats, the *Gullah Gal* and *True Grits.* ✉ *Shelter Cove Marina, 1 Shelter Cove La., Mid-Island* ☎ *843/842–7002* ⊕ *www.hiltonheadislandcharterfishing.com/.*

Integrity. The 38-foot charter boat *Integrity* offers offshore and near-shore fishing. ✉ *Harbour Town Yacht Basin, Mariners Way, Sea Pines, South End* ☎ *843/671–2704, 843/422–1221* ⊕ *www.integritycharterfishing.com.*

Palmetto Bay Charters. This company offers a wide variety of charters on various size boats. ✉ *Palmetto Bay Marina, 86 Helmsman Way, South End, Hilton Head Island* ☎ *843/785–7131* ⊕ *www.palmettobaymarinahhi.com.*

Palmetto Lagoon Charters. Captain Trent Malphrus takes groups for half- or full-day excursions to the region's placid saltwater lagoons. Redfish, bluefish, flounder, and black drum are some of the most common trophy fish. ✉ *Shelter Cove Marina, 1 Shelter Cove La., Mid-Island* ☎ *866/301–4634* ⊕ *www.palmettolagooncharters.com.*

GOLF

Hilton Head is nicknamed "Golf Island" for good reason: the island itself has 24 championship courses (public, semiprivate, and private), and the outlying area has 16 more. Each offers its own packages, some of which are great deals. Almost all charge the highest green fees in the morning and lower fees as the day goes on. Lower rates can also be found in the hot summer months. It's essential to book tee times in advance, especially in the busy spring and fall months; resort guests and club members get first choices. Most courses can be described as casual-classy, so you will have to adhere to certain rules of the greens.

■TIP→ **The dress code on island golf courses does not permit blue jeans, gym shorts, or jogging shorts. Men's shirts must have collars.**

The Heritage PGA Tour Golf Tournament. The most internationally famed golf event in Hilton Head is the annual RBC Heritage PGA Tour Golf Tournament, held mid-April. There is a wide range of ticket packages available. Tickets are also available at the gate. ⊠*Sea Pines Resort, 2 Lighthouse La., South End* ⊕*www.rbcheritage.com.*

TEE OFF ON A BUDGET. Golfing on Hilton Head can be very expensive after you tally up the green fee, cart fee, rental clubs, gratuities, and so on. But there are ways to save money. There are several courses in Bluffton that are very popular with the locals, and some are cheaper to play than the courses on Hilton Head Island. Another way to save money is to play late in the day. At some courses, a round in the morning is more expensive than 18 holes in the late afternoon.

GOLF SCHOOLS

Golf Learning Center at Sea Pines Resort. The well-regarded golf academy offers hourly private lessons by PGA-trained professionals and one- to three-day clinics to help you perfect your game. ⊠*Sea Pines, 100 North Sea Pines Dr., South End* ☎*843/785–4540* ⊕*www.golfacademy.net.*

Palmetto Dunes Golf Academy. There's something for golfers of all ages at this academy: instructional videos, daily clinics, and multiday schools. Lessons are offered for ages three and up, and there are special programs for women. Free demonstrations are held with Doug Weaver, former PGA Tour pro and director of instruction for the academy. Take advantage of the free swing evaluation and club-fitting.

✉ *Palmetto Dunes Oceanfront Resort, 7 Trent Jones La., Mid-Island* ☎ *843/785–1138* ⊕ *www.palmettodunes.com.*

The Island Golf School of Palmetto Hall Plantation. This is a great place to learn golf, perfect your swing, or improve your overall skills. It's administered by qualified and experienced professionals. ✉ *Palmetto Hall Plantation, 108 Fort Hollow Dr., North End* ☎ *843/342–2582* ⊕ *www. palmettohallgolf.com.*

GOLF COURSES

Arthur Hills and Robert Cupp at Palmetto Hall. There are two prestigious courses at Palmetto Hall Plantation: Arthur Hills and Robert Cupp. Arthur Hills is a player favorite, with its trademark undulating fairways punctuated with lagoons and lined with moss-draped oaks and towering pines. Robert Cupp is a very challenging course, but is great for the higher handicappers as well. ✉ *Palmetto Hall, 108 Fort Howell Dr., North End* ☎ *843/689–9205* ⊕ *www. palmettohallgolf.com* 🏷 *$145* ⚐ *Reservations essential* ⚑ *Arthur Hills: 18 holes, 6257 yds, par 72. Robert Cupp: 18 holes, 6025 yds, par 72.*

Country Club of Hilton Head. Although it's part of a country club, the course is open for public play. A well-kept secret, it's rarely too crowded. This 18-hole Rees Jones–designed course is a more casual environment than many of the other golf courses on Hilton Head. ✉ *Hilton Head Plantation, 70 Skull Creek Dr., North End* ☎ *843/681–4653, 866/835–0093* ⊕ *www.clubcorp.com/Clubs/Country-Club-of-Hilton-Head* 🏷 *$85–$105* ⚑ *18 holes, 6543 yds, par 72.*

Golden Bear Golf Club at Indigo Run. Located in the upscale Indigo Run community, Golden Bear Golf Club was designed by golf legend Jack Nicklaus. The course's natural woodlands setting offers easygoing rounds. It requires more thought than muscle, yet you will have to earn every par you make. Though fairways are generous, you may end up with a lagoon looming smack ahead of the green on the approach shot. And there are the fine points—the color GPS monitor on every cart and women-friendly tees. After an honest, traditional test of golf, most golfers finish up at the plush clubhouse with some food and drink at Just Jack's Grille. ✉ *Indigo Run, 100 Indigo Run Dr., North End* ☎ *843/689–2200* ⊕ *www.goldenbear-indigorun.com* 🏷 *$79–$99* ⚑ *18 holes, 6184 yds, par 72.*

★ Fodor'sChoice **Harbour Town Golf Links.** Considered by many golfers to be one of those must-play-before-you-die courses, Harbour Town Golf Links is extremely well known because it has hosted the RBC Heritage Golf Tournament every spring for the last four decades. Designed by Pete Dye, the layout is reminiscent of Scottish courses of old. The Golf Academy at the Sea Pines Resort is ranked among the top 10 in the country. ⊠ *Sea Pines Resort, 11 Lighthouse La., South End* ☎ *843/842–1020, 800/732–7463* ⊕ *www.seapines.com/golf* ⊡ *$215–$272* ⚐ *Reservations essential* ⚑ *18 holes, 7001 yds, par 71.*

Robert Trent Jones at Palmetto Dunes. One of the island's most popular layouts, this course's beauty and character are accentuated by the 10th hole, a par 5 that offers a panoramic view of the ocean (one of only two on the entire island). It's among the most beautiful courses in the Southeast, with glittering lagoons punctuating 11 of the 18 holes. ⊠ *Palmetto Dunes, 7 Robert Trent Jones La., North End* ☎ *843/785–1138* ⊕ *www.palmettodunes.com* ⊡ *$55–$155* ⚐ *Reservations essential* ⚑ *18 holes, 6122 yds, par 72.*

BLUFFTON GOLF COURSES
There are several beautiful golf courses in Bluffton, which is just on the other side of the bridges to Hilton Head Island. These courses are very popular with locals and can often be cheaper to play than the courses on Hilton Head Island.

Crescent Pointe. An Arnold Palmer Signature Course, Crescent Pointe is fairly tough, with somewhat narrow fairways and rolling terrain. There are numerous sand traps, ponds, and lagoons, making for some demanding yet fun holes. Some of the par 3s are particularly challenging. The scenery is magnificent, with large live oaks, pine-tree stands, and rolling fairways. Additionally, several holes have spectacular marsh views. ⊠ *Crescent Pointe, 1 Crescent Pointe, Bluffton* ☎ *843/706–2600* ⊕ *www.crescentpointegolf.com* ⊡ *$70–$95* ⚑ *18 holes, 6773 yds, par 71.*

Eagle's Pointe. This Davis Love III–designed course—located in the Eagle's Pointe community in Bluffton—is one of the area's most playable. Eagle's Pointe attracts many women golfers because of its women-friendly tees, spacious fairways, and large greens. There are quite a few bunkers and lagoons throughout the course, which winds through a natural woodlands setting that attracts an abundance of wildlife. ✉ *Eagle's Pointe, 1 Eagle's Pointe Dr., Bluffton* ☎ *843/757–5900* ⊕ *www.eaglespointegolf.com* 🖂 *$52* ⚑ *18 holes, 6126 yds, par 72.*

Island West Golf Club. Fuzzy Zoeller and golf course designer Clyde Johnston designed this stunningly beautiful course set amid the natural surroundings at Island West. There are majestic live oaks, plenty of wildlife, and expansive marsh views on several holes. Golfers of all skill levels can find success on this succession of undulating fairways. There are several holes where the fairways are rather generous, while others can be demanding. This is a fun and challenging course for golfers of all handicaps. ✉ *Island West, 40 Island West Dr., Bluffton* ☎ *843/689–6660* ⊕ *www.islandwestgolf. net* 🖂 *$35–$45* ⚑ *18 holes, 6208 yds, par 72.*

The May River Golf Club. An 18-hole Jack Nicklaus course, this has several holes along the banks of the scenic May River and will challenge all skill levels. The greens are Champion Bermuda grass and the fairways are covered by Paspalum, the latest eco-friendly turf. Caddy service is always required. No carts are allowed earlier than 9 am to encourage walking. One caveat: The staff can sometimes be unresponsive. ✉ *Palmetto Bluff, 476 Mount Pelia Rd., Bluffton* ☎ *843/706–6500* ⊕ *www.palmettobluffresort.com/ golf* 🖂 *$175–$260* ⚑ *Reservations essential* ⚑ *18 holes, 7171 yds, par 72.*

Old South Golf Links. There are many scenic holes overlooking marshes and the intracoastal waterway at this Clyde Johnson–designed course. It's a public course, but that hasn't stopped it from winning awards. It's reasonably priced, and reservations are recommended. ✉ *50 Buckingham Plantation Dr., Bluffton* ☎ *843/785–5353* ⊕ *www.oldsouthgolf. com* 🖂 *$65–$95* ⚑ *18 holes, 6772 yds, par 72.*

PARASAILING

For those looking for a bird's-eye view of Hilton Head, it doesn't get better than parasailing. Newcomers will get a lesson in safety before taking off. Parasailers are then strapped into a harness, and as the boat takes off, the parasailer is lifted about 500 feet into the sky.

Bay Parasail. You can glide 500 feet in the air over Palmetto Bay Marina and Broad Creek on a trip with Palmetto Bay Parasail. ✉ *Palmetto Bay Marina, 86 Helmsman Way, South End* ☎ *843/686–2200* ⊕ *www.parasailhiltonhead.com.*

CLOSE UP

Fun for Kids

Hilton Head Island is a really fun place for little ones. Check out these kid-friendly sites.

Adventure Cove. With two miniature 18-hole golf courses and a large arcade, Adventure Cove is sure to please the kids. ⊠ *18 Folly Field Rd., Mid-Island* ☎ *843/842–9990* ⊕ *www. adventurecove.com.*

Black Dagger Pirate Ship. The kids get to put on pirate gear, learn how to talk like a pirate, and set sail to search for underwater treasure. The ship sails from Harbour Town. ⊠ *Mariners Way, Sea Pines Resort, South End* ☎ *843/363–7000* ⊕ *www. piratesofhiltonhead.com.*

Island Playground. Near the bridges to Hilton Head, the Island Playground has giant inflatable slides, a fairy-tale castle, toddler exploration area, and snack counter. ⊠ *1538 Fording Island Rd., Bluffton* ☎ *843/837–8383* ⊕ *www. island-playground.com.*

Lawton Stables. Riding lessons, pony rides, horseback excursions through the Sea Pines Forest Preserve are offered at Lawton Stables. The animal farm includes goats, sheep, and pigs. ⊠ *190 Greenwood Dr., Sea Pines Resort, South*

End ☎ *843/671–2586* ⊕ *www. lawtonstableshhi.com.*

Pirate's Island. Two miniature golf courses are set amid tumbling waterfalls in the tropical-themed Pirate's Island. ⊠ *8 Marina Side Dr., Mid-Island* ☎ *843/686–4001* ⊕ *www. piratesislandgolf.com.*

Fodor's Choice ★ The Sandbox, An Interactive Children's Museum. A hands-on place for the youngest members of your family, this museum includes a cockpit where kids can put on a pilot's uniform and pretend to fly the friendly skies. In the Builders of Tomorrow exhibit, children dress up like construction workers and move materials to the building site, raise walls, and maneuver equipment. There's also a Learner's Loft where kids play with a puppet theater, puzzles, games, and toys ⊠ *18A Pope Ave., South End* ☎ *843/842–7645* ⊕ *www. thesandbox.org.*

Station 300. Two dozen state-of-the-art bowling lanes, an arcade, and a restaurant make Station 300 a very welcome addition to the Bluffton area. ⊠ *25 Innovation Dr., Bluffton* ☎ *843/815–2695* ⊕ *station300bluffton.com.*

8

H20 Sports. You can soar above Hilton Head and check out the views up to 25 miles in all directions with this popular company located in Sea Pines. ⊠ *149 Lighthouse Rd., Sea Pines, South End* ☎ *843/671–4386, 877/290–4386* ⊕ *www. h2osports.com.*

TENNIS

There are more than 300 courts on Hilton Head. Tennis comes in at a close second as the island's premier sport after golf. It is recognized as one of the nation's best tennis destinations. Hilton Head has a large international organization of coaches. ■TIP→ **Spring and fall are the peak seasons for cooler play, with numerous tennis packages available at the resorts and through the schools.**

★ Fodor'sChoice **Palmetto Dunes Tennis Center.** Ranked among the best in the world, this facility at the Palmetto Dunes Oceanfront Resort has 25 clay and 2 hard courts (a total of six are lighted for night play). There are lessons geared to players of every skill level given by enthusiastic staffers. Daily round-robin tournaments add to the festive atmosphere. ⊠ *Palmetto Dunes Oceanfront Resort, 6 Trent Jones La., Mid-Island* ☎ *843/785–1152* ⊕ *www.palmettodunes.com.*

Port Royal Racquet Club. The occasional magnolia tree dots the grounds of the Port Royal Racquet Club, which has 10 clay and 4 hard courts. The professional staff, stadium seating, and frequent tournaments are why it is ranked among the best in the world. ⊠ *Port Royal Plantation, 15 Wimbledon Court, Mid-Island* ☎ *843/686–8803* ⊕ *www. portroyalgolfclub.com.*

Sea Pines Racquet Club. The highly rated club has 23 clay courts, as well as instructional programs and a pro shop. There are special deals for guests of Sea Pines. ⊠ *5 Lighthouse La., Sea Pines Resort, South End* ☎ *843/363–4495* ⊕ *www.seapines.com.*

Shipyard Racquet Club. Play on 4 hard courts, 3 indoor courts, and 13 clay courts at this club in Shipyard Plantation. ⊠ *116 Shipyard Dr., Shipyard Plantation, South End* ☎ *843/686–8804* ⊕ *www.vandermeertennis.com.*

Van der Meer Tennis Center. Recognized for its tennis instruction for players of all ages and skill levels, this highly rated club has 17 hard courts, 4 of which are covered and lighted for night play. ⊠ *19 DeAllyon Ave., Shipyard Plantation, South End* ☎ *843/785–8388* ⊕ *www.vandermeertennis.com.*

ZIP LINE TOURS

ZipLine Hilton Head. Take a thrilling tour of Hilton Head on a zip line over ponds and marshes and past towering oaks and pines. This company offers eight zip lines, two suspended sky bridges, and a dual-cable racing zip line. Guests are harnessed and helmeted, and must be at least

10 years old and weigh between 80 and 250 pounds. ⊠ *33 Broad Creek Marina Way, Mid-Island* ☎ *843/682–6000* ⊕ *ziplinehiltonhead.com.*

SHOPPING

Hilton Head is a great destination for those who love shopping, starting with the Tanger outlet malls. Although they're officially in Bluffton, visitors drive by the outlets on U.S. 278 to get to Hilton Head Island. Tanger Outlet I has been completely renovated and reopened with many high-end stores, including Saks OFF 5th, DKNY, Michael Kors, and more.

ART GALLERIES

Walter Greer Gallery. Part of the Arts Center of Coastal Carolina, this modern gallery showcases local artists. ⊠ *Arts Center of Coastal Carolina, 14 Shelter Cove La., Mid-Island* ☎ *843/681–5060* ⊕ *www.artleaguehhi.org.*

★ Fodor's Choice **Images by Ben Ham.** The extraordinary photography of Ben Ham focuses on Lowcountry landscapes. ⊠ *90 Capital Dr., Suite 104, Mid-Island* ☎ *843/842–4163* ⊕ *www.benhamimages.com.*

Morris & Whiteside Galleries. Original art by contemporary artists can be found at this upscale gallery. ⊠ *220 Cordillo Pkwy., Mid-Island* ☎ *843/842–4433* ⊕ *www.morris-whiteside.com.*

GIFTS

Markel's. The very helpful and friendly staff at Markel's is known for wrapping gifts with giant bows. You'll find unique Lowcountry gifts, including hand-painted wineglasses and beer mugs, lawn ornaments, baby gifts, greeting cards, and more. ⊠ *1008 Fording Island Rd., Bluffton* ☎ *843/815–9500.*

Pretty Papers. Fine stationery and gifts are available at Pretty Papers. ⊠ *The Village at Wexford, 100 William Hilton Pkwy., Suite E7, Mid-Island* ☎ *843/341–5116* ⊕ *www. prettypapershhi.com.*

Salty Dog T-Shirt Factory. You can't leave Hilton Head without a Salty Dog T-shirt, so hit this factory store for the best deals. The iconic T-shirts are hard to resist, and there are lots of choices for kids and adults in various colors and styles. ⊠ *69 Arrow Rd., South End* ☎ *843/842–6331* ⊕ *www.saltydog.com.*

8

FAMILY **The Storybook Shoppe.** Charming, whimsical, and sweet describe this children's bookstore. It has a darling area for little ones to read as well as educational toys for infants to teens. ✉ *41A Calhoun St., Bluffton* ☎ *843/757–2600* ⊕ *www.thestorybookshoppe.com.*

Top of the Lighthouse Shop. The Hilton Head Lighthouse is the island's iconic symbol, and this shop celebrates the red-and-white-striped landmark. ✉ *149 Lighthouse Rd., Sea Pines, South End* ☎ *866/305–9814* ⊕ *www.harbourtownlighthouse.com/shop.*

JEWELRY

Forsythe Jewelers. This is the island's leading jewelry store, offering pieces by famous designers. ✉ *71 Lighthouse Rd., Sea Pines, South End* ☎ *843/671–7070* ⊕ *www.forsythejewelers.biz.*

Goldsmith Shop. Classic jewelry, much of it with island themes, is on sale at the Goldsmith Shop. ✉ *3 Lagoon Rd., South End* ☎ *843/785–2538* ⊕ *www.thegoldsmithshop.com.*

MALLS AND SHOPPING CENTERS

Coligny Plaza. Things are always humming at this shopping center, which is within walking distance of the most popular beach on Hilton Head. Coligny Plaza has more than 60 shops and restaurants, including unique clothing boutiques, souvenir shops, and the expansive Piggly Wiggly grocery store. There are also bike rentals and free family entertainment throughout summer. ✉ *Coligny Circle, 1 North Forest Beach Dr., South End* ☎ *843/842–6050.*

Harbour Town. Distinguished by a candy-striped lighthouse, Harbour Town wraps around a marina and has plenty of shops selling colorful T-shirts, casual resort wear, and beach-themed souvenirs. ✉ *Sea Pines, 32 Greenwood Dr., South End* ☎ *866/561–8802* ⊕ *www.seapines.com/resort_activities/harbour_town.*

Shops at Sea Pines Center. Clothing for men and women, the best local crafts, and fine antiques are the draw at this outdoor shopping center. You can even get a massage at the on-site day spa. ✉ *71 Lighthouse Rd., South End* ☎ *843/363–6800* ⊕ *www.theshopsatseapinescenter.com.*

South Beach Marina. Looking like a New England fishing village, South Beach Marina is the place for beach-friendly fashions. ✉ *232 South Sea Pines Dr., South End* ☎ *843/671–6498.*

KID STUFF. Free outdoor children's concerts are held at Harbour Town in Sea Pines and Shelter Cove Harbor throughout the summer months. Guitarist Gregg Russell has been playing for children under Harbour Town's mighty Liberty Oak tree for decades. He begins strumming nightly at 8 in the summer, except on Saturday. It's also tradition for kids to get their pictures taken at the statue of Neptune at Harbour Town. At Shelter Cove, longtime island favorite Shannon Tanner performs a fun, family show at 6:30 pm and 8 pm weekdays from Memorial Day through Labor Day.

Old Town Bluffton. A charming area, Old Town features local artist galleries, antiques, and restaurants. ⊠ *Downtown Bluffton, May River Rd. and Calhoun St., Old Town, Bluffton* ☎ *843/706–4500* ⊕ *www.oldtownbluffton.com.*

★ Fodor's Choice **Tanger Outlets.** There are two halves to this popular shopping center: Tanger Outlet I has more than 40 upscale stores, as well as popular eateries like Olive Garden, Panera Bread, and Longhorn Steakhouse. Tanger Outlet II has Abercrombie & Fitch, Banana Republic, the Gap, and Nike, along with 60 others stores. There are also several children's stores, including Gymboree, Carter's, and Baby Gap. Dine at Food Network star Robert Irvine's restaurant, Nosh. ⊠ *1414 Fording Island Rd., Bluffton* ☎ *843/837–5410, 866/665–8679* ⊕ *www.tangeroutlet. com/hiltonhead.*

The Village at Wexford. Upscale shops, including Lilly Pulitzer and Le Cookery, as well as several fine-dining restaurants can be found in this shopping area. There are also some unique gift shops and luxe clothing stores. ⊠ *1000 William Hilton Parkway, Hilton Head* ☎ *843/686–3090* ⊕ *www. villageatwexford.com.*

SPAS

Spa visits have become a recognized activity on the island, and for some people they are as popular as golf and tennis. In fact, spas have become one of the top leisure-time destinations, particularly for golf "widows." And this popularity extends to the men as well; previously spa-shy guys have come around, enticed by couples massage, deep-tissue sports massage, and even the pleasures of the manicure and pedicure.

There are East Indian–influenced therapies, hot-stone massage, Hungarian organic facials—the treatments span the globe. Do your research, go online, and call or stop by the

8

various spas and ask the locals their favorites. The quality of therapists island-wide is noteworthy for their training, certifications, and expertise.

Auberge Spa at Palmetto Bluff. Dubbed the "celebrity spa" by locals, this two-story facility is the ultimate pamper palace. The names of the treatments, which often have a Southern accent, are almost as creative as the treatments themselves. There are Amazing Grace and High Cotton body therapies, sensual soaks and couples massage, special treatments for gentlemen and golfers, and the soothing Belles and Brides package. Nonguests are welcome. ⊠ *Palmetto Bluff, 1 Village Park Sq., Bluffton* ☎ *843/706–6500* ⊕ *www.palmettobluffresort.com/spa.*

Faces. This place has been pampering loyal clients for more than three decades, thanks to body therapists, stylists, and cosmetologists who really know their stuff. Choose from the line of fine cosmetics, enjoy a manicure and pedicure, or have a professional do your evening makeup for that special occasion. ⊠ *The Village at Wexford, 1000 William Hilton Pkwy., South End* ☎ *843/785–3075* ⊕ *www.facesdayspa.com.*

★ Fodor'sChoice **Heavenly Spa by Westin.** This is the quintessential spa experience on Hilton Head. Known internationally for its innovative treatments, the beautifully renovated Heavenly Spa incorporates local traditions. Prior to a treatment, clients are told to put their worries in a basket woven from local sweetgrass; de-stressing is a major component of the therapies here. The relaxation room with its teas and healthy snacks and the adjacent retail area with products like sweetgrass scents are heavenly, too. In-room spa services are available, as are romance packages. ⊠ *Westin Resort Hilton Head Island, 2 Grasslawn Ave., Port Royal Plantation, North End* ☎ *843/681–4000* ⊕ *www.westinhiltonheadisland.com.*

Spa Soleil. A wide variety of massages and other treatments are offered at Spa Soleil. The tantalizing teas and snacks make your time here a soothing, therapeutic experience. This is an amazing island treasure. ⊠ *Hilton Head Marriott Resort & Spa, 1 Hotel Circle, Palmetto Dunes, Mid-Island* ☎ *843/686–8420* ⊕ *www.csspagroup.com.*

BEAUFORT

*38 miles north of Hilton Head via U.S. 278 and Rte. 170;
70 miles southwest of Charleston via U.S. 17 and U.S. 21.*

Charming homes and churches grace this old town on Port
Royal Island. Come here on a day trip from Hilton Head,
Savannah, or Charleston, or to spend a quiet weekend at a
B&B while you shop and stroll through the historic district.
Beaufort continues to gain recognition as an art town and
supports a large number of galleries for its diminutive size.
Visitors are drawn equally to the town's artsy scene and to
the area's water-sports possibilities. The annual Beaufort
Water Festival, which takes place over 10 days in July, is the
premier event. For a calendar of Beaufort's annual events,
check out ⊕ *www.beaufortsc.org.*

More and more transplants have decided to spend the rest
of their lives here, drawn to Beaufort's small-town charms,
and the area is burgeoning. A truly Southern town, its picturesque backdrops have lured filmmakers here to shoot
The Big Chill, The Prince of Tides, and *The Great Santini,*
the last two being Hollywood adaptations of best-selling
books by author Pat Conroy. Conroy has waxed poetic
about the Lowcountry and calls the Beaufort area home.

To support Beaufort's growing status as a tourist destina-
tion, it has doubled the number of hotels in recent years.
Military events like the frequent graduations (traditionally
Wednesday and Thursday) at the marine base on Parris
Island tie up rooms.

GETTING HERE AND AROUND
Beaufort is 25 miles east of Interstate 95, on U.S. 21. The
only way to get here is by private car or Greyhound bus.

ESSENTIALS
Well-maintained public restrooms are available at the Beaufort Visitors Center. You can't miss this former arsenal; a
crenellated, fortlike structure, it is now beautifully restored
and painted ocher.

The Beaufort County Black Chamber of Commerce
(⊕ *www.bcbcc.org*) puts out an African American visitor's
guide, which takes in the surrounding Lowcountry. The
Beaufort Visitors Center gives out copies.

Visitor Information **Beaufort Visitors Center** ✉ *713 Craven St.* ☎ *843/525–8500* ⊕ *www.beaufortsc.org.* **Regional Beaufort Chamber of Commerce** ✉ *1106 Carteret St.* ☎ *843/525–8500* ⊕ *www. beaufortchamber.org.*

EXPLORING

TOP ATTRACTIONS

★ Fodor'sChoice **Henry C. Chambers Waterfront Park.** Off Bay Street, this park is a great place to survey the scene. Trendy restaurants and bars overlook these seven beautifully landscaped acres along the Beaufort River. At night everyone strolls along the river walk. ✉ *1006 Bay St.* ☎ *843/525–7000* ⊕ *www.cityofbeaufort.org.*

Johnson Creek Tavern. There are times when you just want a cold one accompanied by some raw oysters. Head to Johnson Creek Tavern and sit outside to take advantage of the marsh views. Or opt for a seat in the sporty bar, where every surface is covered with dollar bills. You may even feel compelled to add one of your own—ask for the staple gun and try to find an empty spot for your George Washington. ✉ *2141 Sea Island Pkwy., Harbor Island* ☎ *843/838–4166* ⊕ *www.johnsoncreektavern.com.*

St. Helena Island. About 9 miles southeast of Beaufort, St. Helena Island is a stronghold of the Gullah culture. Several African American–owned businesses in its tightknit community of Frogmore make this quite the tourist magnet. ✉ *Rte. 21, St. Helena Island* ⊕ *www.beaufortsc.org/area/ st.-helena-island.*

FAMILY **York W. Bailey Museum.** The museum at the Penn Center has displays on the heritage of Sea Island African Americans; it also has pleasant grounds shaded by live oaks. Dating from 1862, the Penn Center was the first school for the newly emancipated slaves. These islands are where Gullah, a musical language that combines English and African languages, developed. This museum and the surrounding community of St. Helena Island are a major stop for anyone interested in the Gullah history and culture of the Lowcountry. ✉ *30 Penn Center Circle W, St. Helena Island* ☎ *843/838–2432* ⊕ *www.penncenter.com* ⌸ *$5* ⊙ *Mon.–Sat. 9–4.*

Barefoot Farm. Check out this farm stand for perfect watermelons, rhubarb, and strawberry jam. ✉ *939 Sea Island Pkwy., St. Helena Island* ☎ *843/838–7421.*

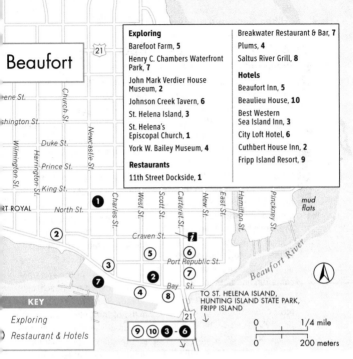

Beaufort

Exploring
Barefoot Farm, **5**
Henry C. Chambers Waterfront Park, **7**
John Mark Verdier House Museum, **2**
Johnson Creek Tavern, **6**
St. Helena Island, **3**
St. Helena's Episcopal Church, **1**
York W. Bailey Museum, **4**

Restaurants
11th Street Dockside, **1**

Breakwater Restaurant & Bar, **7**
Plums, **4**
Saltus River Grill, **8**

Hotels
Beaufort Inn, **5**
Beaulieu House, **10**
Best Western Sea Island Inn, **3**
City Loft Hotel, **6**
Cuthbert House Inn, **2**
Fripp Island Resort, **9**

KEY
Exploring
Restaurant & Hotels

TO ST. HELENA ISLAND,
HUNTING ISLAND STATE PARK,
FRIPP ISLAND

0   1/4 mile
0   200 meters

WORTH NOTING

John Mark Verdier House Museum. Built in the Federal style, this 1804 house has been restored and furnished as it would have been prior to a visit by Marquis de Lafayette in 1825. It was the headquarters for Union forces during the Civil War. ✉ *801 Bay St., Downtown Historic District* ☎ *843/379–6335* ⊕ *historicbeaufort.org* 💲 *$10* ⊙ *Mon.–Sat. 10–4.*

St. Helena's Episcopal Church. The 1724 church was turned into a hospital during the Civil War, and gravestones were brought inside to serve as operating tables. While on church grounds stroll the peaceful cemetery and read the fascinating inscriptions. ✉ *505 Church St.* ☎ *843/522–1712* ⊕ *www.sthelenas1712.org* ⊙ *Mon.–Wed. and Fri. 10–4, Thurs. 1–4, Sat. 10–1.*

WHERE TO EAT

$$$ ✕ **11th Street Dockside.** *Seafood.* Start with the fried green tomatoes or jalapeno-stuffed shrimp at this friendly eatery, then succumb to the succulent fried oysters, shrimp, and fish. More healthful options are also available, including a

CLOSE UP

Writer Pat Conroy on Beaufort

Many fans of best-selling author Pat Conroy consider Beaufort *his* town because of his autobiographical novel *The Great Santini*, which was set here. He, too, considers it home base: "We moved to Beaufort when I was 15. We had moved 23 times. (My father was in the Marines.) I told my mother, 'I need a home.' Her wise reply was: 'Well, maybe it will be Beaufort.' And so it has been. I have stuck to this poor town like an old barnacle. I moved away, but I came running back in 1993."

A number of Hollywood films have been shot here, not just Conroy's. "The beautiful white house on the Point was called the 'Big Santini House' until the next movie was shot and now it is known as 'The Big Chill House.' If a third movie was made there, it would have a new name.

"One of the great glories of Beaufort is found on St. Helena Island," he says. "You get on Martin Luther King Jr. Boulevard and take a right at the Red Piano Too Art Gallery to the Penn Center. Before making the right turn, on the left, in what was the Bishop family's general store, is Gullah Grub, one of the few restaurants that serve legitimate Gullah food."

He continues: "At the end of St. Helena, toward the beach, take Seaside Road. You will be in the midst of the Gullah culture. You end up driving down a dirt road and then an extraordinary avenue of oaks that leads to the Coffin Point Plantation, which was the house where Sally Field raised Forrest Gump as a boy."

steamed seafood hot pot filled with crab legs, oysters, mussels, and shrimp. Everything is served in a classic wharfside environment, where you can eat on a screened porch with water views from nearly every table. [$] *Average main: $21* ✉ *1699 11th St. W, 6 miles southwest of Beaufort, Port Royal* ☎ *843/524–7433* 🌐 *www.11thstreetdockside.com* ✍ *Reservations not accepted* 🕒 *No lunch.*

$$$$ ✕ **Breakwater Restaurant & Bar.** *Eclectic.* This downtown restaurant offers small tasting plates such as tuna tartare and fried shrimp, but if you prefer not to share there are main dishes like lamb meat loaf and filet mignon with a truffle demi-glace. The presentation is as contemporary as the decor. There's also an impressive and affordable wine list. [$] *Average main: $25* ✉ *203 Carteret St., Downtown Historic District* ☎ *843/379–0052* 🌐 *www.breakwatersc.com* 🕒 *Closed Sun. No lunch.*

$$$ ✕**Plums.** *American.* This hip restaurant began its life in 1986 in a homey frame house with plum-color awnings shading the front porch. The namesake awnings are still around, but the dining room has been expanded to make it a more contemporary space. An oyster bar that looks out to Bay Street, Plums still uses old family recipes for its soups, crab-cake sandwiches, and curried chicken salad. At lunch you can chow down on inventive burgers, po'boys, and wraps. Dinner is more sophisticated with creative pairings and artistic presentations, particularly with the pasta and seafood dishes. There's live music Tuesday through Saturday evening. Ⓢ *Average main: $22* ✉ *904 Bay St., Downtown Historic District* ☎ *843/525–1946* ⊕ *www.plumsrestaurant.com.*

★ Fodor'sChoice ✕**Saltus River Grill.** *American.* The hippest eatery
$$$$ in Beaufort, Saltus River Grill wins over diners with its sailing motifs, breezy patio, and modern Southern menu. The bar opens at 4 pm, as does the raw bar with its tempting array of oysters and sushi spacials. Take in the sunset from the outdoor seating area overlooking the riverfront park. A flawless dinner might start off with the signature crab bisque, then segue to the seared sea scallops with green pea and pancetta risotto. The wine list is admirable, and desserts change nightly. Ⓢ *Average main: $30* ✉ *802 Bay St., Downtown Historic District* ☎ *843/379–3474* ⊕ *www.saltusrivergrill.com* ⌕ *Reservations essential* ⊗ *No lunch.*

WHERE TO STAY

Even though accommodations in Beaufort have increased in number, prime lodgings can fill up fast, so do call ahead.

$$ 🏨**Beaufort Inn.** *B&B/Inn.* This 1890s Victorian inn charms you with its handsome gables and wraparound verandas. **Pros:** in the heart of the historic district; beautifully landscaped space; light afternoon refreshments are complimentary. **Cons:** atmosphere in the main building may feel too dated for those seeking a more contemporary hotel; no water views. Ⓢ *Rooms from: $165* ✉ *809 Port Republic St., Downtown Historic District* ☎ *843/379–4667* ⊕ *www.beaufortinn.com* ⌗ *7 rooms, 7 suites, 8 cottages, 1 apartment, 1 house* ⦿ *Breakfast.*

$$$ 🏨**Beaulieu House.** *B&B/Inn.* From the French for "beautiful place," Beaulieu House is the only waterfront bed-and-breakfast in Beaufort—it's a quiet, relaxing inn with airy rooms decorated in Caribbean colors. **Pros:** great views; scrumptious gourmet hot breakfast; short drive to Beau-

8

The World of Gullah

In the Lowcountry, Gullah refers to several things: a language, a people, and a culture. Gullah (the word itself is believed to be derived from *Angola*), an English-based dialect rooted in African languages, is the unique language, more than 300 years old, of the African Americans of the Sea Islands of South Carolina and Georgia. Most locally born African Americans of the area can understand, if not speak, Gullah.

Descended from thousands of slaves who were imported by planters in the Carolinas during the 18th century, the Gullah people have maintained not only their dialect but also their heritage. Much of Gullah culture traces back to the African rice-coast culture and survives today in the art forms and skills, including sweetgrass basket making, of Sea Islanders. During the colonial period, when rice was king, Africans from the West African rice kingdoms drew high premiums as slaves. Those with basket-making skills were extremely valuable because baskets were needed for agricultural and household use. Made by hand, sweetgrass baskets are intricate coils of marsh grass with a sweet, hay-like aroma.

Nowhere is Gullah culture more evident than in the foods of the region. Rice appears at nearly every meal—Africans taught planters how to grow rice and how to cook and serve it as well. Lowcountry dishes use okra, peanuts, *benne* (a word of African origin for sesame seeds), field peas, and hot peppers. Gullah food reflects the bounty of the islands: shrimp, crabs, oysters, fish, and such vegetables as greens, tomatoes, and corn. Many dishes are prepared in one pot, a method similar to the stewpot cooking of West Africa.

On St. Helena Island, near Beaufort, Penn Center is the unofficial Gullah headquarters, preserving the culture and developing opportunities for Gullahs. In 1852 the first school for freed slaves was established at Penn Center. You can delve into the culture further at the York W. Bailey Museum.

On St. Helena, many Gullahs still go shrimping with hand-tied nets, harvest oysters, and grow their own vegetables. Nearby on Daufuskie Island, as well as on Edisto, Wadmalaw, and John's islands near Charleston, you can find Gullah communities. A famous Gullah proverb says, *If oonuh ent kno weh oonuh dah gwine, oonuh should kno weh oonuh come f'um.* Translation: If you don't know where you're going, you should know where you've come from.

fort historic district. **Cons:** thin walls; hot water can be a problem; a bit off the beaten path. [$] *Rooms from: $205* ✉ *3 Sheffield Ct.* ☎ *843/770–0303* 🌐 *beaulieuhouse.com* 🛏 *4 rooms, 1 suite* 🍴 *Breakfast.*

$$ 🏨 **Best Western Sea Island Inn.** *Hotel.* This well-maintained motel in the heart of the Historic District puts you within walking distance of many shops and restaurants. **Pros:** only swimming pool in downtown Beaufort; directly across from marina and an easy walk to art galleries and restaurants; breakfast included. **Cons:** air-conditioning is loud in some rooms, breakfast room can be noisy. [$] *Rooms from: $153* ✉ *1015 Bay St.* ☎ *843/522–2090, 800/528–1234* 🌐 *www.sea-island-inn.com* 🛏 *43 rooms* 🍴 *Breakfast.*

$$ 🏨 **City Loft Hotel.** *Hotel.* This 1960s-era motel was cleverly transformed by its hip, young owners to reflect their high-tech, minimalist style. **Pros:** stylish decor; use of the adjacent gym; very accommodating staff. **Cons:** the sliding Asian screen that separates the bathroom doesn't offer full privacy; no lobby or public spaces. [$] *Rooms from: $179* ✉ *301 Carteret St., Downtown Historic District* ☎ *843/379–5638* 🌐 *www.citylofthotel.com* 🛏 *22 rooms, 1 suite.*

$$ 🏨 **Cuthbert House Inn.** *B&B/Inn.* Named after the original Scottish owners, who made their money in cotton and indigo, this 1790 home is filled with 18th- and 19th-century heirlooms and retains the original Federal fireplaces and crown and rope molding. **Pros:** owners are accommodating; complimentary wine and hors d'oeuvres service; great walk-about location. **Cons:** some furnishings are a bit busy; some artificial flower arrangements; stairs creak. [$] *Rooms from: $200* ✉ *1203 Bay St., Downtown Historic District* ☎ *843/521–1315* 🌐 *www.cuthberthouseinn.com* 🛏 *7 rooms, 3 suites* 🍴 *Breakfast.*

8

FRIPP ISLAND

$$$ 🏨 **Fripp Island Resort.** *Resort.* On the island made famous
FAMILY in *Prince of Tides,* with 3½ miles of broad, white beach and unspoiled scenery, this resort has long been known as one of the more affordable and casual on the island. **Pros:** fun for all ages; the beach bar has great frozen drinks and live music. **Cons:** far from Beaufort; some dated decor; could use another restaurant with contemporary cuisine. [$] *Rooms from: $201* ✉ *1 Tarpon Blvd., 19 miles south of Beaufort, Fripp Island* ☎ *843/838–1558, 888/741–8974* 🌐 *www.frippislandresort.com* 🛏 *210 units* 🍴 *No meals.*

CLOSE UP

Writer Pat Conroy on Fripp Island

"What has Fripp Island meant to me?" Pat Conroy, one of the Lowcountry's famous writers, answered: "The year was 1964. I was living in Beaufort. And when the bridge to Fripp Island was built, I was a senior in high school. My English teacher *and* my chemistry teacher moonlighted as the island's first security guards. It was a pristine island; there were no houses on it yet, and it was as beautiful as any desert island.

"In 1978, my mother moved over there, and all our summers were spent on the island. It was to be her last home. That sealed the island in our family's history. In 1989, I bought a house there, both because it is a private island and thus good for a writer, but also so that our family—my brothers and sisters—could always have a home on Fripp to come to."

PRIVATE VILLAS ON FRIPP ISLAND

There are more than 200 private villas for rent on Fripp Island (but no hotels). Fripp Island Golf & Beach Resort (⊕ *www.frippislandresort.com*) offers a range of rental options, including homes, villas, and golf cottages, many with oceanfront or golf views.

NIGHTLIFE AND PERFORMING ARTS

Emily's. This fun hangout is populated with locals who graze on tapas while eyeing one of the four wide-screen TVs. The piano sits idle until a random patron sits down and impresses the crowd. The bar is full of local characters. ⊠ *906 Port Republic St., Downtown Historic District* ☎ *843/522–1866* ⊕ *www.emilysrestaurantandtapasbar.com.*

Luther's. A late-night waterfront hangout, Luther's is casual and fun, with a young crowd watching the big-screen TVs or dancing to live rock music bands on Thursday, Friday, and Saturday nights. Luther's also has a terrific late-night menu. The decor features exposed brick, pine paneling, and old-fashioned posters on the walls. ⊠ *910 Bay St., Downtown Historic District* ☎ *843/521–1888* ⊕ *www. luthersrareandwelldone.com.*

SPORTS AND THE OUTDOORS

BEACHES

Hunting Island State Park. This secluded park 18 miles southeast of Beaufort has 4 miles of public beaches—some dramatically eroding. The light sand beach decorated with driftwood and the subtropical vegetation is breathtaking. The state park was founded in 1938 to preserve and promote the area's natural wonders, and it harbors 5,000 acres of rare maritime forests. You can kayak in the tranquil lagoon; stroll the 1,300-foot-long fishing pier (among the longest on the East Coast); and go fishing or crabbing. For sweeping views, climb the 167 steps of the 1859 **Hunting Island Lighthouse**. Bikers and hikers can enjoy 8 miles of trails. The nature center has exhibits, an aquarium, and lots of turtles; there is a resident alligator in the pond. **Amenities:** none. **Best for:** solitude; sunrise; swimming; walking. ⌂ *2555 Sea Island Pkwy., off St. Helena Island, Hunting Island* ☎ *843/838–2011* ⊕ *www. southcarolinaparks.com* 🏷 *$5* ⊙ *Park: Apr.–Oct., daily 6 am–9 pm; Nov.–Mar., daily 6–6. Lighthouse daily 10–4:45.*

BIKING

Beaufort looks different from two wheels. In town, traffic is moderate, and you can cruise along the waterfront and through the historic district. However, if you ride on the sidewalks or after dark without a headlight and a rear red reflector, you run the risk of a city fine of nearly $150. If you stopped for happy hour and come out as the light is fading, walk your bike back "home." Some inns lend or rent out bikes to guests, but alas, they may not be in great shape and usually were not the best even when new.

Lowcountry Bicycles. If you want a decent set of wheels, contact Lowcountry Bicycles. Bikes are $8 an hour or $25 a day. ⌂ *102 Sea Island Pkwy.* ☎ *843/524–9585* ⊕ *www. lowcountrybicycles.com.*

BOATING

Beaufort is where the Ashepoo, Combahee, and Edisto rivers form the A.C.E. Basin, a vast wilderness of marshes and tidal estuaries loaded with history. For sea kayaking, tourists meet at the designated launching areas for fully guided, two-hour tours.

Barefoot Bubba's. Less than 1 mile from Hunting Island, Barefoot Bubba's rents bikes and kayaks and will deliver them to the park or anywhere in the area. ⌂ *2135 Sea Island Pkwy., St. Helena* ☎ *843/838–9222* ⊕ *barefootbubbasurfshop.com.*

8

Sea Monkeys

CLOSE UP

There is a colony of monkeys living on Morgan Island, a little isle near Fripp Island. If you are in a boat cruising or on a fishing charter and think you might be seeing monkeys running on the beach, you are not hallucinating from sun exposure. The state of South Carolina leases one of these tiny islands to raise monkeys, both those that are used for medical research and also rare golden rhesus monkeys sold as exotic pets. This deserted island and the subtropical climate and vegetation have proved ideal for their breeding. But you can't land on the island or feed the monkeys, so bring binoculars or a long-lens camera.

Beaufort Kayak Tours. Owner-operators Kim and David Gundler of Beaufort Kayak Tours are degreed naturalists and certified historical guides. The large cockpits in the kayaks make for easy accessibility, and the tours go with the tides, not against them, so paddling isn't strenuous. The tours, which cost $50 per person, meet at various public landings throughout Beaufort County. ☎ 843/525–0810 ⊕ www.beaufortkayaktours.com.

GOLF

Most golf courses are about a 10- to 20-minute scenic drive from Beaufort.

Dataw Island. This upscale island community is home to Tom Fazio's Cotton Dike golf Course, with spectacular marsh views, and Arthur Hill's Morgan River Golf Course, with ponds, marshes, and wide-open fairways. The lovely 14th hole of the latter overlooks the river. To play you must be accompanied by a member or belong to another private club. ✉ 100 Dataw Club Rd., 6 miles east of Beaufort, Dataw Island ☎ 843/838–8250 ⊕ www.dataw.org 🖾 $69–$120 ⚓ Cotton Dike: 18 holes, 6787 yds, par 72. Morgan River: 18 holes, 6657 yds, par 72.

Fripp Island Golf & Beach Resort. This resort has a pair of championship courses. Ocean Creek Golf Course, designed by Davis Love, has sweeping views of saltwater marshes. Designed by George Cobb, Ocean Point Golf Links runs alongside the ocean the entire way. This is a wildlife refuge, so you'll see plenty of animals, particularly the graceful marsh deer. In fact, the wildlife and ocean views may make it difficult for you to keep your eyes on the ball. To play, nonguests must belong to a private golf club. ⊠ *2119 Sea Island Pkwy., Fripp Island* ☎ *843/838–3535, 843/838–1576* ⊕ *www.frippislandresort.com* ⊡ *$75–$99* ⚊ *Ocean Creek: 18 holes, 6643 yds, par 71. Ocean Point: 18 holes, 6556 yds, par 72.*

Sanctuary Golf Club at Cat Island. This is a semiprivate club, so members get priority. Its scenic course is considered tight with plenty of water hazards. ⊠ *Cat Island, 8 Waveland Ave.* ☎ *843/524–0300* ⊕ *www.sanctuarygolfcatisland.com* ⊡ *$40–$80* ⚊ *18 holes, 6673 yds, par 71.*

SHOPPING

ART GALLERIES

Longo Gallery. The colorful designs of Suzanne and Eric Longo decorate the Longo Gallery. Suzanne creates ceramic sculpture—couples dancing and mothers with children are among her favorite motifs. Eric's whimsical paintings often feature fish. ⊠ *103 Charles St., Downtown Historic District* ☎ *843/522–8933.*

★ Fodor'sChoice **Red Piano Too Gallery.** More than 150 Lowcountry artists are represented at the Red Piano Too Gallery, considered one of the area's best (if not the best) art spaces. It carries folk art, books, fine art, and much more. Much of the art at the gallery represents the Gullah culture. ⊠ *870 Sea Island Pkwy., St. Helena* ☎ *843/838–2241* ⊕ *redpianotoo.com.*

Rhett Gallery. The Rhett Gallery sells Lowcountry art by four generations of the Rhett family, including remarkable wood carvings. There are also antique maps, books, Civil War memorabilia, and Audubon prints. ⊠ *901 Bay St., Downtown Historic District* ☎ *843/524–3339* ⊕ *rhettgallery.com.*

DAUFUSKIE ISLAND

13 miles (approximately 45 minutes) from Hilton Head via ferry.

From Hilton Head you can take a 45-minute ferry ride to nearby Daufuskie Island, the setting for Pat Conroy's novel *The Water Is Wide*, which was made into the movie *Conrack*. The boat ride may very well be one of the highlights of your vacation. The Lowcountry beauty unfolds before you, as pristine and unspoiled as you can imagine. The island is in the Atlantic, nestled between Hilton Head and Savannah. Many visitors do come just for the day, to play golf and have lunch or dinner; kids might enjoy biking or horseback riding. On weekends, the tiki hut at Freeport Marina whirrs out frozen concoctions as a vocalist sings or a band plays blues and rock and roll. The famous Jack Nicklaus signature golf course at Melrose on the Beach is one of the highlights of Daufuskie Island. For tee times, call ☎ 843/422–6963. The golf club has an arrangement with Harbourtown Adventures for charter ferry service for golfers (www.melroseonthebeach.com). The island also has acres of unspoiled beauty. On a bike, in a golf cart, on horseback, you can easily explore the island. You will find remnants of churches, homes, and schools—some reminders of antebellum times. Guided tours include such sights as an 18th-century cemetery, former slave quarters, a "praise house," an 1886 African Baptist church, the schoolhouse where Pat Conroy taught, and the Haig Point Lighthouse. There are a number of small, artsy shops like the Iron Fish Gallery.

GETTING HERE AND AROUND

The only way to get to Daufuskie is by boat, as it is a bridgeless island. The public ferry departs from Broad Creek Marina on Hilton Head Island several times a day. On arrival to Daufuskie you can rent a golf cart (not a car) or bicycle or take a tour. Golf carts are the best way to get around the island. Enjoy Daufuskie (enjoydaufuskie.com) offers golf cart rentals to tourists when they come to visit. If you are coming to Daufuskie Island for a multiday stay with luggage and/or groceries, and perhaps a dog, be absolutely certain that you allow a full hour to park and check in for the ferry, particularly on a busy summer weekend. Whether you are staying on island or just day-tripping, the ferry costs $34 round-trip. Usually the first two pieces of luggage are free, and then it is $10 apiece.

TOURS

Freeport Marina, where the public ferry disembarks on Daufuskie Island, includes the Freeport General Store, a restaurant, overnight cabins, and more. A two-hour bus tour of the island by local historians will become a true travel memory. The ferry returns to Hilton Head Island on Tuesday night in time to watch the fireworks at Shelter Cove at sundown.

Live Oac, based on Hilton Head, is an owner-operated company that offers Lowcountry water adventures such as nature tours, fishing excursions, and dolphin cruises. On its first-class hurricane-deck boats you are sheltered from sun and rain; tours, usually private charters, are limited to six people. Captains are interpretive naturalist educators and U.S. Coast Guard licensed.

Take a narrated horse-drawn carriage tour of historic Beaufort with Southurn Rose Buggy Tours and learn about the city's fascinating history and its antebellum and Victorian architecture.

Tour Contacts **Daufuskie Island Adventures** ✉ *421 Squire Pope Rd., Hilton Head* ☎ *843/384-4354* 🌐 *www.daufuskiediscovery.com.* **Live Oac** ✉ *43 Jenkins Rd., North End, Hilton Head Island* ☎ *888/254-8362* 🌐 *www.liveoac.com.* **Southurn Rose Buggy Tours** ✉ *1002 Bay St., Downtown Historic District, Beaufort* ☎ *843/524-2900* 🌐 *www.southurnrose.com.*

WHERE TO EAT

$$ 🍴 **Old Daufuskie Crab Company Restaurant.** *Seafood.* Everyone calls this restaurant the Freeport Marina because of its location. A cold beer may be in order at the colorful bar that plays reggae and rock tunes, especially after a warm-water boat ride. This outpost, with its rough-hewn tables facing the water, serves up surprisingly good fare. The specialties are deviled crab and chicken salad on buttery grilled rolls. Many also enjoy the Lowcountry buffet with its pulled pork and sides like butter beans and potato salad. Dinner entrées include shrimp, rib eyes, and the catch of the day. [$] *Average main: $17* ✉ *Freeport Marina, 1 Cooper River Landing Rd.* ☎ *843/342-8687* 🌐 *www.enjoydaufuskie.com/#!restaurant/cesh* ⏲ *Closed Mon.*

WHERE TO STAY

$$$$ 🏨 **Sandy Lane Villa.** *Rental.* A luxurious, oceanfront low-rise condominium complex, the twin Sandy Lane Villa buildings look out to the simple boardwalk that leads directly to a nearly deserted beach. **Pros:** spacious and private; unobstructed ocean views. **Cons:** not a homey beach cottage; 20 minutes from Freeport Marina. [$] *Rooms from: $400* ✉ *Sandy Lane Resort, 2302 Sandy La.* ☎ *843/785-8021* 🌐 *www.daufuskievacation.com* 🛏 *3 rooms* 🍽 *No meals.*

SPORTS AND THE OUTDOORS

FAMILY **Seagrass Stables at Melrose on the Beach.** There are trail rides, hayrides, and romantic drives in a 200-year-old surrey at Seagrass Stables. It also offers an equestrian center. ⊠ *47 Ave. of the Oaks* ☎ *843/341–2894* ⊕ *www.melroseonthe-beach.com/.*

TRAVEL SMART
CHARLESTON

GETTING HERE AND AROUND

When you're headed to Charleston, you can fly into Charleston International Airport or one of the nearby private airports. The city is reachable by train or bus as well, but you'll certainly need a car if you want to explore beyond the historic downtown, where it's more convenient to get around on foot. Taxis or pedicabs can take you around the city and may be more convenient than driving, especially if your lodging offers free parking.

If Hilton Head is your destination, choose between the Savannah/Hilton Head Island International Airport or the smaller Hilton Head Island Airport. You'll need a car to get around if you want to explore more of the island.

▌ AIR TRAVEL

Charleston International Airport is served by American Eagle, Delta, JetBlue, Southwest, United Express, and US Airways. You'll find more frequent flights in high season.

Airlines and Airports **Airline and Airport Links.com.** You'll find links to many of the world's airlines and airports here. ⊕ *www. airlineandairportlinks.com.*

Airline-Security Issues **Transportation Security Administration.** Check in for answers to almost every question that might come up, particularly regarding security issues. Available 24 hours a day. ☎ *866/289–9673* ⊕ *www.tsa.gov.*

AIRPORTS

Charleston International Airport is about 12 miles west of downtown. Charleston Executive Airport on John's Island is used by noncommercial aircraft, as is Mount Pleasant Regional Airport.

Airport Information **Charleston Executive Airport** ✉ *2742 Fort Trenholm Rd., Johns Island* ☎ *843/559–2401, 843/746–7600* ⊕ *www.atlanticaviation.com.* **Charleston International Airport** ✉ *5500 International Blvd., North Charleston* ☎ *843/797–7000* ⊕ *www. chs-airport.com.* **Mt. Pleasant Regional Airport** ✉ *700 Faison Rd., Mount Pleasant* ☎ *843/884–8837.*

GROUND TRANSPORTATION

Several cab companies serve the airport. Most companies, including Yellow Cab, average $25. Green Taxi, which offers hybrid vehicles, charges a minimum of $35 for an airport run. To ride in style, book a limo or other luxury vehicle through Charleston Black Cab Company or Charleston Downtown Limo.

Charleston International Airport Ground Transportation arranges shuttles for $12 per person to downtown. You can arrange to be picked up by the same service when returning to the airport by making a reservation with the driver.

Airport Transfers **Charleston Black Cab Company** ✉ *7281 Cross County Rd., North Charles-*

on ☎ 843/216–2627. **Charleston
Downtown Limo** ☎ 843/723–1111,
843/973–0990 ⊕ charleston-
downtownlimo.com. **Charleston
International Airport Ground
Transportation** ✉ 5500 International Blvd., North Charleston
☎ 843/767–7026 ⊕ www.chs-airport.
com/Transportation-and-Parking/
Subpage-1.aspx.

▌ BOAT AND
FERRY TRAVEL

Boaters—many traveling the intracoastal waterway—dock at Ash-
ey Marina and City Marina, in
Charleston Harbor. The Charleston Water Taxi is a delightful way
to travel between Charleston and
Mount Pleasant. Some people take
the $10 round-trip journey just for
fun. It departs from the Charleston Maritime Center. Do not con-
fuse its address at 10 Wharfside
as being near the area of Adger's
Wharf, which is on the lower peninsula. The water taxi departs daily
every hour from 9 am to 8 pm Sunday to Thursday, and 9 am to 11
pm Friday and Saturday. It also
offers dolphin cruises and harbor
boat rides.

**Boat and Ferry Contacts Ash-
ey Marina** ✉ 73 Lockwood
Dr., Medical University of South
Carolina ☎ 843/722–1996 ⊕ www.
theharborageatashleymarina.com.
Charleston City Marina ✉ 17
Lockwood Dr., Medical University of
South Carolina ☎ 843/723–5098
⊕ www.charlestoncitymarina.com.
Charleston Water Taxi ✉ Charles-
ton Maritime Center, 10 Wharfside
St., Upper King ☎ 843/330–2989
⊕ www.charlestonwatertaxi.com.

▌ CAR TRAVEL

You'll probably need a car in
Charleston if you plan on visiting
destinations outside the city's Historic District or have your heart
set on trips to Walterboro, Edisto
Island, Beaufort, Bluffton, or Hilton Head.

Although you'll make the best
time traveling along the inter-
states, keep in mind that smaller
highways offer some delightful
scenery and the opportunity to
stumble upon funky roadside diners, leafy state parks, and historic
town squares. The area is rural, but
it's still populated, so you'll rarely
drive for more than 20 or 30 miles
without passing roadside services,
such as gas stations, restaurants,
and ATMs.

GASOLINE

Gas stations are not hard to find,
either in the city limits or in the
outlying areas. Prices are charac-
teristically less expensive than up
north. Similarly, outside Charleston, in North Charleston and the
suburbs, gas is usually cheaper than
at the few gas stations downtown.

PARKING

Parking within Charleston's Historic District can be difficult.
Street parking can be aggravat-
ing, as meter readers are among
the city's most efficient public
servants. Public parking garages
are $1 per hour, with a $16 maximum per day. Some private
parking garages and lots charge
around $2 for the first hour and
then $1 for each additional hour;
the less expensive ones charge a
maximum of $10 to $12 a day if

you park overnight. Some private lots charge a flat rate of around $10 per day, so it's the same price whether you're there 45 minutes or six hours. Most of the hotels charge a valet-parking fee.

RENTAL CARS

All of the major car-rental companies are represented in Charleston, either at the airport or in town. Enterprise has both an airport and a downtown location, good prices, and will pick you up.

RENTAL CAR INSURANCE

Everyone who rents a car wonders whether the insurance that the rental companies offer is worth the expense. No one—including us—has a simple answer. If you own a car, your personal auto insurance may cover a rental to some degree; always read your policy's fine print. If you don't have auto insurance, then seriously consider buying the collision- or loss-damage waiver (CDW or LDW) from the car-rental company, which eliminates your liability for damage to the car. Some credit cards offer CDW coverage, but it's usually supplemental to your own insurance and rarely covers SUVs, minivans, luxury models, and the like. If your coverage is secondary, you may still be liable for loss-of-use costs from the car-rental company. But no credit-card insurance is valid unless you use that card for *all* transactions, from reserving to paying the final bill. It's sometimes cheaper to buy insurance as part of your general travel insurance policy.

ROADSIDE EMERGENCIES

Discuss with the rental agency what to do in the case of an emergency, as this sometimes differs between companies, and make sure you understand what your insurance covers. It's a good rule of thumb to let someone at your accommodation know where you are heading and when you plan to return. Keep emergency numbers with you, just in case.

ROADS

Interstate 26 traverses the state from northwest to southeast and terminates at Charleston. U.S. 17, the coastal road, also passes through Charleston. Interstate 526, also called the Mark Clark Expressway, runs primarily east–west, connecting the West Ashley area, North Charleston, Daniel Island, and Mount Pleasant.

❙ CRUISE SHIP TRAVEL

Cruise ships sailing from Charleston depart from the Union Pier Terminal, which is in Charleston's historic district. If you are driving, however, and need to leave your car for the duration of your cruise, take the East Bay Street exit off the new, majestic Ravenel Bridge on I–17 and follow the "Cruise Ship" signs. On ship embarkation days police officers will direct you to the ship terminal from the intersection of East Bay and Chapel streets. Cruise parking is located adjacent to Union Pier.

Information **Port of Charleston** ✉ *Union Pier, 280 Concord St., Market area* ☎ *843/958–8298 for* cruise information ⊕ www.port-of-charleston.com.

AIRPORT TRANSFERS

Several cab companies service the airport; expect to pay between $25 and $35 for a trip downtown. Airport Ground Transportation arranges shuttles, which cost $12 to $15 per person to the downtown area, double for a return trip to the airport. CARTA's bus No. 11, a public bus, now goes to the airport for a mere $1.75; it leaves downtown from the Meeting/Mary St. parking garage every 50 minutes, from 5:45 am until 11:09 pm.

PARKING

Parking costs $17 per day ($119 per week) for regular vehicles, $40 per day ($280 per week) for RVs or other vehicles more than 20 feet long. A free shuttle bus takes you to the cruise-passenger terminal. Be sure to drop your large luggage off at Union Pier before you park your car; only carry-on size luggage is allowed on the shuttle bus, so if you have any bags larger than 22 inches by 14 inches, they will have to be checked before you park. Also, you'll need your cruise tickets to board the shuttle bus.

PUBLIC TRANSPORTATION

The Charleston Area Regional Transportation Authority, the city's public bus system, takes passengers around the city and to the suburbs. Bus 11, which goes to the airport, is convenient for travelers. CARTA buses go to James Island, West Ashley, and Mount Pleasant. From Mount Pleasant you can catch

CARTA's Flex Service to the beach at Sullivan's Island for $3.

CARTA operates DASH, which runs free buses that look like vintage trolleys along three downtown routes that crisscross at Marion Square.

Contacts **Charleston Area Regional Transportation Authority** ⊠ 36 Johns St., Daniel Island, North Charleston ☎ 843/747–0922 ⊕ www.ridecarta.com.

▌ TAXI TRAVEL

Circling the Historic District, pedicabs are a fun way to get around in the evening, especially if you are barhopping. Three can squeeze into one pedicab; the average cost is $5 per person for a 10-minute ride.

Contacts **Charleston Bike Taxi** ☎ 843/532–8663 ⊕ www.biketaxi.net. **Charleston Rickshaw Company** ☎ 843/723–5685 ⊕ www.charlestonrickshaw.com. **Green Taxis** ☎ 843/819–0846 ⊕ www.charlestongreentaxi.com. **Yellow Cab** ☎ 843/577–6565 ⊕ www.yellowcabofcharleston.com.

▌ TRAIN TRAVEL

Amtrak has service from such major cities as New York, Philadelphia, Washington, Richmond, Savannah, and Miami. Taxis meet every train; a ride to downtown averages $35.

Contacts **Charleston Amtrak Station** ⊠ 4565 Gaynor Ave., North Charleston ☎ 843/744–8264, 800/872–7245 ⊕ www.amtrak.com.

ESSENTIALS

▌ COMMUNICATIONS

INTERNET

Most area lodgings have in-room Wi-Fi for their guests. Internet cafés are rare, but many coffee shops, including Starbucks, have wireless available for free or a minimal fee.

Contacts **Cybercafés** ⊕ *www.cybercafes.com.*

▌ EMERGENCIES

The Medical University of South Carolina Hospital and Roper Hospital have 24-hour emergency rooms. Rite Aid Pharmacy, across from MUSC, closes at 10 pm daily; on weekends the pharmacy counter closes at 8 pm.

Hospitals **Medical University of South Carolina Hospital** ⊠ *171 Ashley Ave., Medical University of South Carolina* ☎ *843/792–2300* ⊕ *www.muschealth.com.* **Roper Hospital** ⊠ *316 Calhoun St., Upper King* ☎ *843/724–2000* ⊕ *www.rsfh.com.*

Late-Night Pharmacy **Rite Aid Pharmacy** ⊠ *261 Calhoun St., Upper King* ☎ *843/805–6022* ⊕ *www.riteaid.com.*

▌ HOURS OF OPERATION

Like most American cities, Charleston businesses generally operate on a 9-to-5 schedule. Shops downtown will often open at 10 am and close at 6 pm, with some conveniently staying open until 7. Around the market area, clothing stores stay open as late as 9, and candy shops and souvenir stores may remain open even later.

▌ MAIL

The main post office is downtown on Broad Street, and there is a major branch in West Ashley. For overnight shipping, FedEx and the UPS Store have downtown branches.

Post Offices **Downtown Station** ⊠ *83 Broad St., South of Broad* ☎ *843/577–0690* ⊕ *www.usps.com.* **West Ashley Station** ⊠ *78 Sycamore St., West Ashley* ☎ *843/766–4031* ⊕ *www.usps.com.*

Parcel Shipping **FedEx** ⊠ *73 St. Philip St., Radcliffeborough* ☎ *843/723–5130* ⊕ *www.fedex.com.* **UPS Store Downtown Charleston** ⊠ *164 Market St., Mount Pleasant* ☎ *843/723–1220* ⊕ *charleston-sc-2386.theupsstorelocal.com.* **UPS Store Mount Pleasant** ⊠ *1000 Johnnie Dodds Blvd., Mount Pleasant* ☎ *843/856–9099* ⊕ *www.theupsstorelocal.com/2130* ⊠ *1643 Savannah Hwy., Floor B, West Ashley* ☎ *843/763–6894* ⊕ *www.theupsstorelocal.com/2114.*

▌ MONEY

As in most cities, banks are open weekdays 9 to 5. There are countless branches in the downtown area, all with ATMs.

CREDIT CARDS

Reporting Lost Cards **American Express** ☎ 800/528–4800 ⊕ www.americanexpress.com. **MasterCard** ☎ 800/627–8372 ⊕ www.mastercard.com. **Visa** ☎ 800/847–2911 ⊕ www.visa.com.

SAFETY

Downtown Charleston is considered a very safe area. Historic District (from Broad Street, to Upper King Street, Mary Street, and slightly beyond) is bustling until midnight during the week and later on weekends. A lot of late-night crime is directed at those who drink too much, so if you'd had a few you might consider taking a taxi to your hotel. Lock your car doors, and don't leave valuables in sight.

■TIP→ **Distribute your cash, credit cards, IDs, and other valuables between a deep front pocket, an inside jacket or vest pocket, and a hidden money pouch. Don't reach for the money pouch once you're in public.**

TAXES

In Charleston, sales tax on most purchases is 8.5%. Hotels are taxed at 13.5% (12.5% in Mount Pleasant). In Charleston area restaurants, the tax is 10.5% for food, beer, and wine.

TIPPING

In upscale restaurants, tip 15% to 20%. In less expensive family restaurants, 15% is the norm. For taxis, a tip of 10% to 15% is typical. Passengers are often more generous in pedicabs, as the drivers are working up a sweat.

▌ TOURS

In a city known for being pedestrian-friendly, walking tours around Charleston are very popular. Many newcomers opt for horse-and-buggy tours, mostly on large wagons holding a dozen or so people, but private horse-drawn carriage trips by day or night are definitely a romantic option.

BICYCLE TOURS

Charleston has relatively flat terrain—they don't call this the Lowcountry for nothing—so a bicycle is a pleasant way to explore the region. The affable owners of Charleston Bicycle Tours lead a maximum of a dozen people on a variety of trips.

Contacts **Charleston Bicycle Tours** ✉ 164 Market St., Suite 104, Historic District ☎ 843/881–9878 ⊕ charlestonbicycletours.com.

BOAT TOURS

Charleston Harbor Tours offers tours that give the history of the harbor. In business since 1908, the company offers a great overview of the areas. Spiritline Cruises, which runs the ferry to Fort Sumter, also offers harbor tours and dinner cruises ($50 to $60). The dinner cruises leave from Patriots Point Marina in Mount Pleasant and include a three-course dinner and dancing to music by a local DJ. Sandlapper Tours focuses on regional history, coastal wildlife, and nocturnal ghostly lore. All harbor cruises range between $20 and $50. On the 84-foot-tall schooner *Pride* you can enjoy an eco-friendly sail and the natural sounds of Charleston harbor on a two-hour harbor cruise, a dolphin cruise, a sunset cruise, or romantic full-moon sails. Tours range from $28 to $46.

Contacts Charleston Harbor Tours ⊠ *Charleston Maritime Center, 10 Wharfside St., Upper King* ☎ *843/722–1112, 800/344–4483* ⊕ *www.charlestonharbortours.com.* **Sandlapper Tours** ⊠ *Charleston Maritime Center, 10 Wharfside St., Upper King* ☎ *843/849–8687* ⊕ *www.sandlappertours.com.* **Schooner Pride** ⊠ *Aquarium Wharf, 360 Concord St., Upper King* ☎ *800/344–4483, 843/722–1112* ⊕ *www.schoonerpride.com.* **Spiritline Cruises** ⊠ *Aquarium Wharf, 360 Concord St., Upper King* ☎ *843/881–7337, 800/789–3678* ⊕ *www.spiritlinecruises.com.*

BUS TOURS

Adventure Sightseeing leads bus tours of the Historic District. The Historic Charleston Foundation pairs local guides with visiting tour groups. Gullah Tours focuses on sights significant to African American culture. Tour guide Alfonso Brown is fluent in the Gullah language.

Contacts Adventure Sightseeing ⊠ *1090 Fort Sumter Dr., Historic District* ☎ *800/722–5394, 843/762–0088* ⊕ *www.touringcharleston.com.* **Gullah Tours** ⊠ *375 Meeting St., Market area* ☎ *843/763–7551* ⊕ *www.gullahtours.com.* **Historic Charleston Foundation** ⊠ *108 Meeting St., Market area* ☎ *843/723–1623 Main office, 843/722–3405 Ticket office* ⊕ *www.*

historiccharleston.org. **Sites and Insights** ☎ *843/552–9995* ⊕ *www.sitesandinsightstours.com.*

CARRIAGE TOURS

Carriage tours are a great way to see Charleston. The going rate is about $25 per person. Carolina Polo and Carriage Company, Old South Carriage Company, and Palmetto Carriage Works run horse- and mule-drawn carriage tours of the Historic District. Each follows one of four routes and lasts about one hour. Most carriages queue up at North Market and Anson streets. Carolina Polo and Carriage, which picks up passengers at the Doubletree Guest Suites Historic Charleston on Church Street, has an authentic carriage that is sought after for private tours and wedding parties. Palmetto Carriage Works offers free parking if you book ahead online.

Contacts Carolina Polo and Carriage Company ⊠ *Doubletree Guest Suites Historic Charleston, 181 Church St., Market area* ☎ *843/577–6767* ⊕ *www.cpcc.com.* **Old South Carriage Company** ⊠ *14 Anson St., Market area* ☎ *843/723–9712* ⊕ *www.oldsouthcarriagetours.com.* **Palmetto Carriage Works** ⊠ *8 Guignard St., Market area* ☎ *843/723–8145* ⊕ *www.palmettocarriage.com.*

ECOTOURS

Barrier Island Ecotours, at the Isle of Palms Marina, runs three-hour pontoon-boat tours to a barrier island. Coastal Expeditions has half-day and full-day naturalist-led kayak tours on local rivers.

Contacts **Barrier Island Eco-
Tours** ⊠ *Isle of Palms Marina,
50 41st Ave., off U.S. 17, Isle of
Palms* ☎ *843/886–5000* ⊕ *www.
nature-tours.com.* **Coastal Expeditions** ⊠ *514-B Mill St., Mount
Pleasant* ☎ *843/884–7684* ⊕ *www.
coastalexpeditions.com.*

HELICOPTER TOURS

You can also fly high with helicopters, which offers exquisite views of
the city. For three people, 30 minutes costs about $400.

Contacts **LowCountry Helicopters**
⊠ *2742 Fort Trenholm Rd., Johns
Island* ☎ *843/580–6567* ⊕ *www.
lowcountryhelicopters.com.*

PRIVATE GUIDES

The Charleston Convention &
Visitors Bureau has a lengthy list
of Charleston's best private tour
guides. Charleston's Finest Historic Tours offers a variety of private tours where you can see some
of the finest private homes and gardens in the city.

Contacts **Charleston's Finest
Historic Tours** ⊠ *Charleston Visitors Center, 375 Meeting St., Upper
King* ☎ *843/577–3311* ⊕ *www.
historictoursofcharleston.com.*

WALKING TOURS

Walking tours on various top-
ics—horticulture, slavery, or
women's history—are given by
Charleston Strolls and the Original Charleston Walks. Bulldog
Tours has walks that explore the
city's supernatural side. Listen to
tales of lost souls with Ghosts of
Charleston, which travel to historic graveyards.

Let Mary Coy, a fourth-generation
Charlestonian and former teacher,
bring the history and architecture
of Charleston's back alleys and
noble streets to life on her two-
hour Charleston 101 Tour. Pay
attention—there may be a quiz at
the end.

Culinary Tours of Charleston is a
foodie adventure that stops at a
variety of restaurants in the Historic District, where you'll experience the area's rich culinary
history and Southern hospitality.

Contacts **Bulldog Tours** ⊠ *40 N.
Market St., Market area* ☎ *843/722–
8687* ⊕ *www.bulldogtours.com.*
Charleston 101 Tours ⊠ *Powder
Magazine, Cumberland St., 1 block
from the City Market, Market
area* ☎ *843/556–4753* ⊕ *www.
charleston101tours.com.* **Charleston Strolls** ⊠ *40 N. Market St.,
Market area* ☎ *843/766–2080*
⊕ *www.charlestonstrolls.com.*
Culinary Tours of Charleston
⊠ *40 N. Market St., Market area*
☎ *843/722–8687, 800/918–0701*
⊕ *www.bulldogtours.com.* **Ghosts of
Charleston** ⊠ *184 E. Bay St., Market area* ☎ *800/854–1670 Office,
843/606-6025 Reservations* ⊕ *www.
tourcharleston.com.* **Original
Charleston Walks** ⊠ *45 S. Market
St., Market area* ☎ *843/408–0010*
⊕ *www.charlestonwalks.com.*

▌ TRIP INSURANCE

Comprehensive travel policies let
you cancel or cut your trip short
because of a personal emergency
or illness. Such policies also cover
evacuation and medical care in
case you are injured or become

ill on your trip. Some also cover you for trip delays because of bad weather or mechanical problems as well as for lost or delayed baggage. Another type of coverage to look for is financial default—that is, when your trip is disrupted because a tour operator, airline, or cruise line goes out of business. Generally you must buy this when you book your trip or shortly thereafter.

Expect comprehensive travel insurance policies to cost about 4% to 7% or 8% of the total price of your trip (it's more like 8% to 12% if you're over age 70). Always read the fine print of your policy to make sure that you are covered for the risks that are of most concern to you. Compare several policies to make sure you're getting the best price and range of coverage available.

■TIP→ **When traveling to the Carolina Lowcountry during hurricane season, there's a chance that a severe storm will disrupt your plans. The solution? Look for hotels and resorts that let you rebook if a storm strikes.**

Comprehensive Travel Insurers
Allianz Travel Insurance ☎ *866/884–3556* ⊕ *www. allianztravelinsurance.com.* **CSA Travel Protection** ☎ *800/873–9855* ⊕ *www.csatravelprotection.com.* **HTH Worldwide** ☎ *610/254–8700* ⊕ *hthworldwide.net.* **Travel Guard** ☎ *800/826–4919* ⊕ *www. travelguard.com.* **Travel Insured International** ☎ *800/243–3174* ⊕ *www.travelinsured.com.*

Insurance Comparison Sites
InsureMyTrip.com ☎ *800/487–4722* ⊕ *www.insuremytrip.com.* **Square Mouth.com** ☎ *800/240–0369* ⊕ *www.squaremouth.com.*

▌ VISITOR INFORMATION

The Charleston Area Convention & Visitors Bureau runs the Charleston Visitor Center, which has information about the city as well as Kiawah Island, Seabrook Island, Mount Pleasant, North Charleston, Edisto Island, Summerville, and the Isle of Palms. The Preservation Society of Charleston has information on house tours.

Contacts **Charleston Visitor Center** ⊠ *375 Meeting St., Market area* ☎ *843/853–8000, 800/868–8118* ⊕ *www.charlestoncvb. com.* **Preservation Society of Charleston** ⊠ *147 King St., Market area* ☎ *843/722* ⊕ *www. preservationsociety.org.*

NDEX

A

dler Lane Beach Park, 177
dventure Cove, 185
iken-Rhett House, 18, 34–35
ir tours, 213
ir travel
  Charleston, 14, 206–207
  Hilton Head, 154–155
lligators, 176
lluette's Cafe ✕, 59, 63
loft Charleston Airport & Convention Center 🖫, 102–103
ndrew Pinckney Inn 🖫, 90
nsonborough Inn 🖫, 90
ntiques, 56, 137, 145, 148, 149
quarium, 34
quaSafaris, 123–124
rt galleries
  Beaufort, 201
  Charleston, 140–141, 146, 147
  Hilton Head, 187
rts Center of Coastal Carolina, 176
shley River, 12, 44–46
udubon-Newhall Preserve, 162
very Research Center for African American History & Culture, 21, 35

B

akehouse ✕, 30
allet, 109
arefoot Farm, 192
ars and pubs, 111–113, 114–115, 116, 174–175
aseball, 119
asil ✕, 59
asket makers, 42–43, 138

Battery, 37
BB&T Charleston Food + Wine Festival, 16, 106–107
Beach House Hilton Head Island 🖫, 169
Beaches, 18, 51, 119–122, 177–178, 199
Beaufort, 153, 191–201
  dining, 193–195
  exploring, 192–193
  nightlife and the arts, 198
  lodging, 195, 197–198
  shopping, 201
  sports and the outdoors, 199–201
  transportation, 191
  visitor information, 192
Beaufort Inn 🖫, 195, 208
Beaulieu House 🖫, 195, 197
Bed & breakfasts, 88, 95
Belmond Charleston Place 🖫, 90, 94
Belmont, The (bar), 113–114
Best Western Sea Island Inn 🖫, 197
Biking, 18–19, 53, 121, 122–123, 179, 199, 211
Black Dagger Pirate Ship, 185
Black Marlin Bayside Grill ✕, 162
Blind Tiger ✕, 78
Blossom ✕, 59, 62
Bluffton, 160, 172, 183–184
Boat and ferry travel
  Charleston, 207
  Hilton Head, 155
Boat tours, 31, 32, 179, 200, 211–212
Boating, *kayaking and sailing, 121, 123–125, 179, 199–200*
Book shops, 144, 146

Boone Hall Plantation & Gardens, 18, 19, 31, 40–41
Bowen's Island ✕, 81
Bowling, 185
Brasserie, *Gigi* ✕, 62
Breakwater Restaurant & Bar ✕, 194
Brewvival, 107
Bull Street Gourmet & Market ✕, 62
Burkes Beach, 177
Bus tours, 212
Bus travel
  Charleston, 14, 209
  Hilton Head, 155
Business hours, 210

C

Candlewood Suites 🖫, 172
Cannonboro Inn 🖫, 103
Canoe and boat tours, 179, 211–212
Cape Romain National Wildlife Refuge, 43
Captain Woody's ✕, 162, 164
Car rental, 208
Car travel
  Charleston, 14, 207–208
  Hilton Head, 155
Carmine's Trattoria ✕, 55
Carriage tours, 31, 212
Cemeteries, 39–40
Charles Pinckney National Historic Site, 43
Charles Towne Landing State Historic Site, 46
Charleston Fashion Week, 16, 107
Charleston Grill ✕, 62, 113
Charleston Harbor Resort & Marina 🖫, 101

Charleston Heritage
  Passport, *34*
Charleston Marriott
  ☒ , *103*
Charleston Museum, *26*
Charleston Visitors Cen-
  ter, *27*
Chez Nous ✕ , *63–64*
Children
  Beaufort, 192, 197
  *Charleston, 22, 26, 27,
  30–31, 34, 37, 40–42,
  43, 44–45, 46, 49, 51,
  63, 65, 83, 91, 94,
  104, 107–108, 109,
  119, 120*
  Daufuskie Island, 204
  *Hilton Head, 160, 162,
  164, 166–167, 169,
  171, 176, 177, 178,
  180, 185, 188*
Children's Museum of
  the Lowcountry, *27*
Churches, *18, 27, 32,
  33–34, 38, 49, 193*
Circa 1886 ✕ , *64*
Circular Congregational
  Church, *27*
City Hall (Charles-
  ton), *38*
City Loft Hotel ☒ , *197*
City Market, *18, 20, 27,
  35, 137*
Civil War sites, *30–31*
Claude & Uli's Bistro
  ✕ , *169*
Climate, *16, 154*
Clothing shops,
  *138–139, 141,
  144–145, 146, 148*
Coast Bar & Grill ✕ , *64*
Coastal Discovery
  Museum, *160*
Coda del Pesce ✕ , *81*
Coligny Beach, *177*
College of Charles-
  ton, *30*
Colleton Museum &
  Farmers Market, *55*
Communications, *210*
Confederate
  Museum, *35*
Conroy, Pat, *39, 198*

Cooking classes, *166*
Cooper River Bridge
  Run, *16*
Courtyard by Marriott
  Charleston Historic
  District ☒ , *94*
CQs ✕ , *164*
Credit cards, *10*
Cru Café ✕ , *64–65*
Cruises, *44, 208–209*
Cuisine, *66, 73, 77*
Cupcake ✕ , *65*
Cuthbert House Inn ☒ ,
  197
Cypress Gardens, *48*
Cypress Lowcountry
  Grill ✕ , *65*

D

Dance, *109*
Dance clubs, *115*
Daufuskie Island, *153,
  201–204*
Dining, *10.* ⇨ See also
  Restaurants
  Beaufort, 192, 193–195
  best bets, 63
  *Charleston, 20–21, 30,
  58–86*
  Daufuskie Island, 203
  Edisto Island, 52
  *Hilton Head, 156,
  162–169*
  price categories, 58, 157
  Walterboro, 55–56
Disney's Hilton Head
  Island Resort ☒ , *169,
  171*
Diving, *131*
Dixie Supply Bakery
  and Café ✕ , *65, 67*
Dock Street Theatre, *30*
Doksa, Eric, *70*
Doubletree by Hil-
  ton Hotel & Suites
  Charleston–Historic
  District ☒ , *94*
Drayton Hall, *18, 46*
Driessen Beach, *178*
Dye's Gullah Fixin's
  ✕ , *164*

E

Ecotours, *212–213*
Edisto Beach, *51, 119*
Edisto Beach State
  Park, *51*
Edisto Island, *50–54*
Edisto Island Serpentar-
  ium, *51*
Edmondston-Alston
  House, *38*
Edmund's Oast ✕ , *82*
1843 Battery Carriage
  House Inn ☒ , *100*
1837 Bed & Breakfast
  ☒ , *90*
11th Street Dockside ✕ ,
  193–194
Elliott House Inn ☒ , *94*
Embassy Suites Historic
  Charleston ☒ , *94, 96*
Emergencies, *208, 210*
Etiquette, *173*
Extra Virgin Oven
  (EVO) ✕ , *82*

F

Fall Tours of Homes &
  Gardens, *107*
Family Circle Cup, *16*
Family Circle Tennis
  Center, *132*
Farmer's Market, *33*
Festival of Houses &
  Gardens, *107*
Festivals and annual
  events, *16, 19,
  106–109, 176*
Fiery Ron's Home Team
  BBQ ✕ , *82–83*
FIG ✕ , *67*
Film, *109*
Fish ✕ , *67*
Fishing, *123–124, 125,
  180*
Folly Field Beach Park,
  178
Folly Beach, *119–120*
Food shops, *141–143,
  145*
Fort Moultrie, *41–42*
Fort Sumter National
  Monument, *30–31*

Fort Sumter Visitor Education Center, 32
Francis Marion Hotel ⬚, 96
Francis Marion National Forest, 48–49
Frankie Bones ✕, 164
French Protestant (Huguenot) Church, 32
French Quarter Inn ⬚, 96
Fripp Island, 197–198
Fripp Island Resort ⬚, 197
Front Beach, 120
Fulton Five ✕, 67
Fulton Lane Inn ⬚, 96
Furniture shops, 143, 146, 148

G
Gardens, 18, 37, 40–41, 44–45, 48, 49
Gasoline, 207
Gaulart and Maliclet Café ✕, 78–79
Geechie Boy Market and Mill, 51–52
Gibbes Museum of Art, 32
Gifts
Charleston, 143, 145, 148
Hilton Head, 187–188
Glass Onion ✕, 83
Glazed ✕, 68
Golf, 19
Beaufort, 200–201
Charleston, 125–130
Edisto Beach, 53–54
Hilton Head, 181–184
Governors House Inn ⬚, 100
Grill 225 ✕, 68
Grocery ✕, 68
Guided tours, 213
Gullah history, 19
Gullah tours, 19
Gullah world, 194

H
Hall's Chophouse ✕, 68–69
Hampton House Bed & Breakfast ⬚, 56
Hampton Inn Charleston-Historic District ⬚, 97
Hampton Inn on Hilton Head Island ⬚, 171
Hank's Seafood ✕, 69
Harbour Town, 162
Harbour Town Golf Links, 183
HarbourView Inn ⬚, 97
Heart Woodfire Kitchen ✕, 83
Heavenly Spa by Westin, 190
Helicopter tours, 213
Henry C. Chambers Waterfront Park, 192
Heyward-Washington House, 37
High Cotton ✕, 70
Hilton Garden Inn Charleston Waterfront ⬚, 103
Hilton Head and the Lowcountry, 151–204
Beaufort, 153, 191–201
Daufuskie Island, 153, 201–204
dining, 156
Hilton Head Island, 153, 158–190
lodging, 156
transportion, 154–156
when to go, 153–154
Hilton Head Island, 153, 158–190
dining, 156, 162, 164–169
lodging, 156, 169, 171–174
nightlife & the arts, 174–176
shopping, 187–189
sightseeing, 160, 162
sports and the outdoors, 177–188
transportation, 159

Hilton Head Island Gullah Celebration, 176
Hilton Head Marriott Resort & Spa ⬚, 171
Hinoki ✕, 165
Hiott's Pharmacy ✕, 55
Holiday Inn Mt. Pleasant ⬚, 101–102
Homes, historic
Beaufort, 193
Charleston, 18, 19, 32–33, 34–35, 37, 38, 40–41, 43, 44–45, 46
Hominy Grill ✕, 70–71
Horseback riding, 131, 185, 204
Hunley (submarine), 35
Hunting Island State Park, 199
Husk ✕, 71

I
Images by Ben Ham, 187
Indaco ✕, 71
Indigo Inn ⬚, 97
Inn at Harbour Town ⬚, 171
Inn at Middleton Place ⬚, 103
Inn at Palmetto Bluff ⬚, 171
Insurance, 208, 213–214
Internet, 210
Irvin-House Vineyards, 46
Island Playground, 185
Isle of Palms County Park, 120
Itinerary ideas, 17

J
Jack's Cosmic Dogs ✕, 83
Jakes, John, 31
Jasmine Inn ⬚, 97
Jazz clubs, 113, 175
Jazz Corner (club), 175
JB's Smokeshack ✕, 83–84

Jewelry
Charleston, 139, 145
Hilton Head, 188
John Mark Verdier
House Museum, *193*
John Rutledge House Inn
🏨, *101*
Johnson Creek Tavern
✕, *192*
Joseph Manigault
House, *32–33*

K
Kayaking, *121,
123–125, 134, 179,
199–200*
Kiawah Beachwalker
Park, *121–122*
Kiawah Island Golf
Resort 🏨, *104*
King Street, *137*
Kings Courtyard Inn 🏨,
97–98

L
Langdon's ✕, *79*
Lawton Stables, *185*
Leon's Oyster Shop ✕,
71–72
Leyla ✕, *72*
Lodging, *10*
*Beaufort, 195,
197–198*
best bets, 91
Charleston, 87–104
Daufuskie Island, 203
Edisto Island, 53
*Hilton Head, 156,
169–174*
price categories, 89, 157
types, 95
Walterboro, 56

M
Macintosh ✕, *72*
Magnolia Cemetery,
39–40
Magnolia Plantation and
Gardens, *18, 44–45*
Magnolias ✕, *72*
Mail and shipping, *210*
Main Street Grille ✕, *56*

Market Hall, *35*
Market Pavilion Hotel
🏨, *98*
Martha Lou's Kitchen
✕, *73*
Martin Gallery, *147*
May River Sandbar, *178*
McCrady's ✕, *73*
Meeting Street Inn
🏨, *98*
Mepkin Abbey, *49*
Mi Tierra ✕, *166*
Michael Anthony's ✕,
165–166
Middleton Place, *18,
19, 45*
Mills House 🏨, *98*
Mitchelville Beach Park,
178
Moe's Tavern ✕, *73–74*
MOJA Arts Festival, *16,
19, 107*
Moncks Corner, *48–49*
Money, *15, 210–211*
Monkeys, *200*
Monza ✕, *74*
Mount Pleasant, *12,
40–43, 116*
Mount Pleasant Memo-
rial Waterfront Park,
19, 42
Mount Pleasant Pal-
metto Islands County
Park, *43*
Muse Restaurant & Wine
Bar ✕, *74*
Museums
Beaufort, 192, 193
*Charleston, 18, 19, 26,
27, 32–33, 34–35, 36,
37, 38, 40, 41–42,
49, 55*
Hilton Head, 160
Walterboro, 55
Music, *109, 176*
Music clubs, *113,
115–116, 175, 198*
Mystery Tree, *52*

N
Nathaniel Russell
House, *18, 38*

Nightlife & the arts
Beaufort, 198
Charleston, 105–116
Hilton Head, 174–176
Nine-O-Seven 🏨, *56*
North of Broad, *12,
26–27, 30–36*

O
Oak Steakhouse ✕, *74*
Obstinate Daughter
✕, *84*
Ocean Course (golf),
129–130
Old Citadel building, *33*
Old Daufuskie Crab
Company Restaurant
✕, *203*
Old Exchange Building/
Provost Dungeon, *40*
Old Fort Pub ✕, *166*
Old Post Office Restau-
rant ✕, *52*
Old Santee Canal
Park, *49*
Old Slave Mart Museum,
18, 33
Old Town Bluffton, *160,
189*
Old Village, *43*
Old Village Post House
✕ 🏨, *80, 102*
Omni Hilton Head
Oceanfront Resort 🏨,
171–172
One Hot Mama's ✕,
166–167
Ordinary, The ✕, *75*

P
Palmetto Dunes Tennis
Center, *186*
Parasailing, *184–185*
Park Lane Hotel & Suites
🏨, *172*
Parking, *207–208*
Parks, *19, 34, 42, 43, 49,
51, 192*
Patriots Point Naval and
Maritime Museum, *42*
Pavilion Bar, *112*
Peninsula Grill ✕, *75*

Piccolo Spoleto Festival, 16, 107–108
Pirate's Island, 185
Plantations, 18, 19, 31, 40–41, 44–45, 162
Planters Inn ⬚, 98–99
Plums ✕, 195
Po' Pigs Bo-B-Q ✕, 52
Poe's Tavern ✕, 84
Powder Magazine, 36
Preservation, 47
Pressley's at the Marina ✕, 52
Price categories, 10
   Charleston, 58, 89
   Hilton Head and the Lowcountry, 157
Private guides, 213
Prudential-Kapp/Lyons Realty ⬚, 53
Public transportation, 209

Q
Queen Street Grocery ✕, 75–76

R
Recovery Room ✕, 76
Red Drum ✕, 80
Red Fish ✕, 167
Red Piano Too Gallery, 201
Renaissance Charleston Hotel Historic District ⬚, 99
Rental agents, 174
Reservations, 15
Restaurants
   American, 62, 72, 73–74, 75–76, 77, 78, 83, 84–85, 167, 168, 195
   Asian, 59
   bakery, 65, 68
   barbecue, 166–167
   eclectic, 65, 67, 85–86, 164
   European, 166, 169
   French, 59, 62, 63–64, 78–79
   Italian, 67, 71, 77–78, 81, 84, 164, 165–166

   Japanese, 164
   Lebanese, 72
   Mediterranean, 74
   Mexican, 76, 166
   modern American, 68
   modern Hawaiian, 79
   pizza, 74, 82
   seafood, 64, 69, 80–81, 162, 164, 193–194, 203
   southern, 59, 62, 64–65, 67, 70–71, 72, 73, 75, 76, 80, 82–83, 84, 85, 164
   southwestern, 80, 167
   steak, 68–69, 74, 168–169
Restoration on King ⬚, 99
Revolutionary War sites, 36, 40, 41–42
Running, 19

S
Safety, 120, 211
Sailing, 121, 123–124
St. Helena Island, 192
St. Helena's Episcopal Church, 193
St. Michael's Church, 38
St. Philip's Episcopal Church, 18, 33–34
Saltus River Grill ✕, 195
Salty Dog Café, 175
Sand dollars, 178
Sandbox, An Interactive Children's Museum, 185
Sandy Lane Villa ⬚, 203
Santa Fe Café ✕, 167
Scuba diving, 131
Sea Pines Forest Preserve, 160
Seabrook Island ⬚, 104
Seeking Indigo (spa), 147
SeeWee Restaurant ✕, 80
Sesame Burgers & Beer ✕, 84–85

Sewee Visitor & Environmental Education Center, 43
Shoes & accessories, 139, 145
Shopping
   Beaufort, 201
   Charleston, 20, 135–149
   Hilton Head, 187–189
   Walterboro, 56
Shrimp boats, 165
Signe's Heaven Bound Bakery & Café ✕, 168
Skull Creek Boathouse ✕, 168
Slightly North of Broad ✕, 76
Soccer, 131–132
Sonesta Resort ⬚, 172
South Carolina Aquarium, 34
South Carolina Artisans Center, 55
South of Broad, 12, 36–40
Southeastern Wildlife Exposition, 16, 108–109
Southern General ✕, 85
Spas, 140, 143–144, 147, 189–190
Spoleto Festival USA, 16, 108
Sports and the outdoors, 18–19
   Beaufort 199–201
   Charleston, 18–19, 117–134
   Daufuskie Island, 204
   Edisto Island, 53–54
   Hilton Head, 177–187
Station 300, 185
Stoney-Baynard Ruins, 162
Sullivan's Island Beach, 18, 116, 122
Surfing, 134
Sweetgrass baskets, 42–43, 138
Symbols, 10

T

Taco Boy ×, 76
Tanger Outlets, 189
Tattooed Moose ×, 77
Taxes, 211
Taxi travel
Charleston, 209
Hilton Head, 156
Ted's Butcherblock
  ×, 77
Tennis, 19, 132–133, 186
Theater, 110
39 Rue de Jean ×, 59
Tipping, 211
Tomato Shed Café ×, 85
Tours
Beaufort, 200
Daufuskie Island,
  202–203
Edisto Island, 50
Charleston, 211–213
Gullah, 19
Hilton Head, 157–158
Train travel
Charleston, 14, 209
Hilton Head, 156
Transportation
Beaufort, 191
Charleston, 14, 206–209
Daufuskie Island, 202
Hilton Head, 154–156,
  159

Trattoria Lucca ×,
  77–78
Trip insurance, 213–214
Truffles Café ×, 168
Two Boroughs Larder
  ×, 78
Two Meeting Street Inn
  🏨, 101

V

Vacation home rentals,
  88–89
Vendue, The 🏨, 99
Venues, 110
Villa rentals, 173–174,
  198
Visitor information, 14,
  27, 158, 214
Voodoo Tiki Bar &
  Lounge ×, 85–86

W

Walking tours, 213
Walterboro, 54–56
Walterboro Wildlife
  Sacctuary, 55
Water sports, 133–134
Waterfront Park, 34
Weather, 16, 154
Web sites, 214
Wells Gallery, 141

Wentworth Mansion 🏨,
  99–100
Westin Hilton Head
  Island Resort & Spa
  🏨, 172
When to go, 16,
  153–154
Wild Dunes Resort 🏨,
  104
Wildlife refuges, 43, 55,
  160, 162
William Aiken House
  Cottage and Lowndes
  Grove 🏨, 100
Wise Guys ×, 168–169
Wreck of the Richard
  & Charlene, The ×,
  80–81
Wyndham Ocean Ridge
  Resort 🏨, 53

Y

Yachting, 123–124
York W. Bailey Museum,
  192

Z

Zen Dog, 99
Zip Line Tours,
  186–187

PHOTO CREDITS

NOTES

NOTES

NOTES

NOTES

NOTES

NOTES

NOTES

NOTES

NOTES

Fodor's InFocus CHARLESTON

Publisher: Amanda D'Acierno, *Senior Vice President*

Editorial: Arabella Bowen, *Editor in Chief*; Linda Cabasin, *Editorial Director*

Design: Tina Malaney, *Associate Art Director*; Chie Ushio, *Senior Designer*; Ann McBride, *Production Designer*

Photography: Jennifer Arnow, *Associate Director of Photography*; Jennifer Romains, *Researcher*

Production: Linda Schmidt, *Managing Editor*; Evangelos Vasilakis, *Associate Managing Editor*; Angela L. McLean, *Senior Production Manager*

Maps: Rebecca Baer, *Senior Map Editor*; Ed Jacobus, David Lindroth, and Mark Stroud (Moon Street Cartography), *Cartographers*

Sales: Jacqueline Lebow, *Sales Director*

Marketing & Publicity: Heather Dalton, *Marketing Director*; Katherine Punia, *Publicity Director*

Business & Operations: Susan Livingston, *Vice President, Strategic Business Planning*; Sue Daulton, *Vice President, Operations*

Fodors.com: Megan Bell, *Executive Director, Revenue & Business Development*; Yasmin Marinaro, *Senior Director, Marketing & Partnerships*

Editorial Contributors: Anna Evans, Kinsey Gidick, Stratton Lawrence, Sally Mahan

Editor: Mark Sullivan

Production Editor: Jennifer DePrima

4th Edition

ISBN 978–1–101–87810–1

ISSN 1943–0167

SPECIAL SALES

This book is available at special discounts for bulk purchases for sales promotions or premiums. For more information, e-mail specialmarkets@penguinrandomhouse.com

PRINTED IN THE UNITED STATES OF AMERICA

10 9 8 7 6 5 4 3 2 1

ABOUT OUR WRITERS

Anna Evans has spent the last 10 years telling stories of the "Holy City" through work in *Charleston Home*, *Charleston Weddings*, and *Charleston*, for which she currently serves as managing editor. The Georgia native moonlights as a freelance writer as well as the editor of a children's book series. She updated the Exploring chapter.

Kinsey Gidick is a South Carolina–based writer and the managing editor of *Charleston City Paper*, where she writes about food and art. A Washington state native, she's lived in the South for 12 years. She updated the Where to Eat, Sports and the Outdoors, and Shopping chapters.

Stratton Lawrence settled in Charleston after college. A former staff writer at *Charleston City Paper*, he's a frequent contributor to *Charleston Magazine* and the *Post and Courier*'s *Charleston Scene*. He lives with his wife on Folly Beach. For this edition he updated the Where to Stay and Nightlife and the Arts chapters.

Sally Mahan Detroit native fell in love with the Lowcountry several years ago when she moved to work at *The Savannah Morning News*. She left to work as an editor in Key West then returned to Michigan to work at *The Detroit Free Press*. However, her heart remained in the Lowcountry. In 2004, she settled in Bluffton, Hilton Head Island. She updated the Hilton Head chapter and Travel Smart for this edition.

EUGENE FODOR

Hungarian-born Eugene Fodor (1905–91) began his travel career as an interpreter on a French cruise ship. The experience inspired him to write *On the Continent* (1936), the first guidebook to receive annual updates and discuss a country's way of life as well as its sights. Fodor later joined the U.S. Army and worked for the OSS in World War II. After the war, he kept up his intelligence work while expanding his guidebook series. During the Cold War, many guides were written by fellow agents who understood the value of insider information. Today's guides continue Fodor's legacy by providing travelers with timely coverage, insider tips, and cultural context.